Sport Governance

Books in the Sport Management Series

Sport Governance
Russell Hoye and Graham Cuskelly

Sport and the Media
Matthew Nicholson

Sport Funding and Finance
Bob Stewart

Managing People in Sport Organizations
Tracy Taylor, Alison J. Doherty and Peter McGraw

Sport Governance

Russell Hoye and Graham Cuskelly

Routledge
Taylor & Francis Group

LONDON AND NEW YORK

First published by Butterworth-Heinemann
This edition published 2012 by Routledge
2 Park Square, Milton Park, Abingdon, Oxon OX14 4RN
711 Third Avenue, New York, NY 10017, USA

Routledge is an imprint of the Taylor & Francis Group, an informa business

Notice
No responsibility is assumed by the publisher for any injury and/or damage to persons
or property as a matter of products liability, negligence or otherwise, or from any use or
operation of any methods, products, instructions or ideas contained in the material herein.
Because of rapid advances in the medical sciences, in particular, independent verification
of diagnoses and drug dosages should be made

British Library Cataloguing in Publication Data
A catalogue record for this book is available from the British Library

Library of Congress Control Number:
A catalogue record for this book is available from the Library of Congress

ISBN-10: 0 7506 6999 3
ISBN-13: 978 0 7506 6999 3

Trademarks/Registered Trademarks

All brand names mentioned in this book are protected by their respective trademarks
and are acknowledged

Typeset by Charon Tec Ltd (A Macmillan Company), Chennai, India
www.charontec.com

Contents

Contents

List of Figures

Series Editor

Dr Russell Hoye is Senior Lecturer in Sport Management, School of Sport, Tourism and Hospitality Management, La Trobe University, Victoria, Australia.

Russell has taught sport management courses since 1993 in Australia at La Trobe University, Griffith University, and Victoria University as well as the University of Hong Kong and Tsinghua University in China. His main teaching areas are sport management, organizational behavior, sport policy, and sport governance. Russell serves as the Coordinator of Honours and Postgraduate Studies for the School of Sport, Tourism, and Hospitality Management at La Trobe University. He is a former Board Member of the Australian and New Zealand Association for Leisure Studies (ANZALS) and a current Board Member of the Sport Management Association of Australia and New Zealand (SMAANZ). He was the Guest Editor for the inaugural special issue of *Sport Management Review* on professional sport in Australia and New Zealand published in 2005.

Russell's areas of expertise include corporate governance, organizational behavior, volunteer management, and public sector reform within the sport industry. He has acted as a consultant for the Australian Sports Commission, Sport and Recreation Victoria, and a number of local government and nonprofit organizations. His research interests focus on examining how governance is enacted with sport organizations and how volunteers engage with and are managed by sport organizations. He has published articles on these topics in journals such as *Nonprofit Management and Leadership, Sport Management Review, European Sport Management Quarterly, Society and Leisure, International Gambling Studies, Third Sector Review, Sporting Traditions, Managing Leisure, Football Studies, Annals of Leisure Research*, and the *Australian Journal on Volunteering*.

Sport Management Series Preface

Many millions of people around the globe are employed in sport organizations in areas as diverse as event management, broadcasting, venue management, marketing, professional sport, and coaching as well as in allied industries such as sporting equipment manufacturing, sporting footwear and apparel, and retail. At the elite level, sport has moved from being an amateur pastime to a significant industry. The growth and professionalization of sport has driven changes in the consumption and production of sport and in the management of sporting organizations at all levels of sport. Managing sport organizations at the start of the twenty-first century involves the application of techniques and strategies evident in the majority of modern business, government, and nonprofit organizations.

The *Sport Management Series* provides a superb range of texts for the common subjects in sport business and management courses. They provide essential resources for academics, students and managers, and are international in scope. Supported by excellent case studies, useful study questions, further reading lists, lists of websites, and supplementary online materials such as case study questions and PowerPoint slides, the series represents a consistent, planned, and targeted approach which:

- provides a high-quality, accessible, and affordable portfolio of titles which match management development needs through various stages;
- prioritizes the publication of texts where there are current gaps in the market, or where current provision is unsatisfactory;
- develops a portfolio of both practical and stimulating texts in all areas of sport management.

The *Sport Management Series* is the first of its kind, and as such is recognized as being of consistent high quality and will quickly become the series of first choice for academics, students, and managers.

Preface

The focus of this book is the governance of nonprofit sport organizations and the practices employed by their boards to carry out their governance role. Books on corporate governance are generally written from a legal, financial accounting or organizational behaviour perspective. The complexity of governance in nonprofit sport organizations that are traditionally governed by a volunteer board lends itself to an examination from the perspective of organizational behaviour. This book explores how the issues of structure, culture, strategy, leadership, change and performance are considered by volunteer boards and their paid staff in governing sport organizations. The principles and ideas in this book are relevant to large community sport clubs; sport governing bodies at the regional, state or provincial, national and international level; professional sport franchises that operate on a nonprofit basis; and allied sport organizations that deliver events, manage stadia or facilities or deliver services to sport participants and consumers.

The boards of nonprofit sport organizations must deal with many challenges in the discharge of their governance responsibilities. The changing nature of the relationship between government and the nonprofit sector, an increasingly demanding regulatory environment, the influence of government sport policy, the impact of globalization processes and increased competition, the expectations of diverse stakeholder groups, and the imposition of prescribed governance guidelines all impact on the governance of nonprofit sport organizations. To varying degrees these challenges are the raison d'être for sport organizations to re-examine their governance structures and practices in striving to meet ever-increasing expectations and standards of transparency, accountability and performance from a wide range of stakeholders. The importance of good governance in achieving high levels of organizational performance has become increasingly recognized by the government agencies that provide significant and ongoing funding to sport organizations.

Boards are crucial for the continued effective delivery of sport opportunities to participants and spectators. Boards are the core decision-making authorities which approve organizational strategies and manage the risks faced by sport organizations. They also have a significant impact on the development of organizational culture, leadership and ultimately organizational performance. It is important that we have a greater understanding of the way sport organization boards work. The structural attributes of sport organization boards, the roles and responsibilities of board and staff members, representation systems and voting rights for members, the performance of individual board members, the sharing of leadership between volunteers and paid staff all impact ultimately on organizational performance.

This book uses a sport team metaphor to encapsulate the idea that the governing board of a nonprofit sport organization should act as a team and that there are certain rules and strategies that teams are expected to follow in order to achieve high levels of performance. With any sporting contest, the internal workings of a team can influence the outcome, which itself is affected by the field of play or the environment in which the game is played. Thus, this book explores both the internal workings of the governance team and the issues and pressures the team must confront in order to be successful in governing a nonprofit sport organization.

This book is divided into three parts. Part One, comprising Chapters 1 and 2, focuses on explaining what sport governance is all about and identifies the external environmental and internal organizational factors that influence how sport governance should be executed. Chapter 1 explores the nature of corporate and nonprofit governance, defines sport governance and reviews the main theories that have been applied to the study of corporate, nonprofit and sport governance behaviour.

Chapter 2 outlines the significant and dynamic factors in the external environment that influence the execution of the governance function within nonprofit sport organizations. It reviews changes in the relationship between government and the nonprofit sector, the regulatory environment in which nonprofit sport organizations operate, the emergence of elite sport development as a priority in government sport policy, governance guidelines developed by government for sport organizations, and the impact of globalization processes on sport. The chapter explains the impact of these dynamics on the governance of nonprofit sport organizations. The chapter extends the argument that the unique features of nonprofit sport organizations at community, state/provincial, national and international levels and the environment in which they operate require governance systems that differ from corporate or public sector organizations.

Part 2, comprising Chapters 3 through 11, covers the fundamentals of the sport governance game. Chapter 3 explores the governance structures of nonprofit sport organizations and the related issues for those who work and volunteer in sport. It describes the elements that comprise the governance structure of nonprofit sport organizations through the use of several examples, discusses a number of issues related to nonprofit sport organization governance structures. It reviews the empirical research that has attempted to categorize and analyse the governance structures of nonprofit sport organizations from the perspectives of organizational theory, governance models and inter-organizational relationships.

Chapter 4 explores the role of the board and the individuals involved in governance roles. It reviews the roles of nonprofit boards, board members and paid staff including a discussion of the reported research on board roles, prescribed governance guidelines and examples from nonprofit sport organizations. A key focus of the chapter is to answer the questions of what do governing boards for nonprofit sport organizations do and how should these roles and responsibilities be allocated within the organization?

In Chapter 5, the question of board member and CEO selection, orientation, training and development is addressed. Much of the prescriptive literature, including governance guides developed specifically for nonprofit sport organizations recommend a shift away from the traditional delegate or representative model towards the appointment of independent board members. The issues and challenges of working within democratic processes to ensure stakeholder representation while striving to have skilled and experienced people in governance roles is a significant focus of this chapter. The findings of the limited amount of published research on nonprofit board member selection issues are compared to prescribed governance guidelines. Several examples of board selection processes are provided in order to illustrate the complexities of selecting individuals to fulfil governance roles within nonprofit sport organizations.

Chapter 6 describes and analyses how boards should work together, both within and beyond the boardroom. A model of board behaviour is presented along with a discussion of the issues of the manifestation of board culture, its impact on board behaviour and how board culture might best be managed. The impact of board culture and other governance matters on board member commitment are also explored through an examination of empirical research on nonprofit organizations and nonprofit sport organizations.

Chapter 7 examines the strategic contribution of the board, specifically in the areas of strategy formulation, implementation and monitoring. The pressures on boards to engage with strategy are reviewed along with a number of prescribed guidelines on how boards should address this important role. Empirical evidence from both corporate and nonprofit sectors on the engagement of boards with strategy is reviewed along with a discussion of the issues involved with enhancing the strategic contribution of nonprofit sport organization boards.

Chapter 8 examines risk management and how boards can ensure compliance with legislative and other regulatory requirements. The pressures on boards to manage risks are reviewed along with a number of standards and prescribed guidelines on how boards should undertake the role of risk management. The chapter also outlines the principles for enhancing the ability of boards to institute compliance monitoring procedures in meeting the requirements of a range of stakeholders.

Chapter 9 focuses on the challenges of dual leadership within nonprofit sport organizations. The chapter discusses the effects of professionalization on leadership and the nature of the relationship between boards and the CEOs. The distribution of power within boards and who has influence over decision-making within boards is explored, along with a discussion of the duality of leadership within nonprofit sport organizations.

Preface

In Chapter 10 issues associated with organizational, board, board member and CEO performance are reviewed. The chapter presents the empirical evidence on board performance evaluation. It also provides a review of the empirical evidence on the correlates of board performance, a brief discussion on organizational performance and reviews the debate surrounding the relationship between board and organizational performance. The chapter concludes with a discussion of the guidelines for how to conduct individual board member performance and CEO evaluations.

Chapter 11 explores the ethical dimensions of governance, the pressures to improve the ethical behaviour of boards and board members, and the range of mechanisms for delivering such improvements. The chapter includes a discussion of the implications of poor ethical behaviour. It reviews the statutory obligations of board members, the development of various corporate governance codes of practice, standards and guidelines, and other influences on ethical governance in sport organizations and overviews several examples of codes of conduct developed by sport organizations.

Part 3 is made up of two chapters that address issues of change and future challenges for sport governance. Chapter 12 explores the drivers of governance change in sport organizations as well as the effects of change on the governance roles of boards and individual board members. It discusses how sport organizations might manage the impacts and processes of instituting governance reforms which are introduced by government sport agencies and through the amalgamation of separate nonprofit sport organizations into one entity. The final chapter of this book discusses the major governance issues that are likely to confront nonprofit sport organizations at the international, national and state/provincial levels.

It would be remiss of us not to acknowledge the outstanding support of Francesca Ford, Commissioning Editor at Elsevier Butterworth Heinemann, who encouraged us to develop the idea for this book and has championed the development of the Sport Management Series within which this book is published. We would also like to thank Melissa Read, Project Manager at Elsevier for managing the production of this book. Finally, we would like to acknowledge the wonderful support and understanding provided by our respective families for the time they gave us to complete this project.

Russell Hoye
Graham Cuskelly

Abbreviations

ASC	Australian Sports Commission
ASIC	Australian Securities and Investments Commission
ASX	Australian Stock Exchange
BASA	Basketball Association of South Australia
BSAQ	Board Self Assessment Questionnaire
CAB	Citizens Advice Bureau
CARA	Canadian Amateur Rowing Association
CCA	Canadian Cycling Association
CCLSR	Centre for Corporate Law and Securities Regulation
CEO	Chief Executive Officer
CGA	Commonwealth Games Association
CGF	Commonwealth Games Federation
COC	Canadian Olympic Committee
EOC	European Olympic Committee
EU	European Union
FA	Football Association
FFA	Football Federation Australia
FGRC	Football Governance Research Centre
FIA	Fédération Internationale de l'Automobile
FMO	Federated Management Organization
GMIP	Governance and Management Improvement Program
IAS	ICC Administrative Services
ICC	International Cricket Council
IDI	ICC Development International Limited
IEL	ICC Events Limited
IOC	International Olympic Committee
IOR	Inter-organizational Relationship
IRB	International Rugby Board
ISF	International Sport Federation
LIRC	Leisure Industries Research Centre
LMX	Leader-Member Exchange
LSE	London Stock Exchange
NBL	National Basketball League
NCAA	National Collegiate Athletic Association
NCVO	National Council for Voluntary Organizations
NFL	National Football League
NGB	National Governing Body
NSL	National Soccer League
NSO	National Sport Organization

Abbreviations

NYSE	New York Stock Exchange
NZOF	New Zealand Orienteering Federation
NZSC	New Zealand Securities Commission
OECD	Organization for Economic Co-operation and Development
ORS	Office for Recreation and Sport
RCA	Rowing Canada Aviron
SA	Soccer Australia
SCORS	Standing Committee on Recreation and Sport
SLSA	Surf Life Saving Australia
SPARC	Sport and Recreation New Zealand
UEFA	Union of European Football Associations
VGA	Victorian Golf Association
VSO	Voluntary Sport Organization
WNBL	Women's National Basketball League
YMCA	Young Mens' Christian Association

**PART
ONE**

Sport
Governance
Concepts

1

The sport governance game

Overview

This chapter explores the nature of corporate and nonprofit governance, defines sport governance and reviews the main theories that have been applied to the study of corporate, nonprofit and sport governance behaviour.

Introduction

Organizational governance is the system by which the elements of an organization are directed, controlled and regulated. Effective governance is necessary for all groups to function properly, whether they are corporations, schools, charitable institutions, universities, religious organizations, nation states, voluntary associations, professional sport franchises or non-profit sport organizations. A system of organizational governance not only provides a framework in which the business of organizations are directed and controlled but also 'helps to provide a degree of confidence that is necessary for the proper functioning of a market economy' (OECD, 2004: 11). In other words, an appropriately functioning governance system assures stakeholders that the organization in which they have invested money, time, effort or their reputations, is subject to adequate internal checks and balances, and that the people empowered to make decisions on behalf of the organization (the board) act in the best interests of the organization and its stakeholders.

One of the most influential authors on corporate governance, Bob Tricker, outlined the importance of governance and its implied influence on organizational performance. He wrote 'if management is about running a business, governance is about seeing that it is run properly' (Tricker, 1984: 7). Governance deals with issues of policy and direction for the enhancement of organizational performance as well as ensuring statutory and fiduciary compliance. Governance is more than day-to-day operational management decision-making.

Interest in corporate governance as a field of research was first sparked by a series of failures in corporate governance in the UK in the early 1980s and later around the world (Clifford & Evans, 1996). As a result of these corporate failures, a number of committees of inquiry were convened around the globe. In the UK, the 1993 Cadbury Committee on the Financial Aspects of Corporate Governance 'focussed attention on the way companies are governed and on the importance of strong, independent non-executive participation at board level' (Tricker, 1994: 1). The recommendations of the Cadbury Committee concentrated on improving the conformance aspects of board operations, with an increased focus on ensuring compliance of management to its fiduciary responsibilities. In contrast, the 1993 Hilmer Report on improving corporate governance in Australia recommended that the board's key role is to ensure that corporate management continuously and effectively strives for above average performance (Hilmer, 1993). In 1994 the Dey Committee on Corporate Governance in Canada of the Toronto Stock Exchange recommended that Canadian corporations adopt 14 best practice guidelines, including the use of a majority of independent directors and for separating the roles of chairman and chief executive officer (CEO).

An important focus of researchers and practitioners in the field of corporate governance in recent years has been the balance between management conformance and the enhancement of organizational performance, and how boards achieve these outcomes. The well-publicized corporate governance failures of corporations such as Enron in the USA, and HIH and OneTel in Australia in the early 2000s continue to highlight the need for effective organizational governance to protect the rights and interests of stakeholders. As a result of these corporate governance failures, the major stock exchanges and most government regulatory agencies developed standards of corporate governance that listed companies must either comply with or at least are encouraged to use to improve their corporate governance practices.

Shortcomings in the organizational governance of sport organizations are no less prevalent, nor are the implications for organizational performance any less serious. One of the first efforts by government to identify governance issues within sport organizations was a 1997 report to the Australian Standing Committee on Recreation and Sport (SCORS). The SCORS report identified that a major concern amongst the sporting community was a 'perceived lack of effectiveness at board and council level in national and state sporting organizations' (SCORS Working Party on Management Improvement, 1997: 10). Subsequently, the government initiated governance reviews of national sport organizations (NSOs) such as the Australian Soccer Association (now Football Federation of Australia) and Athletics Australia in 2003 and 2004 respectively. These reviews have highlighted the negative impacts that poor governance structures and practices have on organizational performance. Independent reviews of how Football Association clubs are governed in the UK, such as those conducted by the Football Governance Research Centre (FGRC) at the University of London, also highlight the importance of developing and implementing sound governance practices in both nonprofit and professional sport organizations. The New Zealand Rugby Football Union Board undertook and independent review of its governance in 2000 as did New Zealand Cricket in 1995 (Ferkins, Shilbury & McDonald, 2005).

Awareness of poor or ineffective governance practices in sport organizations is not a new phenomenon. Governments and sport organizations themselves have recognized the problem for more than a decade, but coordinated responses in the form of guidelines or other assistance for sport from government have been relatively slow to materialize. Aside from a 1999 publication produced by the Australian Sports Commission (ASC, 1999a) entitled *Governing Sport: The role of the board and CEO*, governments in Australia, New Zealand, South Africa and the UK have only recently developed comprehensive guidelines and resources to assist sport organizations assess and improve their governance. The ASC produced a set of governing principles for NSOs in 2002 which was followed by a good practice guide in 2005 (ASC, 2002, 2005). Sport and Recreation New Zealand (SPARC) produced their *Nine Steps to Effective Governance* guide in 2004, the same year the UK Sport published their *Good Governance Guide for National Governing Bodies*. The South African Department of Sport and Recreation also published a set of *Best Practice Principles of Good Governance in Sport* on their website in 2004.

Clearly the importance of sport organizations adopting good governance practices has become increasingly recognized by governments which often provide significant amounts of funding to these organizations. The guidelines and resources developed by governments have tended to draw on the expertise of corporate governance experts, such as the UK Institute of Chartered Secretaries and Administrators and the Australian Institute of Company Directors, or consultants from the nonprofit field. Subsequently, these guidelines are based on a combination of principles from the governance of corporations and the governance of nonprofit entities. It is important to clarify the differences between these two schools of thought.

5

Corporate and nonprofit governance

Corporate governance deals with the governance of profit-seeking companies or corporations that focus on protecting and enhancing shareholder value. In contrast, nonprofit governance is concerned with the governance of voluntary organizations that seek to provide a community service, promote a charitable cause, raise funds or facilitate the involvement of individuals in a variety of activities. Both categories of organizations share similar governance elements as well as having some important differences. Corporate and nonprofit organizations both have boards of elected or appointed individuals to govern their activities and are the subject of a variety of accountability mechanisms to their stakeholders. However, there are a number of important differences in how corporate and nonprofit organizations are governed and consequently the research efforts in these areas have focussed on different issues.

Corporate governance research has covered 'concepts, theories and practices of boards and their directors, and the relationships between boards and shareholders, top management, regulators and auditors, and other stakeholders' (Tricker, 1993: 2). The prescriptive literature as well as research efforts, have concentrated on the two primary roles of the board. First, ensuring conformance by management, and second, enhancing organizational performance. Best practice guides for corporate governance outline how the board should go about supervising and monitoring the work of managers and ensuring that adequate accountability measures are in place to protect the interests of shareholders. Research in this area has sought to identify how conformance in these areas can best be achieved and why the behaviour of managers and boards may deviate from prescribed practices. In addition, corporate governance guidelines provide recommendations on how to enhance organizational performance through the development of strategy and policies that create the direction and context within which executives and managers will work. Research efforts have focussed predominantly on examining the role of the board in developing strategy and how the board can influence organizational outcomes.

The practices of ensuring conformance and enhancing performance appear to be directly applicable to nonprofit organizations. However, the unique characteristics of nonprofit organizations have created a governance framework different to that of the corporation. Nonprofit organizations exist for reasons quite distinct from their profit-orientated counterparts, and generally involve a greater number of stakeholders in their decision-making structures and processes. The relationships that exist between decision-makers who must decide how the nonprofit organization is to be directed, controlled and regulated will therefore be different to that found within profit-seeking corporations (Drucker 1990b). Aside from this major difference in stakeholders and ownership, Drucker (1990b: x) highlighted the following characteristics that distinguish nonprofit organizations from profit-oriented firms: organizational mission; the outcomes of the organization; strategies employed to market their services and obtain funds; the need to attract, develop and manage volunteers; managing a diversity of constituent groups; fund raising and fund development; problems of individual burnout due to commitment to a 'cause'; and importantly, the 'very different role that the board plays in the nonprofit institution'.

Alexander and Weiner (1998: 224) also highlighted that nonprofit governance 'stresses the values of community participation, due process and stewardship (whereas) the corporate model stresses the value of strategy development, risk taking and competitive positioning'. While the management processes employed by CEOs and executive staff to carry out the tasks of the corporate and nonprofit organizations are similar, the governance frameworks are very different. Nonprofit organizations may not be able to adopt corporate governance models because of 'strong pressures to adhere to traditional values of voluntarism, constituent representation and stewardship' (Alexander and Weiner, 1998: 240).

Categorization of sport organizations as either profit-seeking firms or nonprofit organizations on the basis of their governance systems is not as straightforward as it seems. The variety of organizational forms that exist within the sport industry defies simple categorization. Organizations such as government-funded trusts that operate major sporting stadia, statutory authorities that regulate sporting activity or government trading enterprises that operate sporting activities are subject to a variety of corporate as well as public sector governance requirements. These may include reporting to either a Parliament or a Minister, being subject to the scrutiny of an independent Auditor-General, operating according to specific legislation, or working under the direction of an advisory body appointed by the government. While many sports organizations such as sporting goods manufacturers, athlete management companies, retail companies and many venues can be categorized as profit seeking, the majority of sport organizations that provide participation and competition opportunities can be considered to be nonprofit. Sport organizations such as local community clubs, regional associations or leagues, state or provincial governing bodies and national or international sport organizations are generally operated on a nonprofit basis. Their focus tends to be developing opportunities for individuals and teams to participate in sport with any surplus finds used to enhance facilities and services for organizational members. Smith (1993) defined these types of organizations as member-benefit organizations that are created and maintained by the members who consume the services provided by the organization.

It is somewhat difficult to ascertain how many nonprofit sport organizations there are within the sporting system of any individual country.

Doherty (2005) identified that there are more than 33,000 sport and recreation organizations in Canada that comprise 21% of all voluntary non-profit organizations and that 71% of sport and recreation organizations operate at a local level. The Leisure Industries Research Centre (LIRC) (2003) estimated that there were at least 106,000 volunteer run sports clubs in England, in addition to regional and national governing bodies (NGBs). The ASC (1999b) stated that there were more than 30,000 nonprofit sport organizations in Australia. If it is assumed that approximately 70% of these organizations operate at a local level with little or no staff, then there could be as many as 50,000 nonprofit sport organizations that employ at least one paid staff member within the UK, Canada and Australia alone.

Kikulis (2000: 306) highlighted the institutionalized nature of the governance structures of nonprofit sport organizations where there is universal acceptance of the 'volunteer board at the top of the hierarchy of authority'. She also argued that the permanency of such structures is based on a shared 'agreement on the value of the volunteer board and its legitimate decision-making authority has been established and widely adopted across national, regional and local sport organizations' (Kikulis, 2000: 306). This book therefore focuses on the operation of volunteer boards as they have become 'recognized as the legitimate solution for the governance and decision-making structure' (Kikulis, 2000: 307) of nonprofit sport organizations. In addition, this book focuses almost exclusively on nonprofit sport organizations that deliver sport participation or consumption opportunities. It is predominantly concerned with organizations that have at least one paid staff member, though many of the larger nonprofit sport organizations have a great deal more staff. Thus, the principles and ideas in this book are relevant for large community sport clubs; sport-governing bodies of sport at the regional, state or provincial, national and international level; professional sport franchises that operate on a nonprofit basis; and allied sport organizations that deliver events, manage stadia or facilities or deliver services to sport participants and consumers. A further focus of this book is the governance of sport NGBs. UK Sport (2003: 8) defined a sport NGB as an organization that performs the following functions:

- prepares and implements a vision and strategic plan for the sport;
- promotes the sport;
- manages the rules and regulations of the sport, including anti-doping;
- administers officials of the sport;
- establishes and maintains links with the international governing body/ federation;
- encourages participation;
- develops talent;
- develops elite athletes; and
- organizes and hosts competitions.

Fishel (2003) described a number of internal characteristics of nonprofit organizations that are shared by nonprofit sport organizations which have implications for their governance:

■ The organization is not driven solely by financial motives and may have imprecise objectives, consequently making it more difficult to monitor performance than commercial organizations.
■ Nonprofit sport organizations are accountable to many stakeholders including their members, users, government, sponsors, volunteers and staff.
■ Organizational structures can be complex, especially if they have adopted a federated or representative model to facilitate the involvement of a wide range of diverse stakeholders.
■ These organizations rely heavily on the input of volunteers for both service delivery and governance roles.
■ Nonprofit sport organizations are created and maintained on the basis of a set of values or beliefs about the service or opportunities the organization provides. Conflict over direction or priorities can arise through differing interpretations of these values, making it difficult to govern.
■ The relationship between the board and paid staff is potentially difficult if there remains uncertainty over who is in control of the organization.

Anheier (2005: 230) also suggests that nonprofit organizations in general must operate within a 'combination of different motivations, standards, challenges and practices' including a core of professional managers who work with a governing board of experts and constituent representatives. These organizations also have a definable membership or user base, a set of relations with key funding agencies, contractual obligations to government, a set of business contracts with other commercial, nonprofit or public sector organizations and a volunteer base (Anheier, 2005). These internal organizational characteristics and their implications for how nonprofit sport organizations are governed will be explored throughout this book.

Defining sport governance

While there is no universally agreed definition of sport governance there have been several attempts to define it (SPARC, 2004). The ASC (2004) defined governance as 'the structures and processes used by an organization to develop its strategic goals and direction, monitor its performance against these goals and ensure that its board acts in the best interests of the members'. SPARC described governance as 'the process by which the board; sets strategic direction and priorities, sets policies and management performance expectations, characterizes and manages risks, and monitors and evaluates organizational achievements in order to exercise its accountability to the organization and owners' (SPARC, 2004: 16).

These definitions encapsulate the concepts of direction, control and regulation. Governing sport organizations involve establishing a direction or overall strategy to guide the organization and ensuring that organizational members have some say in how that strategy is developed and articulated. Governance also involves controlling the activities of the organization, its members and staff so that individuals are acting in the best interests of the organization and working towards an agreed strategic direction. Regulating behaviour is the third element of governance and entails setting guidelines or policies for individual members or member organizations to follow. These concepts suggest that good organizational governance aims to ensure that the board and management seek to deliver outcomes for the benefit of the organization and its members and that the means used to attain these outcomes are monitored effectively.

Poor governance performance has been attributed to 'director inexperience, conflicts of interest, failure to manage risk, inadequate or inappropriate financial controls and generally poor internal business systems and reporting' (ASC, 2002: 1). SPARC (2004) identified 20 common governance challenges for sport organizations:

1. Complex and confusing governance structures which fail to ensure accountability or cope with changes to the operating environment.
2. Lack of a systematic approach for governing boards to do their work.
3. A lack of training for board members.
4. Boards focussing too much on operational rather than strategic issues.
5. A failure to tackle major policy issues.
6. Being reactive rather than proactive.
7. Boards focussing on reviewing decisions instead of making decisions.
8. Failing to define appropriate accountability measures for the board and staff.
9. Failing to define the results which an organization is striving to achieve.
10. Poor delineation of the roles of the board and staff.
11. Appointing the wrong people to the board.
12. Focusing on compliance issues at the expense of enhancing organizational performance.
13. Failing to define the responsibilities of the board and staff.
14. Having low performance expectations of board members.
15. Poorly skilled and inexperienced board members.
16. Failing to manage the relationship between the board and staff.
17. Developing expectations that exceed the organization's capability.
18. Poor succession planning for board members or key staff.
19. Ad hoc attempts to address governance problems.
20. Failing to provide a clear framework for board members to carry out their duties.

UK Sport (2004) identified that governance problems in sport organizations have emerged as a result of a lack of adequate controls, monitoring and reporting lines, individuals having inadequate skills and a lack of succession planning. These governance failures have resulted in withdrawal of sponsorship, decline in membership numbers and participation, and possible intervention from government-funding agencies (UK Sport, 2004). Sport organizations need to ensure their respective governance systems reflect good practice in order to achieve organizational outcomes.

Governance theories

Cornforth (2003b: 2) identified that a number of theories have been applied to the study of organizational governance and argued that 'each of these theories only gives a partial and limited account of governance'. Cornforth (2003b: 6) also noted that the 'governance of nonprofit organizations is relatively under-theorized in comparison with the governance of business corporations'. Some of the major theories proposed to shed light on how the governance function is enacted within sport, corporate and nonprofit organizations include: agency theory, stewardship theory, institutional theory, resource dependence theory, network theory, stakeholder theory, a democratic perspective and managerial hegemony theory (Hung, 1998; Cornforth, 2003c; Clarke, 2004). Each of these theories is examined, in turn, to identify their relevance in understanding the governance of sport organizations. Figure 1.1 provides a summary of these theories that outlines the assumptions each theory has for the interests of board members, stakeholders and managers, the recommended source of board members and the role of the board. As noted earlier, much of the writing and research on organizational governance has been based on corporations rather than nonprofit entities, and there has been relatively little completed research on the governance of nonprofit sport organizations. Each of the theories presented here offer a perspective on illuminating something of the governance assumptions, processes, structures and outcomes for sport organizations.

Both principal-agent theory (agency theory) and stewardship theory focus on the internal monitoring issues of governance. Agency theory assumes that owners of an organization will have different interests to those that manage the organization and proposes that shareholders' interests should prevail in decisions concerning the operation of an organization. Managers (agents) who have been appointed to run the organization should be subject to extensive checks and balances by the governing board in order to reduce the potential for mismanagement or misconduct by agents that may threaten shareholders' interests. Agency theory has been the predominant theoretical approach to the study of corporate governance. It has focussed on exploring the best ways for boards to maximize control of

Theory	Interests	Board members	Board role
Agency theory	Owners and managers have different interests	Owner's representatives	Compliance and conformance
Stewardship theory	Owners and managers have the same interests	Experts	Enhance performance
Institutional theory	Stakeholders and the organization have different interests	Influenced by external organizations	Compliance and conformance
Resource dependence theory	Stakeholders and the organization have different interests	Selected for ability to influence other organizations	Build relationships with other organizations
Network theory	Stakeholders and the organization have different interests	Selected for ability to influence other organizations	Secure resources to support the organization
Stakeholder theory	Diverse range of interests among stakeholders	Stakeholder representatives	Balancing stakeholder needs
Democratic perspective	Diverse range of interests among stakeholders	Lay representatives	Represent constituents and reconcile differences
Managerial hegemony theory	Owners and managers have different interests	Owner's representatives	Symbolic

Figure 1.1 Theoretical perspectives on organizational governance (*Source*: Adapted from Cornforth (2003b: 12))

managerial actions, and to increase the quality and quantity of information for shareholders in order to provide some assurance that managers will seek outcomes that maximize shareholder wealth and reduce risk. For corporations operating in the sport industry that may have a range of individual, institutional and government shareholders, this theory helps to explain how governance systems work. However, for the majority of non-profit sport organizations, which have diverse stakeholders who do not have a financial share in the organization, this theory has limited application (Hoye, Smith, Westerbeek, Stewart & Nicholson, 2006).

Stewardship theory starts with the opposite assumption of agency theory, proposing that managers are motivated by a need for achievement, responsibility, recognition and respect for authority, rather than seeking to maximize their own interests over those of shareholders. The board therefore needs to focus on enhancing the performance of the organization rather than seeking managerial compliance. This focus seems to be at odds with some of the prescriptive literature such as the UK Sport (2004) guidelines for good governance which emphasize the need for the board to monitor compliance issues.

Institutional theory, resource dependence theory and network theory each seek to explain how organizations relate to their external environments and acquire scarce resources. Institutional theory posits that the governance frameworks adopted by organizations are the result of external pressures to conform to accepted business practice, including legal requirements for incorporation. These pressures are exerted by government agencies in the form of developing governance guidelines and imposing requirements through funding agreements, as well as organizational members concerned that proper governance systems should be employed. If organizations operating in similar environments seek to conform to these pressures they are likely to adopt very similar governance frameworks, a situation known as institutional isomorphism. This is evident in sporting systems in countries such as Australia, Canada, New Zealand and the UK where most national and state or provincial sport governing organizations are currently governed by somewhat traditional federated models.

Resource dependence theory proposes that organizations are dependent on other organizations for survival and therefore need to manage their relationships with other organizations to ensure they 'get the resources and information they need' (Cornforth, 2003b: 8). In managing these relationships, organizations enter into inter-organizational arrangements which frequently require some loss of flexibility and autonomy in exchange for gaining control over other organizations' resources. These inter-organizational arrangements take the form of mergers, joint ventures, co-optation (the inclusion of outsiders in the leadership and decision-making processes of an organization), growth, political involvement or restricting the distribution of information (Pfeffer & Salancik, 1978). The governing board of a nonprofit sporting organization plays a crucial role in establishing and maintaining these relationships and can be considered both part of the organization and its environment as it plays a boundary spanning role (Cornforth, 2003c). The inter-organizational arrangements adopted by the board and the organization are likely to have an impact on the governance structure adopted and the skills required of board members to manage these relationships.

Network theory is the third theory that attempts to explain how organizations relate to their environment. The main premise of network theory is that in addition to legal contracts, organizations enter into socially binding contracts to deliver services which create a degree of interdependency between organizations. This interdependency facilitates the development of informal communication and resource flow between organizations.

Nonprofit sport organizations certainly display such interdependency. For example, many sport organizations are heavily dependent on government financial support for stadia construction, infrastructure development and hosting major sport events, as well as using political connections to garner support from other organizations or form alliances. In this sense, network theory could be considered as merely one facet of resource dependency theory, however, it is highlighted here as it can help to explain how the actions of board members, in using their personal networks, can assist nonprofit sport organizations. The ability of a well-connected board member to secure support from sponsors, governments or other organizations, by whatever means, can have a considerable impact on an organization's performance. Together, institutional theory, resource dependency theory and network theory highlight the value of examining governance in terms of the external pressures faced by sport organizations, and the strategies, structures and processes they put in place to manage these pressures.

Stakeholder theory examines the relationships between organizations and their stakeholders and conceptualizes organizations as a series of relationships and responsibilities for which the governance framework must account. Hung (1998) noted that stakeholder theory highlights that organizations are not only responsible to their shareholders or custodians but also to a wider range of societal groups. Nonprofit sport organizations need to manage relationships with a number of these groups including, for example, sponsors, funding agencies, members, the general public, affiliated organizations, staff, board members, venues, government agencies and suppliers. The implication for governance is that organizations need to assimilate the views of a number of these different stakeholder groups on their boards, so that the board overall is more capable of responding to 'broader social interests that the narrow interests of one group' (Cornforth, 2003b: 9).

The central ideas of Western democracy are enshrined in the governance systems of most nonprofit sport organizations. Cornforth (2003b) identifies these ideas as follows:

- Open elections on the basis of one person one vote.
- Pluralism or the idea that elected representatives will represent interests other than their own.
- Accountability to the electorate.
- The separation of elected representatives who make policy from the executive who implement policy.

Most nonprofit sport organizations are governed in line with these tenets with the elected board's role to decide how individual interests should be weighed against the interests of the collective. Critically, most nonprofit sport organizations provide the opportunity for any member to be elected regardless of skills or experience. Ironically, it is these democratic ideals that sometimes thwart the ability of nonprofit sport organizations to develop good governance structures, processes and systems.

A final theory relevant to understanding organizational governance is managerial hegemony theory. This theory postulates that although the key organizational stakeholders (shareholders or members) are legally in control of their organization, they rarely have effective control because it has 'been ceded to a new managerial class' (Cornforth, 2003b: 10). Such a view is shared by many sport management scholars who argue that the professionalization of the sport industry has led to a reduction in volunteer control of nonprofit sport organizations (cf. Ferkins et al., 2005). The introduction of professional staff who work for volunteer boards has challenged the decision-making processes and systems within nonprofit sport organizations and has been a focus of much research into how governance has changed within these organizations (Thibault, Slack & Hinings, 1991; Amis, Slack & Berrett, 1995; Kikulis, Slack & Hinings, 1995a, 1995b, 1995c; Amis & Slack, 1996; Auld, 1997; Auld & Godbey, 1998).

Conclusion

Cornforth (2003b: 11) argued that attempts to understand organizational governance in the wider corporate and nonprofit sectors have suffered from using a single perspective and that adopting a multi-paradigm approach would allow the 'paradoxes, ambiguities and tensions involved in governance' to be embraced thus shedding new light on how the governance game is played by nonprofit sport organizations. This book applies this approach to the study of nonprofit sport organization governance and explores the ways in which nonprofit sport organizations are and should be governed.

The remainder of this book is about how these organizations should approach the governance game and how the core functions of direction, control and regulation should be carried out within the context of nonprofit sport organizations. A number of specific questions concerning sport governance are addressed.

■ What are the roles of governing boards? How and why are boards best able to influence organizational outcomes?
■ What governance structures and processes are appropriate for sport organizations?
■ What is the relationship between boards, executives and management? What types of relationships are the most effective in achieving organizational compliance and performance? Who is really in control of sport organizations?
■ What are the key influences on boards and board members? How do these influences affect the ways sport organizations are governed?

2

The playing field: influences on sport governance

Overview

This chapter outlines the significant external environmental issues that influence the execution of the governance function within nonprofit sport organizations. It reviews changes in the relationship between government and the nonprofit sector, the regulatory environment in which nonprofit sport organizations operate, the emergence of elite sport development as a priority in government sport policy, governance guidelines developed by government for sport organizations and the impact of globalization processes on sport, and assesses their impact on the governance of nonprofit sport organizations.

The playing field

As noted in the previous chapter a number of environmental factors influence how governance is executed within sport organizations. The importance of understanding the contextual factors in which governance occurs was highlighted by Cornforth (2003a) who argued that much of the theorizing about boards and organizational governance fails to take into account the external and internal context in which specific types of organizations operate. For example, 'board composition, structure and behaviour change over time' (Cornforth, 2003a: 237). These changes may be a result of new regulations or legislation pertaining to legal structures or reporting requirements, shifts in government policy or pressures from affiliated organizations.

Nonprofit sport organizations vary in terms of their size, structures, cultures, traditions and their capacity to respond to external pressures. In writing about the UK sport context, Taylor (2004) identified two types of nonprofit voluntary sport organizations (VSOs) at opposite ends of a spectrum. At one end are the traditional, informal sport organizations which are characterized as having strong collective identities, operate as cooperatives and consider professionalism and external assistance from government as a threat. At the other extreme, contemporary, formal sport organizations are described as systematic, business like and receptive to external assistance. Taylor (2004) also identified a number of issues confronting sport volunteers and nonprofit sport organizations that have implications for the governance of these organizations. These included the trends:

- that not enough people are prepared to volunteer for sports clubs and subsequently volunteer numbers have decreased in the last 5 years;
- more than a third of national governing bodies (NGBs) and clubs report volunteer recruitment difficulties which leads to multi-tasking and merging of key positions within nonprofit sport organizations;
- an increasingly ageing volunteer force, especially for core administrative and governance roles;
- volunteers currently involved in these organizations are devoting more time in response to increased bureaucracy and pressure to implement changes imposed by sport NGBs and legislation;
- a 'pay and play' attitude by organizational members and a 'childminding' attitude by parents of young members.

Taylor (2004: 107) argues that these pressures and the variable capacity of VSOs 'conspire to create considerable constraints to the development potential of VSOs'. Arguably, these pressures could lead the decision-makers of more informal and traditional nonprofit sport organizations to focus on core operational tasks at the expense of strategic developments that deliver improved sporting experiences. These pressures are not new to the sporting system but have increased over the last decade. Based on the research conducted by the Leisure Industries Research Centre (2003), Taylor (2004: 107) identified several underlying societal and institutional reasons the pressures on nonprofit sport organizations, and the volunteers that operate within it (especially board members) are greater than they were 10 years ago:

- Increased choice and competition for people's leisure time and expenditure.
- A 'time squeeze' caused not only by this greater choice of leisure options but also increasing time devoted to paid work and child care, particularly in the higher socio-economic groups who are the ones with the strongest representation in sports participation.
- A lack of time is the most important reason for people giving up volunteering in sport according to the research, as well as the most important constraint preventing interested non-volunteers from volunteering.
- Greater expectations of higher quality service delivery by members of VSOs.
- Central government and Sport England requirements and initiatives (e.g. greater accountability for funds received, social inclusion, equal access, child protection).
- NGB standards and requirements (e.g. coach training, accreditation and registration, and member registration).

Taylor (2004: 108) contends that these pressures may limit the ability of the traditional informal VSOs to contribute to strategic sport development but on the other hand more contemporary formal VSOs 'have the managerial skills and techniques to promote development and respond to external initiatives'. This conclusion is made on the basis that some VSOs report falling volunteer numbers while an equal portion have experienced an increase in volunteer numbers. As such, the greater volunteer workloads are due to increased activity or use of organizational resources (i.e. more people participating in organized sport). Taylor (2004) concluded that there was sufficient evidence to suggest that at least some organizations are well placed to cope with these increasing pressures and that the capability of individual organizations to cope with these pressures should be taken into consideration.

The core organizational unit that is central to all discussions of governance is the board, comprising the volunteers who are elected, appointed or invited to act as the key decision-makers for the organization. Boards act as boundary spanners for the organization, dealing with the external environment and the associated pressures to be accountable to stakeholders as well as providing the organization and its staff with direction. Figure 2.1 illustrates the external influences on governance within nonprofit sport organizations with the board being the central focus of these influences.

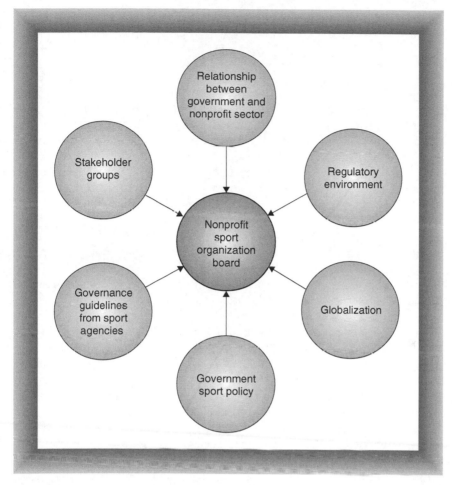

Figure 2.1 Influences on governance within nonprofit sport organizations

The environmental influences on governance within nonprofit sport organizations include:

1. changes in the relationship between government and the nonprofit sector,
2. the regulatory environment in which nonprofit sport organizations operate,
3. the emergence of elite sport development as a priority in government sport policy,
4. governance guidelines developed by government for sport organizations,
5. the impact of globalization processes on sport,
6. the expectations of stakeholder groups.

19

Government and nonprofit sector relationship

Fishel (2003: 6) identified a number of trends that 'impact on the board's business' including the move by governments to look to nonprofit organizations to provide services which in the past were delivered through government departments or specialist agencies. The wave of privatization that has swept through most Western democracies over the last 20 years with governments selling off assets such as power generating and distribution entities, airlines, lotteries and wagering entities, banks, agricultural producers, welfare agencies and other organizations is indicative of a shift to smaller government and less direct ownership of service delivery. Nonprofit organizations have subsequently entered into contractual arrangements to deliver more and more services on behalf of government. Warburton and Mutch (2000: 39) argued that the relationship between government and the nonprofit sector generally has shifted 'towards notions of social contract, mutual obligation and partnerships between individuals, communities and the state'.

The sport sector has not been unaffected by such changes. In exchange for government funding, NGBs are responsible for the delivering of both high-performance programmes for elite athletes and sport development initiatives designed to increase involvement in regular organized sport. The activities of nonprofit sport organizations are becoming increasingly tied to the aims of government policies, requiring the boards of these organizations to decide on the nature and extent of their involvement and subsequent direction of their respective organization. The relationship between nonprofit sport organizations and government differs according to the type of organization involved (e.g. large national organizations compared to regional or local sport organizations) and the level of government involved (Anheier, 2005). The funding arrangements between government and sport organizations take many forms: grants, fee-for-service contracts or government loans and sport organizations may also receive other types of support such as access to facilities or expertise, or even direct organizational support.

Government and nonprofit relationships also differ on the extent to which their respective organizational goals and means overlap (Najam, 2000). Such relationships will be cooperative, complementary, co-optive or confrontational. A cooperative relationship exists when the goals and means are similar. The relationship between an elite sport agency such as the Australian Institute of Sport and NGBs aiming to improve the performance of elite athletes and teams is an example of a largely cooperative relationship. If the goals were similar but the means dissimilar, this would constitute a complementary relationship such as governments promoting higher levels of sport participation via a mass media campaign supported by sport organizations linking with schools and local community groups to promote community sport participation. Organizations with dissimilar goals but with similar means form co-optive relationships such as when government financially supports the construction of a multipurpose sport stadium whereby sport organizations provide their own funds in order to secure access for their own discrete purposes. Confrontational relationships develop when the goals and means are both dissimilar, such as a sports organization lobbying government for more funding to the sport sector or criticizing current government sport policies.

O'Regan and Oster (2002) explored the implications of increased government funding and allied requirements for increased accountability for nonprofit boards. They found that boards of organizations with higher levels of government funding focus more on fiduciary and boundary-spanning activities than other traditional functions such as fund raising and monitoring of service delivery. The implications for nonprofit sport organizations is that while increased government funding may support more or better quality sport development programmes, particularly at the elite level, it may influence the ability of the board to focus on other sport development issues. Thus, boards need to be aware that a trade off for increased funding carries with it increased reporting and accountability requirements that indirectly shape the way governance is enacted within their organization.

Regulatory environment

In their comprehensive book on the principles of corporate governance du Plessis, McConvill and Bagaric (2005: 107) explain that the 'regulation of corporate governance in Australia is achieved through both binding and non-binding rules, international recommendations and industry specific standards, commentaries of scholars and practitioners and the decisions of judges'. The sources of regulation for nonprofit organizations are similar and generally take one of four forms:

1. Government determined set of legal rules supported by monitoring and enforcement;
2. Interpretations of statutory law made by judges;
3. Best practice recommendations such as *The Code of Governance for the Voluntary and Community Sector* developed by the National Council for voluntary organizations in England;
4. Accounting Standards and auditing Standards.

In addition, as highlighted in Chapter 1, specific sport agencies such as the Australian Sports Commission (ASC), Sport and Recreation New Zealand

(SPARC) and UK Sport have developed voluntary governance guidelines for nonprofit sport organizations.

In most western countries, for-profit companies are regulated under Federal law. In Australia for example, companies are regulated by the Commonwealth government agency, the Australian Securities and Investments Commission (ASIC) under the powers of the *Corporations Act (2001)*. In contrast, the legal rules relevant to the governance of nonprofit sport organizations in Australia take the form of state-based regulations, which present problems for NGBs having to work with separately constituted legal entities in each state/province and territory. A similar regulatory framework operates at a provincial level in Canada. The reporting requirements and the financial disclosure regime of these state and provincial-based regulations often vary enormously, making it difficult to promote accountability and good governance practices across the country. A report published on reforming the regulation of nonprofit organizations in Australia (University of Melbourne Centre for Corporate Law and Securities Regulation (CCLSR), 2004) recommended the introduction of a single Commonwealth statutory regime for nonprofit organizations by referral of powers from the states to the Commonwealth. Such a move would make it easier for national level nonprofit sport organizations to adopt unitary structures that operate as a single legal entity with state/provincial offices. This is the preferred model of Federal sport agencies such as the ASC.

The regulatory environment in which nonprofit sport organizations operate has changed dramatically in the last decade. The increasingly litigious society where individuals seek redress through the legal system to solve disputes has forced nonprofit sport organizations to be more cognizant of their legal responsibilities and associated risk management issues. At the same time there has been an increase in the level of professionalization within sport which has raised expectations of service and standards of behaviour by clients and members, the community and the legal system itself. The Canadian Centre for Sport and Law (2005) contended that society is now 'more litigation-oriented and the public is expecting nonprofit organizations to be more accountable and business like in managing their affairs'. Increased professionalism in sport means that nonprofit sport organizations are now engaged in a wider variety of revenue raising and commercial activities, the establishment of contracts with suppliers, sponsors, merchandisers and other business operations and in some cases employing paid personnel, even at the community level of sport.

Collectively these changes impose greater pressures on volunteer board members to be appropriately skilled and experienced to deal with a complex array of issues. In some cases the pressures act as a deterrent to attracting individuals to governance positions. Healey (2005) argued that volunteer recruitment and retention has been adversely affected because of apprehension about the possibility of exposure to personal legal liability and the potential risk for financial loss.

The roles of board members (directors) are explored in more detail in later chapters. At this point it is important to explore the legal duties and potential liability issues faced by individual board members. The Canadian Centre for Sport and Law (2005) identifies the core responsibility of directors as representing the interest of the members in directing the affairs of the organization and to do so within the law. Their duties include: (1) diligence – to act reasonably, prudently, in good faith and with a view to the best interests of the organization and its members; (2) loyalty – to place the interests of the organization first, and to not use one's position as a director to further private interests and (3) obedience – to act within the scope of the governing policies of the organization and within the scope of other laws, rules and regulations that apply to the organization (Canadian Centre for Sport and Law, 2005). A director who fails to fulfil their duties in this manner may be found personally liable in one or more of the following four situations: (1) statute – breaking the law; (2) contract – a contract is breached or violated; (3) tort – an act, or a failure to act, whether intentionally or unintentionally, causes injury or damage to another person or (4) wrongful acts – errors, omissions, actions or decisions that harm others by interfering with their rights, opportunities or privileges (Canadian Centre for Sport and Law, 2005). Such requirements and potential for personal liability can obviously deter individuals from wishing to take on the responsibility of fulfilling a governance role as a board member or director. In order to counter this deterrent, the majority of larger nonprofit sport organizations take out indemnity insurance, the costs of which have escalated in recent years.

In summary, the changes in the regulatory environment and the variety of sources from which the regulation of governance activities emanates, presents nonprofit sport organizations with several governance challenges, irrespective of their organizational capability. These include a relatively complex compliance burden to fulfl reporting requirements, a high level of public scrutiny of governance processes and performance and difficulties in attracting volunteer board or committee members, particularly in lower profile sports. In addition, the voluntary nature of boards and their 'multiple and complex accountability foci (e.g. their accountability to grant makers, members, clients and regulatory bodies) … [are] … significant impediments to good corporate governance practices' (CCLSR, 2004: 16).

Government sport policy

In an examination of British post-war sport policy, Roche (1993) identified three dominant ideologies that drove the development of sport policy – amateurism, welfarism and more recently, pro-market commercialism.

He argued that these ideologies exist contemporaneously among the members of the sport policy community (i.e. national and regional government departments, NGBs, Olympic Councils and specific sport agencies) and that these members do not necessarily share the same ideology on any specific sport policy issue. Nonprofit sport organizations, therefore, operate in a sport policy environment where traditional values of sport (i.e. amateurism, volunteering, community involvement) are promoted but at the same time they are encouraged to become financially self-sufficient in order to reduce their reliance on government assistance by becoming more commercially oriented. Some nonprofit sport organizations are also provided with significant funding for elite athlete programmes and supported to bid for major events in order to secure economic benefits for communities. However, the same organizations receive little direct financial assistance to enhance the quality or quantity of sport experiences available at the community or 'grass roots' level of sport.

Government intervention in sport is generally accepted as having increased in recent years in a number of Commonwealth countries (Oakley & Green, 2001; Green, 2004; Stewart et al., 2004; Thibault & Bibiak, 2005). This intervention has come in the form of increased funding and the development of policies and programmes designed to increase participation rates in organized sport and to improve the performance standards of elite athletes. Oakley and Green (2001: 74) argued that while 'government influence over the sports policy community is increasing' the fragmented nature of government intervention is problematic for nonprofit sport organizations. National sport policies developed by countries such as Australia, Canada, New Zealand and the UK are driven by government agencies with specific responsibility for sport. These agencies may hold little political influence over education or health agencies both of which impact directly on how sport related activities appear in the school curriculum or how sport is used to promote healthy lifestyles. The effect is a fragmented approach to how government as a whole seeks to support, regulate or encourage the activities of nonprofit sport organizations and their boards.

Oakley and Green (2001: 91) concluded that, in the UK at least, there is evidence of the 'emergence of a more discrete and tightly focussed policy community, coalescing around the interests of elite sport (which) suggests the competitive political process has been dominated by narrow performance principles above other interest groups'. In other words, the funding of elite athletes and high-performance programmes has become increasingly accepted as a cornerstone of national sport policy and focus for government intervention. Subsequently the NGBs of the higher profile, mostly Olympic sports, have received the majority of sport funding with a concomitant increase in government expectations being placed on the boards of these organizations to deliver improved elite level performances. Green (2004) explored the impact of these increased expectations on NGBs in England and concluded that the increasing emphasis from government on elite sport performance (supported by increased National Lottery funding) was driving decision-making at the national level of nonprofit sport organizations to the extent that elite sport objectives have assumed 'increasing priority over other conceptions of sports participation' (Green, 2004: 382).

In later work, Green (2005: 161) reaffirmed the view that 'the interests of elite sport development have dominated the sport policy-making process in Australia and Canada over the past 2–3 decades, with a similar scenario emerging in the UK over the past 10 years'. However, the emphasis on elite sport has not been the result of 'sustained bargaining from effective elite sport advocacy coalitions' (Green, 2005: 161). The role of State agencies has been 'crucial in specifying, constructing and maintaining through resource control and dependency the pattern of values and beliefs supportive of elite achievement' (Green, 2005: 161). Nonprofit sport organizations have lobbied for increased funding and support for other areas of sport development such as community sport club development and mass participation programmes. However, Green argues, State agencies have created such a resource dependent relationship with NGBs through the elite sport funding programmes, that other areas of sport policy and the subsequent funding support for them have become marginalized.

The focus of government policy on elite sport has forced nonprofit sport organizations to enter into contractual arrangements with government sport agencies to deliver elite sport or high-performance programme outcomes. The governing boards have therefore had to appoint more paid staff, oversee larger funding pools, monitor a greater range of compliance and reporting requirements and arguably find more appropriately skilled and experienced people to govern their organization. It has also increased the demands for governing boards to find a balance within their organization for meeting their elite sport development goals as well as their obligations to continue to deliver sporting opportunities at the community level.

Governance guidelines

An important element of several Commonwealth countries sport policies has been an effort to improve the governance of National Sport Organizations (NSOs) and their member organizations. As mentioned in Chapter 1, the Australian, New Zealand and UK governments have sought to influence the quality of governance within their respective sport systems by producing governance guidelines (SPARC, 2004; UK Sport, 2004; ASC, 2005). With the significant increases in elite sport funding within these countries, a large proportion of which flows through high-performance programmes managed by NSOs, governments have sought to protect their investment in sport by striving to ensure that NSOs are governed effectively. As a result, the notion of excellence in sport management and governance has become an increasingly prevalent part of government sport policy and is one of the four pillars of the Australian government's sport policy, Backing Australia's Sporting Ability.

In Australia, the ASC operates the Governance and Management Improvement Program (GMIP) designed to direct, assist and support NSOs to address strategic governance and organizational issues. Such assistance takes the form of funding reviews of NSO constitutional and structural arrangements, and board effectiveness; the provision of advice on matters of policy, process and procedures in areas such as financial management, risk management, insurance, information technology and people management and facilitating strategic and business planning, amalgamations, mergers and change management issues. The ASC 2005 publication, *Governing Sport: The role of the board*, provides guidelines for NSOs in areas such as: the role of the board, board responsibilities, carrying out the board's responsibilities, performance monitoring, organizational structures and directors' and officers' insurance.

SPARC operates a programme similar to the ASC's GMIP for its NSOs. Entitled the Leadership and Governance Programme, SPARC published *Nine Steps to Effective Governance* in 2004. The guidelines designed to assist NSOs in areas such as the role of the board, work planning, meeting structures and procedures, strategic planning, the Board – chief executive officer (CEO) relationship, performance monitoring for the organization, board performance, succession planning and the induction process for new board members.

In the UK, the agency responsible for high-performance sport, UK Sport, has undertaken a modernization programme to improve the management and delivery of high-performance sport programmes. A core component of the programme is to improve the governance of NGBs by focussing on three core concepts: leadership and culture, policies and procedures and accountability. In 2004, UK Sport published the *Good Governance Guide for National Governing Bodies*, designed to assist NSOs with a wide range of governance issues. These included: roles, responsibilities and liabilities of board members; the role of the board chair; board member training, performance and evaluation; conflicts of interest; the role of the CEO; Constitution or Articles of Association; the purpose and conduct of meetings; planning and risk management; stakeholder participation and compliance issues.

The governance guidelines promoted by government are based on an assumption that improving the board performance of nonprofit sport organizations will result in better organizational performance. Implicit in these guidelines is the notion that national level organizations influence the activities and performance of member organizations particularly at state/provincial level and to a lesser extent at regional and local levels and that member organizations comply with national directives. Often compliance is not possible as the boards of nonprofit sport organizations must manage one-sided resource exchange relationships between state/provincial and national level sport organizations. However, the compliance sought by NGBs from member organizations is difficult in the absence of real power, as will be discussed in detail in the next chapter.

The nonprofit sport governance guidelines have been either heavily influenced or prepared by organizations operating from a corporate governance frame of reference. For example, the ASC guidelines were based on the Australian Institute of Company Directors governance guidelines and principles. The SPARC guidelines were prepared in partnership with the New Zealand Institute of Company Directors, while the UK Sport guidelines were prepared by the Institute of Chartered Secretaries and Administrators. As argued in Chapter 1, the governance of nonprofit sport organizations is more aligned with the principles nonprofit sector governance than those from corporate governance. It would seem that government agencies seeking to improve the governance of nonprofit sport organizations look first to corporate governance resources, a somewhat ironic situation given the spectacular failures of corporate governance in recent years despite many government reviews and codes of governance introduced for corporate entities.

Globalization

Globalization has been a major force in changing the way sport is produced and consumed. Spectators and television audiences interested in elite sport events such as Olympic and Commonwealth games, world championships and world cups for athletics, swimming, rugby union, cricket and football, the Formula One Grand Prix circuit, as well as high profile competitions such as the English Premier League Football, National Football League and National Basketball Association in North America and Grand Slam tournaments for tennis and golf enjoy unprecedented media coverage. Aside from actually attending the events live at a stadium or competition venue, sport fans can watch these events provided by free to air and pay television networks; listen to them on radio and the internet; access information about favourite players and teams from newspapers and dedicated sport magazines and receive audio and visual progress scores, commentary, highlights packages or real time broadcasts through mobile phone networks. Sport organizations are using technology to expand their marketing reach beyond traditional geographic boundaries, and for the elite events and competitions at least, the global sport marketplace is very competitive.

The impacts of globalization have also resulted in changes to the way elite sport leagues and major international sport events have been governed. It is also evident that the power and influence that some of the leading international governing bodies of sport have acquired in recent years is 'not commensurate with their size and economic contribution' (Westerbeek & Smith, 2003: 31). The impact of the Union of European Football Associations (UEFA) Champions League restructuring and governance reforms in 1992 is an example of globalization having a marked impact on localized sport organizations. The UEFA Champions League provides those clubs who finish near the top of their domestic league competition the opportunity to play in the most financially lucrative football competition in the world. The move to create such a league was made 'in response to commercial forces and the demands of the more economically powerful clubs' (Football Governance Research Centre (FGRC), 2004: 1). This has radically transformed not only the Champions League itself but also had flow on effects on domestic football leagues throughout Europe. The result has been the formation of 'divisions within divisions' where those clubs who regularly play in the Champions League also generate the most profit. The consequences for leading domestic leagues such as the English Premier League and its feeder leagues are profound. According to the FGRC (2004: 2) these changes will 'increase the level of risk as income streams will be more dramatically affected by relegation, and it will also limit the ability of the economically smaller clubs to gain promotion, thus diminishing an element of competitive uncertainty'.

Changes brought about through the forces of globalization such as the UEFA Champions League, for example, present significant challenges for the various governing bodies in football. The leading professional clubs, struggling semi-professional clubs and the amateur clubs and leagues have competing interests and there will 'always be a divergence of interest between the professional game and the amateur game … (on matters such as) … grass roots development, financial stability, or the pursuit of European glory' (FGRC, 2004: 2). Governing bodies for sport therefore need to recognize these competing interests and be 'strong enough to withstand the demands of the more powerful organizations, and be able to govern neutrally and effectively, making decisions that acknowledge the merits of the various respective interests' (FGRC, 2004: 2).

Stakeholder expectations

Sport governing bodies are also confronting environment of heightened expectations from organizational stakeholders for increased transparency and accountability. Sport organizations are subject to scrutiny from their

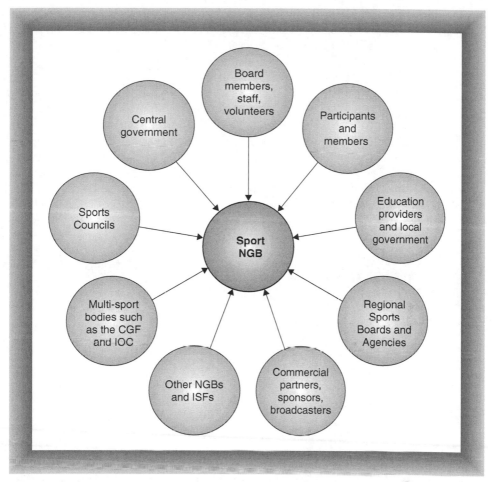

Figure 2.2 Stakeholders for sport NGBs (*Source*: Adapted from UK Sport (2003: 19))

members, sponsors, consumers and government funding agencies who expect the organization to deliver high quality outcomes. The board therefore, must be able to govern the organization in the best interests of the organization and its key stakeholders. UK Sport (2003) identified nine specific groups of stakeholders for sport NGBs (see Figure 2.2).

An illustration of the complexity of governing a national nonprofit sport organization in taking account of stakeholder expectations is provided by the New Zealand Orienteering Federation (NZOF). In a recently developed a set of stakeholder relationship strategies the NZOF identified 29 discrete stakeholder groups with which it aims to develop some form of strategic relationship in order to develop the sport of orienteering on a national basis. The rationale for undertaking this exercise was 'because good governance demands that stakeholder interests be identified and appropriate relationships established' (NZOF, 2005: 4). It is important to note that the NZOF identified both external stakeholders (such as SPARC, Regional Sports Trusts and landowners) and internal stakeholders (such as members, orienteering clubs and affiliated organizations). Finding individuals to act as board members who have the skills, understanding and ability to govern in the interests of all 29 stakeholders highlights the complex nature of governing nonprofit sport organizations.

The FGRC used the stakeholder network concept to analyse the responsibilities of UK football clubs to their various stakeholders and the interaction between stakeholder groups (FGRC, 2005). The network approach facilitated an analysis of 'how the corporate governance of football clubs is affected by multiple stakeholder influences' (FGRC, 2005: 70). The FGRC (2005) identified the typical set of stakeholders that any one football club may have as:

- Football Supporters' Federation
- Federation of Stadium Communities
- Professional Footballers Association
- Supporter's groups
- Football club shareholders
- Supporter's trusts
- Local government authorities
- The Football League
- The Premier League
- Football Association
- Sponsors
- Local community
- The media

While the network approach is helpful in identifying the individual relationships a club may have with its various stakeholders and highlights the myriad of stakeholder demands, it fails to explain the nature, intent or extent of the relationships that might exist or develop between these stakeholders. The FGRC (2005: 71) highlighted the complexity of the stakeholder environment and that it is 'not a series of uncomplicated, individual relationships between a football club and its various stakeholder organizations'.

In summary, stakeholder expectations and the complexity of boards having to deal with these relationships present challenges for individual board members in terms of the requisite skills, experience and understanding needed and for the boards to establish clear systems for communicating with stakeholders. Indeed, the FGRC (2005: 73) found that there is a great deal of evidence to 'suggest that football clubs are not particularly effective at balancing the needs of various stakeholders' with the interests of the organization itself.

Conclusion

In addition to the external influences outlined above, nonprofit sport organization boards must also deal with a range of internal issues that influence the ability of the board to perform their governance function. These include the composition of boards, the processes they use in areas such as conducting meetings or to recruit board members, their governance structure, organizational values and culture, the distribution of leadership within the board and the resource exchange relationships between NGBs and member organizations. The remainder of this book focuses on exploring the internal workings of nonprofit sport organization boards within the context of the external influences outlined in this chapter. In this way the structures, processes and activities undertaken by boards (i.e. the governance system) will be examined in light of what drives boards to adopt and adapt particular systems of organizational governance and their impact on board and organizational performance.

PART TWO

Sport Governance Fundamentals

3

Team structures: governance structures in sport

Overview

This chapter explores the governance structures of nonprofit sport organizations and the related issues for those people working and volunteering in sport. This chapter comprises three parts. First, a description of the elements that comprise the governance structure of nonprofit sport organizations is provided including several examples. Second, the issues related to nonprofit sport organization governance structures are discussed. The final part of the chapter reviews attempts to categorize and analyse the governance structures of nonprofit sport organizations from the perspectives of organizational theory, governance models and inter-organizational relationships (IORs).

Governance structure elements

The governance structure of nonprofit sport organizations generally comprise three elements: the Council, the board, and one or more sub-committees. The Council is made up of the individuals or organizations registered as members and who have been afforded voting rights on the basis of their membership status. The members of a nonprofit sport organization may include individual players or athletes, coaches, officials, administrators, other individuals. In other cases the   are organizations such as clubs that compete in a league run by a regional sports association, or state or provincial sport organizations affiliated to a national governing body. In sports such as squash, basketball or netball organizational members, be they organizations or individuals, may also be commercial facility owners or lessees. Thus, these individual or organizational members form what is more commonly called a Council. Members of the Council are usually responsible for electing, appointing or inviting individuals to act as a director of a board. The board, in turn, is charged with responsibility for making decisions throughout the year on behalf of the Council and the nonprofit sport organization.

The individuals who comprise the board frequently represent and are aligned to the interests of various categories of members categories, geographic regions or sporting sub-disciplines. Increasingly directors in nonprofit sport organizations are independent and not aligned with any particular member category, geographic region or sub-discipline. The board acts as the principal governing forum where the majority of organizational decisions are either made or ratified. To assist the board carry out a range of governance functions, most nonprofit sport organizations operate a system of sub-committees. The remit of sub-committees is to focus on specific issues such as technical rules committees, coach development, financial management, event operations, human resource management or commercial affairs.

Organizations of sufficient size and with requisite resources employ paid staff to manage their day to day affairs. The usual arrangement is for the board to employ a staff member in a Chief Executive Officer (CEO) or similarly titled position that reports directly to the board. Other paid staff report to the CEO and may be employed in positions such as financial managers, marketing personnel, programme, development or support staff. However, the nature of nonprofit sport organizations, often means that paid staff work closely with a network of volunteers who deliver the bulk of the services provided by the organization in areas such as coaching, player and official development, marketing, sport development and event delivery. The volunteers come from within the membership of affiliated or member organizations such as sport clubs and associations.

Watt (2003) outlined eleven characteristics shared by nonprofit sport organizations:

1. They are grant aided with the vast majority of them dependent on national government funding to sustain their operations.
2. They are considered autonomous in the sense that they are largely self-controlling and decide their own strategies despite being dependent on government funding and subject to the views of a myriad of stakeholders.
3. They rely extensively on the time and efforts of volunteers to ensure programmes and services are delivered.
4. National governing bodies (NGBs) fulfil a lobbying role by requesting support and interest in their respective sport on behalf of their participants.
5. Nonprofit sport organizations, especially at club level, rely extensively on member contributions to fund their activities.
6. The volunteers involved in governing the organizations by sitting on committees and performing other duties do so in the spare time, often in addition to their normal form of employment.
7. They rely on their links with public sector bodies such as elite sport institutes and local governments to assist with their activities.
8. As mentioned previously, most of these organizations operate on an individual membership basis but many also have clubs or other organizations as members.
9. Individual members, especially those in key governance roles, are vital for supporting initiatives and ideas that need to be instigated within the member clubs and associations of a sport NGB.
10. They are governed democratically with a general principle of one vote per member but are usually dominated by limited cliques of influential individuals.
11. The decision-making processes are dominated by committees and committee structures, which may be inefficient but enables democratic processes to be enacted.

The following example of how the international sport of cricket is governed illustrates many of the governance structural elements outlined above and the nature of the inter-organizational linkages that exist between club-level, regional, state or provincial, national and an international organization.

International cricket

The international governing body for cricket, the International Cricket Council (ICC), is representative of the complex nature of sport governance

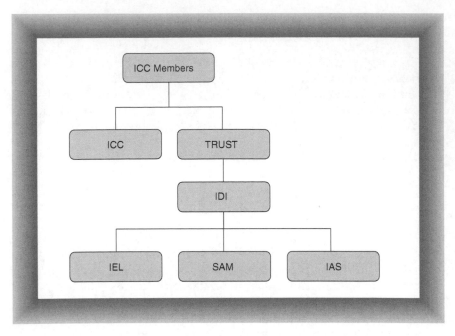

Figure 3.1 Organizational structure of the ICC (*Source*: adapted from ICC (2005: 2))

and the structures of international governing bodies for sport. The ICC began as the Imperial Cricket Conference which was founded in 1909 by Australia, England and South Africa. It changed its name to the International Cricket Conference in 1964, and then to the ICC in 1989. The CEO, Malcolm Speed, stated that 'the ICC is a truly international, multi-cultural and complex business enterprise' (ICC, 2005: 6). With revenues of nearly USD50 million per year, and responsibility for promoting the game as a global sport, protecting the spirit of cricket and optimizing commercial opportunities for the benefit of the game, the ICC governs the sport on behalf of its 96 member countries. The decisions and actions taken by the ICC, as the international governing body, directly impact on the ability of NGBs to develop the game within their respective nations.

The organizational structure of the ICC is outlined in Figure 3.1. The ICC is a company registered in the British Virgin Islands with a share capital of USD1 and undertakes no transactions. The 10 Full Members, 32 Associate Members and 54 Affiliate Members have established a Trust that operates ICC Development (International) Limited (IDI) a company that in turn, has three subsidiary companies: ICC Administrative Services (UK) Limited (IAS); ICC Cricket Management SAM (SAM); and ICC (Events) Limited (IEL). These three companies provide administrative services to the ICC, manage the cricket development activities undertaken around the world, and manage the commercial rights to cricket events owned by ICC members. The IAS is the largest component of the ICC and comprises staff grouped into seven operational areas: the Anti-Corruption and Security Unit, Corporate Affairs, Cricket Operations, Development, Human Resources and Administration, Internal Audit, and Legal. In addition, the IDI operates two divisions: Financial Control and Commercial.

The governance structure of the ICC comprises 9 committees (see Figure 3.2). The three most important committees are the ICC Annual Conference, the ICC Executive Board and IDI Board of Directors (these two comprise the same individuals), and the ICC Chief Executives' Committee. The ICC Annual Conference meets annually. Its major role is to ratify the appointment of the ICC President and acceptance of new member countries. The ICC Executive Board and IDI Board of Directors are the key policy forums for international cricket with its membership comprising the Presidents and Chairman of the 10 Full ICC Member countries plus three elected representatives from the Associate Member countries. The ICC Chief Executives' Committee is 'the key forum for making recommendations on the business of cricket' (ICC, 2005: 52) and comprises the CEOs of the 10 Full ICC Member countries plus three elected representatives from the Associate Member countries. Six further committees fulfil specific governance functions: ICC Cricket Committee, Audit Committee, Code of Conduct Commission, Development Committee, Human Resources, Remuneration and Appointments Committee, and a Governance Review Committee.

The importance of governance within the ICC was highlighted by the ICC President, Ehsan Mani, who said that 'a successful (sport development) framework begins with an effective system of governance' (ICC, 2005: 2). Further, the Governance Review Committee of the ICC had brought in a number of changes to 'improve the professionalism and effectiveness of the ICC's decision-making processes and ensure the ICC has the people in place with the necessary skills and experience to take it forward' (ICC, 2005: 2). The governance structure of the ICC facilitates decision-making by its members. The voting rights and membership of the various committees reflects the relative importance of each of the membership categories within the organization. Most of the ICC committees link directly to the teams of operational staff employed within the subsidiary companies (IAS and IDI). This enables discrete areas of ICC operations to report to and receive instruction from (via the CEO of the ICC) a specific purpose group of stakeholders charged with decision-making responsibility in a particular strategic area.

The ICC maintains relationships with each of the 96 NGBs for cricket that comprise its membership. Cricket Australia, one of three founding members of the ICC, is the national governing body for cricket in Australia. Its members include the six state cricket associations, with the two territory associations having non-member status. Cricket Australia is governed by a

ICC Sub-Committee	Membership	Main functions
ICC Annual Conference	Delegates of all 96 Full, Associate and Affiliate member governing bodies	Ratify major decisions, appoint ICC President, accept new member countries
ICC Executive Board and IDI Board of Directors	Presidents or Chairmen of the 10 Full Members and 3 representatives from the Associate Members	Key policy body for international cricket, responsible for the major financial and commercial policies
ICC Chief Executives' Committee	CEOs of the 10 Full Members and 3 representatives from the Associate Members	Key forum for making recommendations on the business of cricket, refers policy to the Executive Board for approval
ICC Cricket Committee	Five people nominated by the players of Full Member teams, Five people nominated by the boards of Full Member teams, One nominated by the players of Associate Member teams, One nominated by the boards of Associate Member teams, plus the President and CEO of ICC	Makes recommendations to the CEC on matters of the game of cricket
Audit Committee	Representatives from 2 Full Members, an Independent appointment and an Alternate appointment, plus the President and CEO of the ICC	Review the ICC's financial reporting process, internal controls, risk management, audit process and compliance issues
Code of Conduct Commission	A nominated representative from each of the Full Member countries	Oversees formal enquiries into conduct which may be prejudicial to the interests of the game and makes recommendations to the
ICC		Executive Board
Development Committee	One nominated representative from each	Reviews and monitors all policy matters relating to the

Figure 3.2 Sub-committees of the ICC (*Source*: adapted from ICC (2005))

ICC Sub-Committee	Membership	Main functions
	of the five ICC regions, an MCC delegate, an Associate Member delegate, the Chair of the ICC Women's Committee, plus the CEO of the ICC	structure and delivery of the ICC Global Development Program
HR, Remuneration and Appointments Committee	Representatives from two Full Members, a representative from one Associate Member, plus the President and CEO of the ICC	Responsible for reviewing and monitoring all policy matters relating to the ICC's human resources
Governance Review Committee	Representatives from two Full Members, a representative from one Associate Member, plus the President and CEO of the ICC	Reviews the ICC governance structures and makes recommendations to the ICC Executive Board on the effectiveness of organizational decision-making processes

Figure 3.2 (Continued)

board of 14 elected directors who are appointed by their respective state associations, and has more than 60 full-time staff. The number of directors on the board from each of the member associations includes 1 from Tasmania, 2 each from Queensland and Western Australia, and 3 each from New South Wales, South Australia and Victoria (see Figure 3.3). The organizational structure of Cricket Australia comprises seven departments: executive with responsibility for supporting the board and CEO, commercial operations, cricket operations, finance and administration, game development, legal and business affairs, and public affairs. Notwithstanding differences in organizational size and capability, the governing bodies for cricket in other nations largely perform similar functions and many have similar representative-based governance systems in place.

Cricket Australia works closely with its state association members and affiliated territory members. Queensland Cricket is the governing body for cricket in the State of Queensland. Its members include the various organizations that administer cricket competition and participation opportunities throughout the state. These involve junior cricket, public and private school systems, church-based competitions, indoor cricket, country (non-metropolitan) competitions, as well as organizations representing umpires

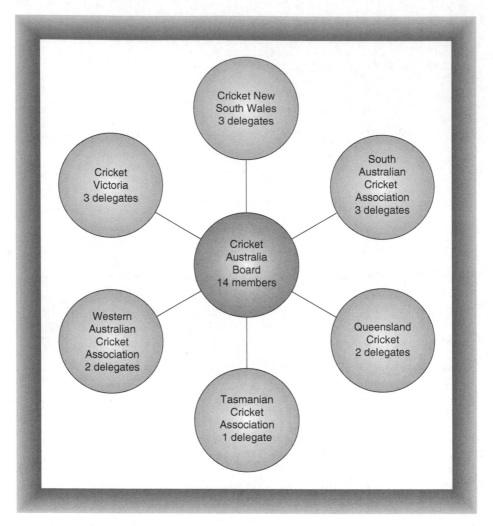

Figure 3.3 Cricket Australia Board of Directors

and scorers and the clubs involved in the premier district club competition. These members form a Delegates Council who elect a board of 9 directors to govern Queensland Cricket on behalf of its individual members and member organizations. The organizational structure of Queensland Cricket comprises six departments: Administration, marketing, game development, finance, information technology and the management of Queensland Cricket office. Most other state associations responsible for governing cricket perform similar functions and have adopted largely representative systems of governance.

In summary, at each level of cricket, individual members and member organizations are, through various means, able to be involved in governance of the sport. Members are able to vote within Council structures to appoint Boards that make decisions, for the term of their appointment or election, on their behalf on a regular basis. The governance of cricket operates as an internationally federated network under the ICC umbrella. The majority of NGBs for cricket also operate as federated networks within their own nations with state or provincial associations as members. The state or provincial associations in turn work with regional and local associations and clubs to deliver the sport cricket at the community level.

Governance structure issues

The ICC example and the various levels of organizations within the governance structure of cricket provide a useful background for exploration and analysis of a number of internal governance issues and IORs that exist within international sport governing bodies. Hoye, Smith, Westerbeek, Stewart and Nicholson (2006: 169) noted that the typical governance structure adopted by nonprofit sport organizations 'has been criticized for being unwieldy and cumbersome, slow to react to changes in market conditions, subject to potentially damaging politics or power plays between delegates, and imposing significant constraints on organizations wishing to change'. Despite these limitations many sport-governing bodies use governance structures with similarities to the ICC because such structures enable members to be directly involved or have their interests represented in decision-making processes. At the same time such governance structures allow sport-governing bodies at various levels (i.e. club, regional, state/provincial and national) to maintain a degree of operational autonomy. However, these structural arrangements raise several issues for nonprofit sport organizations, such as professional staff and volunteer relationships and the challenges of achieving compliance within complex IORs.

The governance structures of nonprofit sport organizations have been conceptualized and analysed largely from three different perspectives: organizational theory, governance models and IORs. Each of these perspectives provides a useful lens to examine significant and recurring issues in the governance structures of nonprofit sport organizations. The organizational theory perspective analyses governance issues through the processes of formalization, centralization, specialization, departmentalization and structural isomorphism. From the governance models perspective issues in the governance of nonprofit sport organizations are analysed through idealized governance policies, systems and processes. Governance structures have also been conceptualized and analysed from the perspective of IORs. The key concepts and published research findings in relation to each of these perspectives is presented in the following sections.

Organizational theory

The application of organizational theory to the analysis of the governance structures within nonprofit sport organizations has focused on the impacts and process of professionalization that has occurred within nonprofit sport organizations, categorizing organizations, and exploring the relationship of structure with size, conflict and organizational change. The vast majority of sport governance research has been conducted on Canadian provincial and national sport organizations (NSOs). Other research has been completed in Australia and the UK. The impacts of introducing paid staff to nonprofit sport organizations was first explored by Slack (1985) and has since been a constant focus of sport management research. While the process and impacts of professionalization are discussed in more detail in Chapter 9, they are briefly addressed here in relation to the governance structures of nonprofit sport organizations. The introduction of paid staff into nonprofit sport organizations has, to a large extent, been in response to increases in government funding for sport. Government sport policy has increasingly led nonprofit sport organizations to develop specialized high performance and elite programmes as well as investing in a range of sport development activities, which in turn, has led sport organizations to employ paid staff to manage these programmes and allied resources. The impact of professionalization on the structure of Canadian provincial sport organizations was explored by Thibault, Slack and Hinings (1991) who found that specialization and formalization increased after the introduction of professional staff. They also found that centralization, after initially increasing, actually decreased over time. This was possibly because volunteer board members initially sought to retain control over decisions, and then allowed professionals to make some decisions as the relationship between board members and staff stabilized. The inherent resistance to changes on the part of volunteers in governance structures was also noted by Kikulis, Slack and Hinings (1995b). Since this work, the nature of the relationship between paid staff and volunteers in governance roles has been studied extensively, and is discussed at length in Chapter 9.

One of the earliest reported studies was conducted by Frisby (1986) who explored the relationship between a range of structural variables and organizational performance of Canadian NGBs. Her findings suggested that 'bureaucracy is an effective method of managerial control' (Frisby, 1986: 69) within nonprofit sport organizations. Kikulis, Slack, Hinings and Zimmermann (1989) developed a taxonomy of eight structural design archetypes for provincial Canadian sport governing bodies using the organizational structure dimensions of specialization, standardization and centralization. They found that 'important relationships among the variables composing structure indeed exist and importantly influence the feasibility of establishing consistent structural designs' (Kikulis et al., 1989: 146). Their work established that the governance structure adopted by nonprofit sport organizations is dependent on the level of professionalization (i.e. employment of paid staff) and the degree of bureaucratization (i.e. use of formalized and standardized processes). They argued that the impacts of these processes were felt differently by organizations that exhibited different structural design archetypes.

Based on organizational values and organizational structure variables, Kikulis, Slack and Hinings (1992) categorized design archetypes of NGBs into three distinct designs – kitchen table, boardroom and executive office. Organizational values included the extent of orientation toward private or public interests, the scope of activities conducted between community and elite sport, the degree of involvement in decision making held by professional staff, and the criteria used by the organization to evaluate effectiveness. The organizational structure variables of specialization, standardization and centralization were the same as used in the earlier study by Kikulis et al. (1989). Organizations of the kitchen table archetype focussed on securing funds through traditional fundraising and membership contributions, delivered both mass and high performance sporting opportunities, had few if any staff in decision making roles, and judged organizational performance by the extent to which they met member expectations. Organizations in this category used few rules and did little planning. Decisions were dominated by a few volunteers and the roles adopted by volunteers were based on their personal interests. At the other extreme, the executive office archetype organizations focussed on securing government grants and corporate sponsorship, emphasized high performance sport, were dominated by professional staff, and judged performance by their level of success in international competition. The executive office design archetype had many specialized staff, used formal roles, rules and programmes, and decisions were decentralized to paid staff. Theodoraki and Henry (1994) adopted a similar approach in their attempt to develop a typology of British NGBs. They identified six clusters of NGBs which they designated titles based on Mintzberg's organizational structures, ranging from machine bureaucracy to simple structure. The majority of the organizations in their study were found to be variations of Mintzberg's simple structure, highlighting the high level of involvement by volunteers in governance roles within these organizations.

Organizational theory suggests that the organizational forms or structures adopted by nonprofit sport organizations tend to become similar to the extent that they are subjected to similar internal and external forces. DiMaggio and Powell (1983) designated this expected similarity as structural isomorphism and argued that such isomorphism may result from coercive (coercion based on power differences), mimetic (imitation of successful organizations) or normative (influence of professionals or experts) influences. As discussed earlier, sport organizations, particularly at the state or provincial and NGB levels, are largely dependent on government funding and are frequently encouraged to adopt governance guidelines developed by government. These coercive forces tend to push these organizations towards adopting similar solutions to governance issues, including similar structural arrangements. Nonprofit sport organizations are frequently made aware of innovative governance practices and the successes of other sport organizations by governments and industry organizations and hence are subject to mimetic forces. These organizations are also becoming more professionalized, employing more paid staff in key positions, and are thus subject to normative pressures which also drive them towards structural isomorphism.

Despite these coercive, mimetic and normative pressures, Henry and Theodoraki (2000: 501) argued that nonprofit sport organizations have not adopted 'a single set of organizational structures or strategies, even within a given national context'. A study of governance reforms within horse racing in Australia by Hoye (2006a) found that while the various state level governing bodies were subject to similar industry and government pressures for reform, there existed six distinctly different organizational forms among the eight organizations. This apparent lack of structural isomorphism evident in nonprofit sport organizations is also evident in the wider nonprofit field. Leiter (2005: 27) found a higher than expected degree of heterogeneity in the structures of Australian nonprofit organizations, concluding that best practice had not become widespread and that 'ultimately efficient and productive organizational methods have not yet been discovered, disseminated, and institutionalized'.

In a study of four Canadian sport NGBs, Amis, Slack and Berrett (1995) found that structural issues were a major contributing factor to conflict. They argued that nonprofit sport organizations are subject to pressures of increased efficiency and specialization. This leads to differentiation and interdependence of organizational sub-units which 'adds considerably to the potential for conflict' (Amis et al., 1995: 14). Nonprofit sport organizations operate under a combination of volunteer leadership and professional expertise, with each party having differing values and expectations. These organizations also have a lower level of formalization and resource provision relative to commercial organizations, which contributes to exacerbating the potential for conflict within sport organizations. Watt (2003) noted that the study by Amis et al. (1995) highlighted that while conflict often manifests as disputes between individuals, it occurs due to their membership or allegiance to conflicting sub-units of the organization, which suggests that the cause of conflict is often structural. This phenomenon is further explored in later chapters.

Organizational theory states that as organizations grow they become more formalized, with more specialist roles and departments and more levels of management compared to smaller organizations. Accordingly, as organizational size increases decision-making should become more decentralized. Amis and Slack (1996) explored this premise within Canadian sport NGBs, and found that as these organizations increased in size, control over organizational decision-making remained centralized at the voluntary board level. Their study concluded that a 'central role of decision making as a means of control and the desire for volunteers to retain this control' (Amis & Slack, 1996: 84) meant that the boards of these organizations were reluctant to relinquish control to professional staff. Amis and Slack (1996: 84) attributed this (in part) to the 'levels of mistrust and antagonism that often exist between the professional workers and their volunteer superiors'.

The final application of organizational theory to the study of structural issues within nonprofit sport organizations has been to the study of change. Kikulis et al. (1995a; 1995b; 1995c) explored the patterns of organizational change influenced by federal government requirements within 36 Canadian NGBs between 1984 and 1988. They utilized the concept of centralization to explain: the structural changes that occurred within the organizations over this period (Kikulis et al., 1995a); the role of values in defining the manner in which the organizations changed (Kikulis et al., 1995b); and, what impact human agents and choices had in determining the nature of structural change (Kikulis et al., 1995c). The key findings from the research were that as organizations move toward the executive archetype outlined earlier, volunteers become less involved in decision-making processes and paid staff become more involved. This may be problematic because while a change in the level of decision making is required for an organization to move into the executive office archetype, the shift in values associated with moving decision making control into the hands of professional staff may not occur at the same time. This highlights the importance of the informal decision-making structures that exist within nonprofit sport organizations. Kikulis et al. (1995a: 297) noted that 'it will take a long time before professionally led decision making displaces values for volunteer-led decision making so deeply embedded in the history of these organizations'.

In summary, the application of organizational theory to the analysis of the structure of nonprofit sport organizations has focused on categorizing organizations, and exploring relationships between structure, size, conflict and change. The issues and challenges posed by the governance structures of nonprofit sport organizations also have implications for issues that are addressed in subsequent chapters such as the relationships between paid staff and volunteers, leadership within the boards of these organizations, and achieving governance reforms.

Governance models

The governance structures of nonprofit sport organizations and associated issues they present have also been conceptualized as models of governance. Governance models can be defined as a set of policies and systems that outline the responsibilities of the various governance elements, and the processes used to carry out the governance function, including matters such as the relationship between the CEO and the board and the role of the board. Three issues are apparent from the literature on governance models. First, is the debate over the merits of nonprofit organizations adopting the corporate model of governance and the differences between corporate and nonprofit systems of governance. Second, is the discussion of differences between three types of nonprofit governance: the traditional model, executive-led model and the policy governance model. Third, are concerns about the application of governance models designed for larger nonprofit organizations with paid staff to the vast array of voluntary sport associations that operate entirely with voluntary labour. Each of these issues is explored in this section.

The corporate model of governance, as outlined by Hodgkin (1993), includes a strong CEO who is a voting member of the board, has complete administrative authority over the organization, and a board that focuses solely on employing and evaluating the performance of the CEO and setting the broad organizational policy direction. Hodgkin (1993: 416) argued that adopting such a 'corporate model would be a dangerous error for nonprofit organizations' and that the governance model of any organization should meet the needs and purposes of the organization. Hodgkin outlined three important differences between corporate and nonprofit organizations that affect their governance, all of which are relevant to the governance of nonprofit sport organizations. First, the lack of a profit motive within nonprofit organizations means the board of a nonprofit organization must continually return to the question of defining its mission and balancing the values and demands of its various constituent members. Accordingly, the measurement of a multi-faceted mission requires boards to make value judgements, to prioritize its strategic focus, to be involved in detailed policy decisions, and to exercise greater control over the decisions made by paid staff to ensure they are made within the policies and priorities set by the board. Second, nonprofit organizations should meet the moral expectations of their members and demonstrate high levels of accountability to stakeholders. Finally, nonprofit organizations have to service a wider range of constituencies than corporations. Hodgkin (1993: 423) argues that 'balancing the organization's response to these constituencies is the job of the nonprofit board, and the balancing process must be incorporated into the governing structure'.

Alexander and Weiner (1998: 237) identified that the 'arguments advanced in support of adopting corporate or business practices are based on the premise that such practices will rescue nonprofit organizations from financial crises or improve their competitive positions in their markets'. However, not all nonprofit organizations will

48

find the corporate governance model appropriate because the priorities and design principles it embodies run counter to the institution's missions, values, and relationships with key stakeholders … (or be in a position to adopt it due to) … strong pressures to adhere to traditional values of voluntarism, constituent representation, and stewardship.

(Alexander & Weiner, 1998: 239).

The example of the ICC provided earlier in this chapter highlighted that nonprofit sport organizations are governed through a high level of voluntary input, a delegate representative system at all levels of the sport, and a sense of stewardship in looking after the code of cricket and the values embodied through participating in the sport. While nonprofit sport organizations should attempt to conduct their affairs in an efficient, effective and even business-like manner, their missions and structures require that their governance policies and systems adhere to a nonprofit governance model rather than the adoption of a corporate model.

The second issue related to governance models concerns discussion of the differences between the traditional governance model outlined by Houle (1960, 1997); the policy governance model developed by Carver (1997); and the executive-led model (after Drucker, 1990a; Herman & Heimovics, 1990a; 1990b; 1994; Block, 1998). The traditional governance model is based on five elements. First, a systematic board member recruitment process is used along with on-going board member development so that the human potential of the board is maximized. Second, the board operates within a set of by-laws and policies and that the minutes of board and committee meetings are consistently reported. Third, the roles of the board, CEO and other paid staff (and the relationships between them) are clearly defined to facilitate clear decision-making. Fourth, the board should work hard to develop a positive culture, adopt an annual work plan, have regular meetings with well-managed agendas and conduct an on-going evaluation of its work and the contributions of individual board members. Finally, the board should focus on maintaining external relationships with its various stakeholders. Fletcher (1999: 435) summarized that in this model 'the work is done by the staff, the administration by management and the policy making by the board; in this traditional model, the board is truly in charge of the organization'. Arguably, this model is used by most nonprofit sport organizations as it clearly separates the tasks of staff and volunteers and highlights volunteer board members as being ultimately accountable for the stewardship of the organization.

Two of the leading researchers into nonprofit governance have criticized this model for the idealistic view that the board alone has ultimate responsibility for the organization (Heimovics & Herman, 1990) and the rather simplistic notion of the board making policy while the staff do the work (Herman & Heimovics, 1990b). Herman and Heimovics (1990b) argued that this does not reflect the reality of the working relationships that occur in most nonprofit organizations and the prominence of the executive or

CEO in providing leadership to nonprofit sport organizations and their boards. Drucker (1990a) argued that the ultimate responsibility for the performance of a nonprofit organization, including its governance, should rest with the executive. Herman and Heimovics' (1990b) study found that the reality of most boards was that they depended on their executive for information almost exclusively and looked to them to provide leadership. Similar conclusions were made by Hoye and Cuskelly (2003b) and Hoye (2004, 2006b) in studies of leadership within the boards of nonprofit sport organizations.

The policy governance model is an alternative to the traditional and executive-led models. Originally developed by Carver (1997) the policy governance model focuses on five elements. First, the board should determine the mission and strategic direction of the organization, with a focus on the desired outcomes, and leave the development of the means to achieve them to the CEO and paid staff. Second, the board should set broad limitations to the decision-making power of the CEO and constraints for the work practices (or means) that staff use to achieve the mission set by the board. Third, the board has to clarify the respective role of the board and CEO and how the relationship will work between them. Fourth, the board should define how key the governance processes such as board member selection and succession and the reporting of activities of the board and staff should operate. Finally, the role of the board should focus more on defining and measuring clear performance criteria related to strategic outcomes rather than simply ensuring organizational compliance with financial management standards and ethical management practices. The policy governance model has attracted criticism for its 'idealized view of the board, operating above the messiness of the board–executive relationship as it really exists in nonprofit organizations' (Fletcher, 1999: 436). While each of the three models of nonprofit governance models focus on different aspects of governance, they clearly provide a better fit with the governance structures of nonprofit sport organizations board than the profit-focussed corporate model.

The final issue in relation to governance models concerns the utility of these models to the vast array of voluntary associations that operate entirely with voluntary labour. Nonprofit sport organizations at the community or 'grass-roots' level of sport such as local sport clubs and associations are run informally and reflect the social nature of the volunteer experience. These organizations are categorized as member-benefit organizations because they are created, developed and maintained by the individuals (i.e. athletes, players or participants) and those most closely connected to them (i.e. family or friends) who both produce and consume the services provided by the organization (Smith, 1993). Organizational members have the opportunity to be involved in governing their organization by being elected, appointed or invited to serve on the board and to vote at elections. Smith (1999) argued that the majority of nonprofit organizations fall into this category as they are predominantly volunteer run, employ few if any staff, and are governed by volunteers. Thus, the utility of governance models focussed on the relationship between the board and paid staff and on the board setting policy rather than dealing with operational issues is limited. Hoye and Inglis (2003) argued that the majority of research on non-profit sport organization structures had focused on larger organizations that employ paid staff, with the result that not much is known about how smaller nonprofit sport organizations are governed or indeed how the governance models might be adaptable to their particular governance structures.

Inter-organizational relationships

The sport system is defined by most people who work within it as a 'pyramid' structure in which the international and NGBs work with their respective affiliated state or provincial, regional and local member organizations. However, this conceptualisation fails to acknowledge the complexity of the IORs that exist within the current system. The relationships between ISFs, NGBs and state or provincial, regional and local level sport organizations do not operate as top-down power hierarchies. Organizations positioned at lower levels in the hierarchy do not always comply fully with the directives and policies of the organizations in which they are a member. The IORs that operate between the various organizational levels in sport require a spirit of cooperation and negotiation in order to operate effectively and efficiently. Thus the volunteers who are elected or appointed to governance roles within nonprofit sport organizations must act in the best interests of the organization they represent. The complexity of the IORs within sport systems is reflected in a range of organizational governance issues including: structural inefficiencies, the nature of paid staff and volunteer relationships, resource exchange between national and state organizations, compliance with national initiatives, decision-making and strategic planning, and meeting government funding requirements.

The IORs within the sport systems of nations such as Australia, Canada, New Zealand and the UK can be conceptualized in the majority of cases as federations, with each NGB acting as a 'unique administrative body or coordinating agency called a federated management organization (FMO)' (Fleisher, 1991: 116). Sport federations represent a unique yet common form of inter-organizational collaborative network. A federation 'differs from other linkage networks with respect to the control and management, or governance, of its activities' (Fleisher, 1991: 117). The federated structural arrangements between NGBs and state or provincial organizations typically take one of three forms: (1) participatory federations where state affiliates maintain an active role in federation management through involvement with the NSO, (2) independent federations where the NGB is not controlled by affiliates or (3) mandated federations in which state organizations may be forced to affiliate with a NGB (Fleisher, 1991). A small number of sports have adopted a unitary structure where state bodies are limited to an advisory role at the national level. Federated networks within nonprofit sport have not been studied extensively apart from early work by Stern (1979) and later by Mitchell, Crosset and Barr (1999), who both examined the operation of the National Collegiate Athletic Association (NCAA) in the USA. Studies of federated networks and IORs within the wider non-profit sector are also limited (see, e.g. Young, 1989; Oster, 1992, 1996; Young, Bania & Bailey, 1996; Grossman & Rangan, 2001).

The complex nature of the IORs between sport governing bodies and allied attempts by government to influence the development of IORs has focussed attention on institutional pressures and resource dependency within sport systems. There has been extensive theorizing (e.g. institutional, resource dependency and agency theory) and empirical research reported in the wider management and organizational theory literature about these concepts and their applications (Eisenhardt, 1989; Oliver, 1990, 1991). The application of these theories to nonprofit sport organizations has been limited to the Canadian sport system and has focused largely on *intra*-organizational research reported earlier in this chapter (cf. Thibault et al., 1991; Slack & Hinings, 1992, 1994; Kikulis et al., 1995a; 1995b; 1995c; Thibault & Harvey, 1997). There has been very little research that has sought to extend the application of these theories to exploring IORs within sport systems.

Research and debate on IORs typically represents the range of compli-ance strategies as a simple dichotomy of sanctions and compensation or rewards (see, e.g. Padilla & Baumer, 1994; Deschriver & Stotlar, 1996; Bridgman & Davis, 2000). Such a simplistic analytical framework fails to address the full range of possible compliance strategies that could be employed as well as contextual governance factors such organizational capabilities, opportunities, perceptions and information flows. Mitchell et al. (1999) identified six possible strategies that sport leagues could use to encourage compliance from member organizations and illustrated their application to the NCAA. Mitchell et al. (1999) described these strategies as: punitive – punish non-compliant organizations; remunerative – reward member organizations for compliance; preventive – threaten to lock member organizations from participating in a programme; generative – create opportunities for involvement in a policy area; cognitive – provide infor-mation to increase awareness of the benefits of compliance; and norma-tive – teach organizations the correct way to operate. The success of national talent identification systems, elite athlete support programmes, volunteer, coach and official education and development programmes, and other sport development programmes are dependent on the ability of NGBs to achieve compliance from their federation members. The majority of sport federations were initially created by state or provincial organizations agreeing to create a national body. However, many of these federations have evolved to a structure where the NGB in responding to various external pressures seeks compliance from its state or provincial members.

Using institutional and resource dependence perspectives Oliver (1991: 145) developed 'a typology of strategic responses that vary in active organizational resistance from passive conformity to pro-active manipulation'. Oliver (1991) proposed that organizations may: (1) conform or acquiesce, (2) compromise, (3) comply symbolically by attempting to conceal nonconformity or minimize external evaluation, (4) actively resist pressures or (5) attempt to manipulate or change the pressure being applied. The response adopted by an organization is dependent on a mix of internal organizational characteristics and IORs. The nature of IORs differs according to the type of federation governance structure within a particular sport which range from affiliates maintaining an active role in federation management (participatory federation), affiliates relinquishing control to the FMO (independent federation) or affiliates being forced to form a federation (mandated federation) (Fleisher, 1991).

Conclusion

This chapter has explored the governance structures of nonprofit sport organizations and the associated issues that they present for those people working and volunteering in sport. Nonprofit sport organizations are reliant to some extent on government funding, and have a variety of membership structures which either facilitate or inhibit involvement in decision-making and governance activities. They also rely on volunteers to govern, manage and administer their operations from international to local levels. However, there are differences in the degree of formalization, specialization and centralization that exist within the structures of these organizations. Attempts to categorize nonprofit sport organizations have illustrated the varied nature of nonprofit sport organizations at all levels of the sport system. The organizations must deal with a number of structural issues such as a heightened potential for conflict, the need to manage professionalization and changes processes within sport, the impacts of government policy, and industry-wide changes as the sport industry becomes more commercially orientated. It also apparent that a number of different governance models exist that can be applied to nonprofit sport organizations. Finally, nonprofit sport organizations must manage a complex array of IORs which further complicates the execution of the governance function.

4

Team positions: governance roles and responsibilities

Overview

Defining the governance roles and responsibilities of the board, individual board members, the board chair and paid staff is important to enable appropriate decision-making to take place within an organization and to ensure accountability. This chapter explores the role of the board and the individuals involved in governing roles through an examination of reported research on board roles, governance guidelines and examples from nonprofit sport organizations. It examines the role of nonprofit sport organization boards and how board roles and responsibilities are allocated within these organizations.

The chapter is presented in four parts. First, the roles of nonprofit boards and widely prescribed board member and paid staff roles within the context of nonprofit organizations are reviewed. Second, the body of published research on the role of the nonprofit boards and board members is examined. Third, the recommended governance roles of nonprofit sport organizations are examined through a review of the limited amount of research on the role of nonprofit sport organization boards together

with examples of how these roles are conducted. Finally, the pre-scribed roles for individuals involved in nonprofit sport organizations are explored along with the debate over the allocation of portfolio responsibilities within boards.

The role of nonprofit boards

There have been many statements developed that articulate a vision for the set of activities in which a nonprofit board should be involved. Summarized by Fishel (2003: 10) these include:

- attending board meetings and organizational activities;
- approval of the mission, participating in the planning process;
- selection and evaluation of the chief executive officer (CEO);
- ensuring legal and financial obligations are being met;
- support and oversight of programmes;
- assistance with fundraising;
- assurance of board effectiveness;
- community relations and advocacy, representing the organization.

This list provides a useful overview of the activities boards should undertake. However, it does not distinguish how the role of a board differs from paid staff in these areas of organizational work, apart from the task of selecting and evaluating the CEO. Nor does this list explain what the board should actually do within each of these areas of activity. Fishel (2003) suggested that in order to fully explain the role of the board it is necessary to define the purpose for which nonprofit organizations exist. Anheier (2005) defined the purpose of a nonprofit board as ensuring that an organization carries out its mission without striving to make a profit as a result of that process and to make sure that the benefits the organization creates accrue to its members or the individuals it purports to serve.

Authors such as Saidel (2002) and Iecovich (2004) have highlighted that the foundation for defining the purpose of boards and therefore the roles they are required to fulfil are largely dictated by law. As discussed in Chapter 2, nonprofit organizations are subject to specific legislative and regulatory frameworks. For example, nonprofit organizations based in Victoria, Australia must comply with the Associations Incorporations Act 1981 and the Association Incorporation Regulations 1998. The only reference the Act makes to the roles of the committee (board) is the stipulation that board members must not knowingly or recklessly make improper use of their position for their own gain or cause detriment to the organization.

The Association Incorporation Regulations further state that the committee (board) shall control and manage the business and affairs of the organization.

The difficulty for nonprofit organizations is that while such legislation and associated regulations define the major responsibilities of boards they do not stipulate how they should be accomplished. Consequently, a number of umbrella groups representing nonprofit organizations in various areas of activity have developed guidelines for the role of the board. A prominent example is the guide entitled *Good governance: A code for the voluntary and community sector* and produced by the UK based National Council for Voluntary Organizations (NCVO) in 2005. This guide defined the board as a board of trustees, that 'have and must accept ultimate responsibility for directing the affairs of their organization, ensuring it is solvent, well-run and delivering the outcomes for which it has been set up' (NCVO, 2005: 10). The guide prescribed six roles of the board:

1. The board should have a statement of its strategic and leadership roles, and of key functions that cannot be delegated. These should include as a minimum:
    (a) ensuring compliance with the objects, purposes and values of the organization, and with its governing document;
    (b) setting or approving policies, plans and budgets to achieve those objectives, and monitoring performance against them;
    (c) ensuring the solvency, financial strength and good performance of the organization;
    (d) ensuring that the organization complies with all the relevant laws, regulations and requirements of its regulators;
    (e) dealing with the appointment (and if necessary the dismissal) of the organization's chief executive;
    (f) setting and maintaining a framework of delegation and internal control; and
    (g) agreeing or ratifying all policies and decisions on matters which might create significant risk to the organization, financial or otherwise.
2. The board must ensure that the organization's vision, mission and values and activities remain true to its objects.
3. Trustees are bound by an overriding duty, individually and as a board, to act reasonably at all times in the interests of the organization and of its present and future beneficiaries or (in the case of a membership organization) members.
4. All trustees are equally responsible in law for the board's actions and decisions, and have equal status as trustees.
5. Each and every trustee must act personally, and not as the representative of any group or organization; this applies regardless of how that person was nominated, elected or selected to become a trustee.

6. The trustees must ensure that they remain independent, and do not come under the control of any external organization or individual. (NCVO, 2005: 10–11).

Such prescriptive lists of roles and responsibilities and guidelines are commonplace. Indeed, Saidel (2002: 8) noted that 'the literature is replete with such lists'. Saidel (2002: 8) also identified a 'gap or disconnect between prescribed roles and actual behaviour' of boards and board members. The behaviour of nonprofit boards and the roles undertaken by board members has attracted a great deal of attention from researchers in recent years. It is this body of research that is now reviewed in order to further explore the role of the board and board members in the governance of nonprofit organizations.

Research on roles within nonprofit boards

Harris (1989) was one of the first authors to articulate the problems that nonprofit boards have in enacting their governance role in the context of prescriptions from legislation, regulations and codes of conduct. She argued that 'despite the existence of these formal documents and pre-scriptions, there is evidence that a number of problems and issues surround the implementation of the governing role in the voluntary sector' (Harris, 1989: 317). In a study of the workings of the UK Citizens Advice Bureau (CAB), Harris (1989) identified 6 main functions of local level CAB management committees that were articulated amongst a variety of internal documents. They were: securing resources, legal responsibilities, representation, policymaking, monitoring and staffing. For each of these six functions, Harris (1989: 325) found there was a 'gap between official agency statements about the management committee role and functions, on the one hand, and the perceptions of the role and the working assumptions formulated by committee members and staff, on the other hand'. While the existence of such a discrepancy is not unusual, this can result in 'misunderstandings and conflicts between groups and individuals' (Harris, 1989: 326) in relation to the performance of governing roles.

The organizational culture of nonprofit voluntary organizations was identified as a distinctive feature facilitating the development of such problems. Harris (1989: 329) argued that the CAB volunteer committee members placed a high degree of trust in paid staff which subsequently discouraged them 'from any kind of monitoring activity' for fear of being perceived as interfering or being ungrateful for their contributions. This same attitude stymied efforts on behalf of paid staff to seek greater input from

57

volunteer board members as they did not wish to overwork them in their voluntary capacity. Harris (1989: 329) suggested that the reluctance of volunteer board members to engage in monitoring activities or to challenge paid staff was based on their 'tendency to draw behaviour guidelines from the private world of informal relationships, rather than from the formal world of bureaucratic organizations that employ staff'. In other words, the culture of nonprofit voluntary organizations influences volunteer board members in their role to focus on ensuring the maintenance of good interpersonal relationships rather than acting as employers and dealing with organizational and staffing issues.

The discrepancy between prescribed roles and actual board member roles was also explored by Widmer (1993: 339), who postulated that board members 'often experience role conflict and confusion that frequently interfere with the work of the board member, the board and the organization'. Board members may experience role ambiguity, role conflict or role overload through the course of their experience as a board member. Role ambiguity occurs 'when an individual is uncertain about the expectations of the role and does not know what to do to enact the role' Widmer (1993: 340). Role ambiguity can create stress for board members, resulting in poor individual performance and poor contributions to the board. Role conflict can develop 'when an individual is confronted with divergent role expectations' (Widmer, 1993: 340). In other words, an individual board member is subject to conflicting choices of what to do in their role. Role conflict can lead board members to feel dissatisfied with the organization, lessen their trust and confidence in other board members, and generally affect performance and interpersonal relationships within the organization. Role overload occurs when 'it is impossible for an individual to fulfil a specific role because of the magnitude of the demands rather than the specific expectations, of that role' (Widmer, 1993: 340). Role overload can also cause board members to become stressed and overwhelmed with their role as a board member. Together, role ambiguity, role conflict and role overload can result in a number of poor organizational outcomes such as deficient board member performance, high board member turnover and may result in general ineffectiveness and inefficiency on the part of the board.

Widmer (1993) identified five roles that board members adopt: trustee, worker, expert, representative and figurehead. The trustee role involves board members fulfilling a set of prescribed duties outlined earlier (cf. NCVO, 2005). Workers act as board members as well as carrying out tasks for the organization. Experts provide skills and specialist knowledge to the board based on their particular qualifications and professional experience. Representative board members are common within the federated structures of nonprofit sport organizations and act as a conduit to other organizations that they represent. Figureheads provide a board with prestige or standing in their interactions with government, industry and other nonprofit organizations. The prescriptive literature reviewed earlier outlined the role of the board and the expectation that board members should act as trustees of the organization. However, Widmer (1993, 1996) argued that the actual behaviour of board members in board roles other than as a trustee may be at odds to the trustee role. Widmer (1993: 351) found that 'some but not all board members play the role of trustee as it is described in the prescriptive literature, that some board members combine the role of trustee with the other roles, and that some play other roles to the exclusion of the role of trustee'. The effect of these various board member behaviours is to create the environment for dysfunctional roles to emerge. The multiplicity of roles, subsequent behaviours adopted by board members in relation to such roles and the implications for board performance have yet to be fully explored.

In an attempt to reconcile discrepancies in the prescriptive and actual roles of board members, Harris (1993) proposed the use of Total Activities Analysis (TAA) to define the role of the board in relation to all the other roles undertaken within nonprofit organizations. The central argument for adopting the TAA approach was the emerging evidence at the time that the roles of the board and staff were both interlinked and interdependent. Conceptualizing the role of the board in isolation from the role of other elements within an organization was deemed incongruous. The first stage of the TAA approach developed by Harris (1993: 272–273) was to define the various functions or activities undertaken by a particular nonprofit organization, viz:

1. Providing services (direct provision and/or advocacy work).
2. Designing and developing services and structures (including setting policies and priorities, planning and monitoring).
3. Developing and maintaining an understanding of need and demand (e.g. in the field of housing, health, human services or the arts).
4. Maintaining good public relations (including publicity and making links with key people, groups and agencies in the field).
5. Fundraising (from a range of sources and using a variety of arrangements, including donations, grants and contracts).
6. Finance work (including collection and disbursement of cash, accounting, budgeting and budgetary control).
7. Staffing and training (including recruitment, induction and staff welfare work).
8. Managerial and coordinative work (including selection and induction of staff, prescription of work, coordination or work and appraisal).
9. Logistical work (including providing premises and equipment, materials and other supporting services).
10. Clerical and secretarial work (including recording and communication of decisions, actions and events).

In order for organizations to develop a clearer sense of the roles of board and staff in each of these areas, Harris (1993) suggested that nonprofit organizations reflect on who plays a part in enabling these activities to occur, to what extent are board members or paid staff are or should be involved in each of the activities, and under what criteria are divisions of responsibility made. Such an analysis enables organizational members to reflect on who is doing what within the organization and importantly, to decide if the roles of paid staff and volunteer board members are appropriate. One advantage of the TAA approach is the lack of prescription of what the board should be doing. Organizations are able to develop a sense of what roles the board and staff should play in all areas of organizational activity in a manner consistent with the specific cultural and structural characteristics of the organization.

Inglis, Alexander and Weaver (1999) defined three broad areas for the roles of the board: strategic activities, operations and resource planning. The strategic activities were 'future focused with an eye to the external community' (Inglis et al., 1999: 163). Strategic roles included developing a mission and vision, establishing policy, developing long-range plans and responding to community needs. The resource planning roles included functions such as annual budget allocations, hiring senior staff and setting financial policy. The roles and responsibilities in the operations area included 'developing and delivering programmes and services, advocating for interests of groups and raising funds for the organization' (Inglis et al., 1999: 163). A similar study of Israeli nonprofit organization boards concluded that roles and responsibilities of nonprofit boards are 'similar across countries, societies and cultural contexts, a finding that in turn implies that there are common behaviours of nonprofit boards' (Iecovich 2004: 19).

Inglis et al. (1999) identified five discrete benefits of developing a framework to define the broad roles and responsibilities of boards. First, a framework enables the role of the board to be more clearly defined for important constituent groups such as the board itself, staff, funding agencies, donors, clients and the wider community. Second, defining the roles and responsibilities enables an assessment of board performance. Third, such a framework provides a starting point for establishing new roles. Fourth, a framework for understanding roles and responsibilities would assist boards to better design meetings. Finally, a framework would assist board determine their training and development needs so that boards and board members could operate more effectively.

A later study by Inglis and Weaver (2000: 67) argued that the board meeting agenda is 'an important link between key board roles and how the board conducts its business'. However, the standard agenda used traditionally by nonprofit organizations failed to allocate sufficient time to the future of the organization. They applied the Inglis et al. (1999) framework to redesign the agenda for board meetings within a nonprofit organization and the results were positive. Board members were subsequently able to make 'a stronger connection between their roles and how the agenda format can help keep them focused on the important items related to their roles, thereby enhancing their ability to govern' (Inglis & Weaver, 2000: 74). The framework can assist board members think more 'strategically about their roles and how they can plan their work to fulfil their roles and responsibilities' (Inglis & Weaver, 2000: 76).

In summary, irrespective of statutory obligations, a determination to meet the demands of regulators or to follow voluntary codes of conduct, the actual behaviour of board members in fulfilling their roles has consistently found to differ from the prescriptive literature. The influence of organizational culture and structure, the existence of a number of role dysfunctions, the unique working environment of paid staff working with volunteer board members that requires governance and management roles to be clearly defined, and the nature of board roles that vary between 'high level' strategy, resource planning and operations have been identified as factors affecting the implementation of board roles.

The discussion so far has not considered the work of authors such as Miller-Millesen (2003) who developed a model of the influences on board member behaviour, or Stephens, Dawley and Stephens (2004b) on the antecedents of board member commitment. Such considerations are addressed in Chapter 6 where the discussion focuses on the culture that exists within boards and the ability of boards to work as a team. The next section explores the recommended roles within nonprofit sport organizations, provides examples of how these roles are carried out, and reviews the limited amount of research that has been completed on the role of nonprofit sport boards.

Roles of nonprofit sport boards

The Australian Sports Commission (ASC, 2005) described the role of a nonprofit sport organization board in legal, strategic, financial, and moral terms as well as having responsibility for the assessment and management of organizational risks, the appointment of the CEO and accountability to stakeholders. The legal responsibilities of the board extend to ultimate accountability for the performance of the organization, ensuring the organization complies with relevant legislation, and that it remains financially solvent at all times. The board's strategic responsibilities include establishing the strategic direction of the organization and the evaluation of progress toward outcomes articulated in the strategic plan. The financial responsibilities of the board include financial governance, planning and reporting. Financial governance 'entails setting financial policies within which the CEO must carry out day-to-day financial management, and monitoring the effective implementation of these policies' (ASC, 2005: 11).

Financial planning by the board should include identification of the desired financial position for the organization and the approval of a broad budget that allows the CEO to make operational adjustments without board approval. Financial reporting should occur monthly and include evidence of compliance with financial policies set by the board. The ASC (2005: 13) defined the moral responsibilities of the board to include remaining 'up to date with the concerns and expectations of stakeholders and to ensure that these receive proper consideration at board or management level'. The board is also bound to keep all organizational members informed of issues of concern, to create a positive working relationship with the CEO and to 'consider matters on the basis of equity and transparency and in the interests of the sport as a whole, and not in preference to any one or more classes of stakeholder' (ASC, 2005: 13).

The board's role in assessing and managing organizational risks is to have a 'broad appreciation of the risks facing the organization and the likelihood of occurrence together with the potential impact of these should they occur' (ASC, 2005: 14). The board should consider risks in areas such as finance, human resource management, governance, stakeholder relations and general areas of organizational activity such as asset management, health and safety, and technology. While the board should approve a risk management plan developed by the CEO, it is the responsibility of the CEO to implement the plan.

In appointing the CEO, the board's responsibility is to ensure that the appointee has the requisite skills and understanding of the organization and that the CEO is compatible with the culture of the organization. The board is also responsible for ensuring the role of the CEO is clearly defined, and that the appointee understands the key strategic issues for the organization, the policy framework within which they must work, reporting expectations and their conditions of employment. The ASC (2005) highlighted the fact that the CEO is the only direct employee of the board with all other staff being responsible to the CEO.

The final area of responsibility extends to the board being held accountable to three types of stakeholders: (1) legal owners such as members; (2) moral owners who are the individuals who benefit from the services provided by the organization, such as players, coaches or officials, but who do not have voting rights as members and (3) the individuals or organizations with whom the organization has a contractual relationship such as employees, funding agencies or suppliers. These stakeholders have varying levels of involvement in the governance of the organization. The board has a responsibility to facilitate stakeholder involvement through voting to elect, appoint or select board members, soliciting information or opinions on decisions, or other forms of communication with the board.

In interpreting these broad areas of responsibility, the ASC (2005: 3) identified eleven key roles for the board of a nonprofit sport organization (see Figure 4.1).

1. Strategic planning – defining, driving and monitoring the organization's strategic direction, priorities and results.
2. Stakeholder involvement – defining key relationships, interacting with stakeholders to inform them of achievements and ensuring that stakeholders have input into determining strategic goals and direction.
3. Enhancing the organization's public image – promoting the organization in a positive light and performing 'ambassadorial' duties.
4. Organizational performance – reviewing, monitoring and ensuring management and organizational performance.
5. Reporting – reporting to members and stakeholders at the annual general meeting.
6. Policy formulation – establishing the board-level policy framework for governing the organization, from which all operational policies and actions are developed.
7. Management of the CEO – appointment, management and review, providing advice and guidance and rewarding the CEO as appropriate.
8. Legal compliance – monitoring organizational compliance with relevant federal, state and local legislation, and the organization's constitution.
9. Management of financial resources – approving the allocation of funds through the annual budget, striving to secure the resources required and ensuring sound financial management of the organization.
10. Risk management – ensuring the risks facing the organization are identified and assessed, ensuring a risk management plan is established, regularly reviewing this plan to ensure its effectiveness and monitoring compliance with it.
11. Board effectiveness – carrying out board business through productive meetings, engaging in regular self-assessment and evaluation, and initiating board development activities, to strengthen its effectiveness.

Figure 4.1 Eleven key roles for the board of a nonprofit sport organization; reprinted with permission of the Australian Sports Commission (*Source*: ASC (2005: 3))

The governance guidelines from other leading sport agencies in New Zealand (SPARC, 2004) and in the UK (UK Sport, 2004) prescribe similar roles and responsibilities for the board. Despite the evidence from the wider nonprofit field that the role of the board in practice differs significantly from prescribed guidelines, there has been a lack of research into the role of nonprofit sport boards. To date there have only been two reported studies that have focused on the role of the nonprofit sport board, both of which focused on state or provincial level sport governing bodies (Inglis, 1997a; Shilbury, 2001).

The study by Inglis (1997a) developed a theoretical framework to conceptualize the roles of the board based on those prescribed for the boards of general nonprofit organizations. The study found that the role of the board could be defined as encompassing four elements: (1) setting and monitoring the mission of the organization; (2) undertaking planning activities such as developing financial policy and setting long-range plans;

(3) appointing and monitoring the activities of the CEO and (4) managing community relations through activities such as fundraising and advocacy. Inglis (1997a) concluded that the board roles within nonprofit sport organizations were very similar to those of general nonprofit organization boards.

Shilbury (2001) explored the differences in how paid staff and volunteer board members were perceived to fulfil a range of board roles and the relative importance of a range of board roles. A key finding from the study was that strategy, developing financial policies and budgeting were perceived as the most important board roles. In addition, Shilbury (2001) concluded that there was evidence of paid staff having increasing influence over matters that were previously the exclusive purview of the board. The issues of board–staff relations and the nature of shared leadership within nonprofit sport organization boards are explored in further detail in Chapter 9.

In terms of what is known of the actual roles undertaken by the boards of nonprofit sport organizations, Inglis (1997a) and Shilbury (2001) highlighted the similarities with the roles performed by other types of nonprofit boards. However, much work remains to be done to investigate the degree of congruence between the actual roles of nonprofit sport boards and the prescribed roles of the board promulgated by agencies such as the ASC (2005). A recurring theme in the prescriptive literature is role boards should play in determining the strategy of nonprofit sport organizations. Ferkins, Shilbury and McDonald (2005) noted that strategy has only recently been a focus of study for sport management research and that there has been no investigation of the explicit role of the board in the development, approval or monitoring of strategy. Similarly, Edwards and Cornforth (2003) noted that empirical studies of the strategic role of nonprofit boards are rare despite the many prescriptive guidelines calling for the board to make such a role a priority. This crucial role of the board in strategy is explored in depth in Chapter 7.

A final issue concerning the role of the board in nonprofit sport organizations is the impact of organizational size on the governance roles adopted by the board. Rochester (2003) was critical of much of the literature on nonprofit governance for treating nonprofit organizations and the contexts within which they operate as homogenous. Specifically, Rochester (2003: 115) noted that:

> the nature of the board's role and the issues faced in implementing it are seen as essentially the same, regardless of variations in the size or function of nonprofit and voluntary sector organizations or of the environments in which they operate.

In a study of small voluntary organizations, Rochester (2003: 121) identified a degree of ambiguity in some of the organization's understanding of the role of the board which he attributed to 'tensions between controlling and partnering the paid staff and between conformance and performance roles'. In other organizations, the role of the board was clear but the board found it difficult to fulfil their functions.

Rochester (2003) concluded that smaller nonprofit organizations had a distinctive approach to governance, which was evident in three ways. First, while authority was 'invested in elected officers or in staff employed to co-ordinate, manage or direct the agency's work, in practice authority was exercised on an individual or personal basis' (Rochester, 2003: 126). Individuals, regardless of their formal position with the organizations, chose to address problems, develop solutions and enact change through political persuasion and reaching consensus rather than via more formal decision-making processes. Second, the roles of the board and staff were intertwined, making it difficult for boards to govern and staff to manage as most guidelines recommend. Rochester (2003: 127) argued that making a clear distinction between governance and management within small nonprofit organizations is not plausible and continuing to conceptualize their roles in such a way is 'unhelpful'. Finally, conceptualizing the governance function as the exclusive domain of the board is misleading as many other elements of small nonprofit organizations are involved in performing governance roles. Rochester (2003) argued that while the board should be considered the primary organizational element charged with responsibility for governance, in small nonprofit organizations the board often is involved intimately in operational aspects of service delivery. The phenomena is evident in the operation of many boards in small sport organizations at local, regional and sometimes state or provincial and national levels.

In summary, based on a limited amount of research it is apparent that sport boards share a high degree of similarity in their role with nonprofit governing boards generally. In addition, a number of government agencies with jurisdiction for sport have developed quite detailed governance guidelines. However, there is limited knowledge about how the role is enacted in light of such guidelines, the execution of the governance role in smaller sport organizations, and the role of the board in important areas such as strategy development and monitoring. There has been a dearth of empirical studies explicitly addressing these issues. However, an examination of sport board roles as they are articulated in a range of governance documents from international, national and state/provincial level nonprofit sport organizations highlights how the role of the board has been defined in practice.

The roles, powers and responsibilities of the Executive Committee (the board) of the International Rugby Board (IRB) are outlined in the By-laws of the board (IRB, 2004) and appear in Figure 4.2. Based in Dublin, Ireland, the IRB is the nonprofit sport organization with sole responsibility for promoting, fostering, developing, extending and governing the game of rugby union throughout the world and for decision-making and the regulatory

The Roles, Powers and Responsibilities of the Executive Committee shall be:

(a) The formulation, in conjunction with management, of the strategic plan to achieve the vision, mission and goals of the IRB;

(b) The approval of the annual business plan and budgets;

(c) The monitoring of the implementation of the strategic plan and annual business plan, operational plan and budgets of the IRB and assessment of performance against key performance indicators;

(d) The co-ordination of the work of Standing committees, Advisory Groups, Working Parties and trading companies, excluding Rugby World Cup Ltd and its associated entities;

(e) The formulation and implementation of good corporate governance principles and practices;

(f) To ensure that the IRB operates as an effective business and member services organization;

(g) To recruit, remove, monitor and evaluate performance of the CEO;

(h) To determine delegations of authority and accountabilities of the CEO;

(i) To approve expenditure, contracts and commitments that fall outside the authority of the CEO;

(j) To ensure that there is a sound system of internal control and risk management policy and process in place to identify and manage risk;

(k) To ensure that appropriate codes and policy frameworks exist to promote effective governance of the IRB through clear written and regular review and updating of:
(i) The policies of the IRB;
(ii) Strategic, business and annual operational plans;
(iii) Standing orders and Terms of Reference for Committees and advisory groups;
(iv) Procedures and protocols for the operation of IRB Companies excluding Rugby World Cup Limited and its associated entities;
(v) Clearly defined and delegated powers/limits of authority for decision making for the Executive, Standing Committees and Staff;
(vi) Risk and audit policies;
(vii) Standard operating policies and procedures;

(l) Between Council Meetings, to deal with matters of an urgent nature that would ordinarily be dealt with by Council under Bye-Law (sic) 9.4 (but excluding changes to Bye-Laws, Regulations Relating to the Game, General Regulations or Laws of the Game);

(m) Subject to paragraph (l) above, to discharge such other responsibilities that do not fall within the constitutional, legal or statutory jurisdiction of the Council or other person/entity under the Bye-Laws required to ensure the effective management and operation of the Board.

(n) To receive and approve the audited financial statements of the Company for the preceding financial year.

Figure 4.2 Roles, powers and responsibilities of the Executive Committee of the International Rugby Board; reprinted with permission of the International Rugby Board (*Source*: IRB (2004: 18–19))

framework in relation to international rugby competitions. The IRB has over 40 fulltime staff working in partnership with 95 national governing bodies throughout the world. The role of the board of an international sport governing body such as the IRB highlights the variety of roles fulfilled by the board and the fact that their roles encompass many of the governance functions articulated by Harris (1993).

As a national governing body for sport, the Canadian Cycling Association (CCA) aims to organize and promote the sport of cycling throughout Canada. The Constitution and By-laws of the CCA (2004) outline five explicit functions of the board: (1) to exercise its powers conferred by the By-laws, including duties and responsibilities as directed by the Annual General Meeting; (2) to establish and regulate committees; (3) to evaluate the performance of permanent employees; (4) to make and enforce policies and procedures relating to discipline of organizational members; and (5) to make and enforce policies and procedures relating to the resolution of disputes within the organization. The roles and responsibilities of the board are specified in a policy on organization structure (CCA, 2003) outlined in Figure 4.3. The CCA has extensively documented the roles and responsibilities of the board which also cover the ten governance functions articulated by Harris (1993) and the prescribed roles for sport boards as they appear in guidelines such as those developed by the ASC (2005).

A recent governance review of the South Australian Cycling Federation (SACF) (Office for Recreation and Sport, 2004) provides an example of how ill-defined the role of the board for a state/provincial level sport governing body can become in practice. Part of the review process involved a comparison of the governance system in place within the SACF to the governance principles provided by the ASC at that time (ASC, 2002). One of the ASC principles stipulated the need for clear delineation of governance roles, with no overlap of powers between organizational elements. The review found that the roles of the board (in this case called an Executive) were neither clearly defined nor understood and that the board did not contribute actively to the development of strategy, Furthermore, there was a lack of clear performance indicators against which the board could assess progress, few opportunities for stakeholder involvement in governance, and no policies in place to address individual board member roles, duties, or conflicts of interest (Office for Recreation and Sport, 2004). The review concluded with a recommendation to redevelop the governance structure of the SACF with clear definitions of responsibilities for the board and staff as a matter of priority.

These examples demonstrate how the role of the board within several nonprofit sport organizations has been defined in practice. They illustrate the wide variety of roles played by boards and the extent to which these roles can be clearly defined in relation to governance guidelines. One final aspect of governance is the roles played by individual board members and CEOs.

The Board of Directors functions as a policy board. The roles and the responsibilities of the board include those described below, but does not exclude any role or responsibility that is consistent with its role as a policy board. It is expected that the board will carry out its responsibilities in a consultative fashion.

A. Management of human resources
1. With respect to the Director General: Hire and ensure succession, monitor performance, approve compensation and provide advice and counsel in the execution of duties.
2. Approve terms of reference for the Director General.
3. Review the Director General's performance, at least annually, against agreed upon written objectives and staff limitation policies.
4. Ensure succession plans are in place, including programmes to train and develop senior staff.

B. Strategy and planning
1. Direct, and participate with programme committees and staff in developing, and ultimately approving CCA's strategic plan.
2. Approve the annual programme and budget plans that support the Strategic Plan.
3. Monitor the association's progress towards its mission, and to revise and alter its direction in the light of changing circumstances.

C. Financial and corporate issues
1. Evaluate and use information provided by the Director General and others (auditors) about the effectiveness of internal control and management information systems.
2. Monitor and review programme and financial performance relative to budgets and plans.
3. Approve financial statements and approve their release by the Director General.
4. Approve contracts, leases and other arrangements or commitments that may have a material impact on the association.
5. Approve banking resolutions and significant changes in banking relationships.
6. Review coverage, deductibles and key issues regarding association insurance policies.
7. Approve commencement or settlement of litigation that has a material impact on the association.
8. Recommend appointment of external auditors to the Annual General Meeting and approve auditors fees.
9. Ensure a policy that allows CCA to acquire, accept, solicit or receive legacies, gifts, grants, settlements, bequests, endowments and donations of any kind.
10. Borrow money on the credit of the association, from any bank, corporation, firm or person, upon such terms, covenants and conditions at such times, in such sums, to such extent and in such manner as the Board may deem expedient.

Figure 4.3 Roles and responsibilities of the board of the Canadian Cycling Association; reprinted with permission of the Canadian Cycling Association (*Source*: CCA (2003: 1–2))

11. Secure any such bond, debenture or other securities, or any other present or future borrowing or liability of the association by mortgage, hypothec, charge or pledge of all or any currently owned or subsequently acquired real and personal, movable and immovable, property of the association, and the undertaking and rights of the association.

D. Business and risk management

1. Ensure that the Director General identifies the principal risks of CCA's business and implements appropriate systems to manage these risks.
2. Receive, at least annually, reports from the Director General and/or its committees on matters relating to, among others, ethical conduct, environmental management, and related party transactions.

E. Policies, procedures and process

1. Approve and monitor observance of all significant policies and procedures by which the association is operated.
2. Direct the Director General to ensure that CCA operates at all times within applicable laws and regulations and to the highest ethical and moral standards.
3. Review annually the policies and procedures governing its own operations, including the board manual.
4. Annually review its own performance and effectiveness and make recommendations for improvement as appropriate.

F. General legal obligations

1. Ensure, through clear direction to the Director General that legal requirements have been met, and that documents and records have been properly prepared, approved and maintained.
2. Review and recommend to the AGM changes in the By-laws and Articles of Incorporation, identify matters requiring approval at the AGM, and approve agendas for the Annual General Meeting.
3. Manage the business and affairs of the association; including the relationships among the association, its affiliates and their members, directors and officers.
4. Act honestly and in good faith with a view to the best interests of CCA.
5. Exercise the care, diligence and skill that reasonably prudent people would exercise in comparable circumstances.
6. Act in accordance with its obligations contained in the Canada Corporations Act, other relevant legislation, regulations and policies, and the Association's Articles and By-laws.

Figure 4.3 (Continued)

Individual board member roles

There has been a great deal of attention paid to defining the role of the board as a group and somewhat less reported research on the role of individuals in the governance of nonprofit organizations. None of this research has focussed on exploring the roles played by individual board members within nonprofit sport organizations. Research into issues related to individual board members other than their roles are discussed in subsequent chapters. These include the impacts of professionalization (Auld, 1997; Auld & Godbey, 1998); the relationship between board members and paid staff (Hoye & Cuskelly, 2003a, 2003b); group cohesion (Doherty & Carron, 2003), committee norms (Doherty, Patterson & Van Bussel, 2004), organizational commitment (Cuskelly, 1995; Cuskelly, McIntyre & Boag, 1998) and leader–member exchange relationships (Hoye, 2004, 2006b).

The ASC (2005) governance guidelines define the role of the board chair and the CEO but not the role of other board members. Guidelines developed by SPARC (2004) outlined the role of board members in terms of their fiduciary responsibilities. The SPARC (2004: 20–21) guidelines specified that board members should:

> exercise a duty of care; act honestly; avoid using their positions for personal advantage; comply with all relevant legislative and constitutional requirements such as employment, trading, occupational health and safety; be aware of the scope and general content of such legislation and its relevance; and act in the best interests of the organization as a whole.

The focus on specifying the fiduciary responsibilities of board members and what they should not do rather then prescribing more roles in proactive language is also evident in the constitutions and governance documents of sport governing bodies. The governance policy of Surf Life Saving Australia (SLSA) (2003: 6) provides eight guidelines for the role of individual board members:

1. Must be committed to ethical, businesslike and lawful conduct including proper use of authority and appropriate decorum when acting as Directors.
2. Must always act in the interests of the Company and the members.
3. Must avoid conflicts of interest.
4. Must not attempt to exercise individual authority over the Company or make decisions outside of their designated scope of authority.
5. Should not publicly voice any negative comments or individual opinions relating to the CEO, staff, fellow Directors or any Company matter or issue.
6. Should only speak to the media as requested by the CEO or President.
7. Should adhere to and support the President in an effort to govern effectively.
8. Should respect the confidentiality of sensitive issues or business items under negotiation or discussion.

These guidelines tends to say more about what board members should avoid doing in their roles rather than the proactive roles board members should play in areas such as strategy, operations and resourcing.

A prominent debate in the literature is whether board members should be allocated responsibility for a discrete portfolio of organizational activity such as coaching, programme delivery, events, officiating, marketing, fundraising, player development. There is a tendency for board members with such portfolio responsibilities to focus increased attention on operational matters within their portfolio and possibly limit their capability or capacity to contribute to more governance related issues within the board. This may also make it difficult for the CEO to retain a reasonable degree of managerial control over operational matters. What may be appropriate and effective in terms of individual board member roles is likely to vary in accordance with organizational size. Requiring board members to take up portfolio roles within smaller sport organizations, particularly those without any paid staff, may be quite appropriate and enable the organization to function with greater efficiency and effectiveness. This issue is debated in more detail in Chapter 6.

The role of the board chair role lends itself to being more readily defined because of its specific nature and its prominence on boards. The ASC (2005) guidelines provide a clear framework for understanding the role of the board chair. The guidelines stipulate that the board chair has six fundamental responsibilities: (1) to represent the board; (2) to set the agenda and ensure board members receive timely and clear information; (3) to manage board meetings so that sufficient time is allocated for agenda items and related decision-making; (4) to liaise with the CEO; (5) to ensure that board members are inducted and developed in their capacity as board members; and (6) to ensure that the board and board members undertake regular performance assessments (ASC, 2005). The Constitution of the Canadian Amateur Rowing Association (CARA) (2005) clearly specifies the duties of the board chair as representing the organization, presiding over meetings, calling and managing the preparation for board meetings, and having responsibility for a number of specific operational areas of the association.

The role of the CEO is generally defined as a management role. For example, the governance policy of SLSA (2003) specifies the role of the CEO to include responsibility for implementing the strategic plan, managing the office, day-to-day management of the organization, employment and human resource management issues, financial management, business development including marketing and sponsorship, implementing the Company business plan, management and execution of contracts, government relations and acting as a spokesperson.

Fishel (2003: 174) noted that the demands on CEOs working in the non-profit sector 'have increased in breadth and sophistication' in recent years. He argued that their role now requires them to be able to:

- Reconcile the conflicting demands of clients, public and private sector partners, donors, volunteers and others and align their energies in pursuit of socially, culturally or educationally useful services.

- Inspire trust, confidence and optimism among those who care about an issue or cause and are willing to volunteer their time and money to help address it.
- Ensure that the organization is financially sound, ethically above reproach, and fully accountable to the community it services.
- Position the organization for the future in the face of severe challenges of limited resources and frequent changes in the external environment; accomplish this through flexibility, innovative strategies, and rapid adaptation to threats and opportunities.
- Help develop leaders on the board, in other parts of the organization, among the volunteers, and in the overall community to carry on the work of the organization (Fishel, 2003: 175–176).

Conclusion

This chapter has discussed the governance roles and responsibilities of the board, individual board members, the board chair and paid staff. It has highlighted the importance of establishing clear roles to enable effective and efficient decision-making processes and accountability to occur within nonprofit organizations. This chapter has compared and contrasted what the governing boards for nonprofit sport organizations should do and what they do in practice. It has also explored how and why governance roles and responsibilities should be allocated within these organizations. The review of research from the wider nonprofit field highlighted the incongruence often evident between the prescriptive literature and practice. The body of research concerned with the role of nonprofit sport boards is less advanced. However, there is evidence that the guidelines prescribed by agencies such as the ASC, SPARC and UK Sport for the allocation of roles and responsibilities may not reflect the current practice within nonprofit sport organizations. Much more research is needed if we are to fully understand how sport boards exercise their governance roles and responsibilities.

5

Team selection: board composition and recruitment issues

Overview

This chapter addresses the issues of board composition including the selection and recruitment of board members and board chairs. Many of the prescriptive governance guides developed for nonprofit sport organizations recommend a shift away from the traditional delegate or representative model towards the appointment of independent board members. The issues and challenges of working within democratic processes to ensure adequate stakeholder representation balanced with a desire to have appropriately skilled and experienced people in governance roles is the focus of this chapter. The findings of the limited amount of published research on nonprofit board member selection issues are compared to prescribed governance guidelines. Several examples of board selection processes are provided in order to illustrate the complexities of selecting individuals to fulfil governance roles within nonprofit sport organizations.

The right to govern

The questions of who should comprise the board and how they get elected, appointed, selected or invited to a position as a board member are central to the governance of nonprofit sport organizations. In the context of for-profit enterprises, Ben-Ner and Van Hoomisen (1994: 395) identified that the ownership of any firm 'consists of three primary rights: to control the firm, to dispose of its returns and to transfer the previous two rights'. The right to control 'is the key right of ownership because it accords the power to determine how inputs are used in the organization and what objectives are pursued, which in turn critically affect the size of organizational returns and their allocation' (Ben-Ner & Van Hoomisen, 1994: 395).

Organizational control includes the power and authority to decide objectives, to employ staff, to acquire and dispose of assets and to make other decisions affecting the conduct of an organization. The right to dispose of its returns entails decisions about the distribution of the financial returns of an organization, how programmes and services are to be delivered, and how individuals are rewarded within an organization.

In the corporate sector these ownership rights are traded through purchasing an organization either in whole or in part via shareholdings. For nonprofit sport organizations ownership rights commonly reside with the members of the organization. As discussed in Chapter 3, nonprofit sport organizations are generally member-benefit organizations in the sense that they are created, developed, operated and maintained by the individuals. Those most closely connected to such organizations both produce and consume the services provided by the organization (Smith, 1993). Organizational members have the opportunity to govern the organization by being elected, appointed, selected or invited to serve on the board and to vote at elections. By establishing a board to represent their interests, organizational members effectively cede the ownership rights to the board in order for the board to make decisions on their behalf.

Smith (1999) defined nonprofit organizations that are predominantly volunteer run as grassroots associations. He suggested that grassroots associations differ from other nonprofit organizations because they are generally locally based, employ few staff, and are governed by volunteers usually without the involvement of paid staff. Following this line of reasoning, Hoye and Inglis (2003) suggested that the application of nonprofit governance guidelines to the governance of nonprofit sport organizations may need some adaptations, arguing that there is a need to consider the member representation in the governance of member-benefit sport organizations. However, issues concerning how member representation systems impact on the governance of these organizations have not been a significant focus of research because the majority of nonprofit organizations are not membership based (Smith, 1999). In terms of nonprofit sport organizations there has been a dearth of studies that have explored the impact of member representation systems impact on governance or issues concerning board composition. The literature from the wider nonprofit sector is briefly reviewed to shed light on how these issues may manifest in nonprofit sport organizations.

Board composition

In a comprehensive review of the nonprofit literature Saidel (2002) identified that although rare, studies of board composition suggest that gender, race and ethnicity impact on organizational structure, processes, politics and culture may be important factors in board performance and the execution of the governance function. To date, such issues have not been explored within nonprofit sport organizations. However, rapidly emerging trends in the cultural and linguistic diversity of societies in Australia and the UK, suggest that these are important areas for future study. Ostrower and Stone (2005) suggested that board composition varies among institutions of different types and especially on the basis of characteristics such as organizational size, prestige and area of activity. Nonprofit sport organizations differ markedly on these characteristics. Significant variation within the sport sector is evident in terms of size (local club level to international federation), prestige (higher profile sports such as football compared to minority sports such as squash), and activity (local clubs versus international sport event organizations), with a concomitant variation in board composition.

Daley and Angulo (1994: 174) argued that greater board diversity can provide boards with greater levels of expertise, offer greater legitimacy and influence to the board with external groups and assist the board communicate a variety of organizational values such as 'citizen participation, consumer involvement, broadly inclusive, open policy making, (and) public accountability'. In a study of the boards of 240 Young Mens' Christian Association (YMCA) organizations, Siciliano (1996: 1319) found that while board member diversity had no impact on organizational efficiency or the 'board's ability or tendency to perform its control function', it did have an impact on the organization's social performance. In other words, having a diverse board membership helped to ensure the social values of the organization were considered in board decisions involving programme and service delivery to minority groups. Brown (2002: 370) identified that previous research efforts have suggested that 'increased heterogeneity of board members facilitates the organizations' representation of and sensitivity to stakeholders'. Callen, Klein and Tinkelman (2003) found that greater diversity in board composition was related to greater organizational efficiency.

This was primarily due to external donors being present on boards who tended to focus on reducing administrative costs in order to maximize the use of donor funds. While these studies point to the value of ensuring diversity in board composition, some nonprofit organizations, and virtually all nonprofit sport organizations, have little control over the diversity of their boards. This is because board membership is frequently reliant on democratic electoral processes.

In a study of board composition within professional associations, Friedman and Phillips (2004) reported that having the entire board directly elected from the membership presented several problems. First, there was reluctance on the part of employing organizations 'to release professional employees from their commitments, and self-employed professionals or those in small partnerships are also less able and willing to give their time' (Friedman & Phillips, 2004: 194). Second, 'associations cannot find the mix of skills necessary to run complex organizations among members who may be highly competent in their own field but lack appropriate experience and expertise' (Friedman & Phillips, 2004: 194). Finally, for a board to operate effectively there must be an appropriate range of personality types willing to play various roles within the board, something that an election result is unlikely to deliver.

Other authors such as O'Regan and Oster (2005) have found no relationship between nonprofit board member's personal demographics and board performance. In other words the demographic 'make up' of the board seems to make little difference to the ability of the board to govern effectively. In the corporate sector, Ingley and van der Walt (2003) argued that attempts to increase board diversity without considering how to manage group dynamics and the processes through which board members interact would be counter productive to good governance. They defined diversity in governance terms as relating to 'board composition and the varied combination of attributes, characteristics and expertise contributed by individual board members in relation to board process and decision-making' (Ingley & van der Walt, 2003: 8). According to Milliken and Martins (1996) diversity can be represented on the board in terms of age, gender, ethnicity, culture, religion, constituency representation, independence, professional background, knowledge, technical skills, commercial and industry experience, career and life experience. Theoretically, increased diversity within a board should enable it to perform better as a wider collective range of attributes, skills and experiences are bought to bear on decisions. Ingley and van der Walt (2003: 16), however, concluded that 'fully utilizing the diversity that offers wider perspectives and experiences for better quality board decision-making is clearly a complex matter that requires sensitive and skilful leadership and ongoing management of group processes'.

Nonprofit sport organizations must grapple with the accepted logic that greater diversity in board composition may yield better governance versus the imperative to ensure traditional stakeholder groups are involved in significant governance roles which may actually diminish diversity within the board. Agencies such as the ASC, SPARC and UK Sport all advocate for boards to comprise entirely of independent directors or at the very least the appointment of some independent directors to work alongside elected board members. The guidelines developed by these agencies and the issues of how nonprofit sport organizations select board members are the focus of the following section.

Guidelines for voting systems and selection

The UK-based NCVO (2005: 21) suggested that nonprofit boards should have a strategy for their own renewal and that the 'recruitment of new trustees (board members) should be open, and focused on creating a diverse and effective board'. The NCVO (2005: 21) specified a number of guidelines for nonprofit organizations to adopt in recruiting and renewing their board:

- The Board should have a strategy for its own renewal, with succession planning arrangements in place to ensure timely replacement of trustees resigning or reaching the end of their terms of office; particular attention should be given to succession planning for replacement of the chair and other honorary officers.
- The Board may wish to delegate implementation of this strategy to a sub-committee or panel.
- Trustees must be recruited and appointed in accordance with the organization's governing document, and with relevant legislation.
- The Board should consider setting maximum terms of office to ensure a steady renewal of trustees; these may be set out in standing orders or in the organization's governing document.
- Before new trustees are appointed, the Board should determine what new attributes and knowledge are needed, and write them down in the form of a role description, or role profile.
- The Board should ensure that the recruitment process is open to all sections of the community, and should consider open advertising and a range of other recruitment methods to attract a wide range of candidates.
- Candidates should, where the organization's governing document permits, be interviewed formally, and appointed on merit.
- In the case of organizations where the trustees are nominated by an external body, or elected by a wider membership, the Board should work in partnership with the organizations or people concerned to ensure

that they are aware of the specific skills and experience required from new trustees.

■ Where permitted by the organization's governing document, using co-options should be used where necessary to recruit individuals with particular skills, experience and qualities that are not fully provided by existing trustees.

■ The Board should ensure that the procedures for joining and leaving the Board are clearly understood by all trustees and others involved.

The ASC (2005: 6) also advocated that nonprofit sport organization board members require certain skills and attributes and that 'whenever possible, the composition of a board should be planned so that the right people with the right skills are elected or appointed'. However, the federated system that prevails within most nonprofit sport organizations precludes the application of such a process. An inability to plan for board composition is widely recognized as a significant governance challenge for nonprofit sport organizations (SPARC, 2004). The boards of nonprofit sport organizations are typically made up of individuals who are elected to represent the interests of an identifiable stakeholder group. Such groups might include coaches, officials or players, a particular discipline within a sport (e.g. show jumping or dressage in equestrian sports), an age or gender group, or a particular geographic region. Individuals elected as board members of international, national or state/provincial governing bodies, leagues or associations may also represent the interests of member organizations.

In addition to setting guidelines for board composition, the ASC (2005) also identified the following set of skills and competencies that board members should possess outlined in Figure 5.1.

The vast majority of nonprofit sport organizations do not explicitly require elected board members to possess or indeed demonstrate such skills as part of the election process. The ASC (2005) suggests that in order to facilitate such a process, nonprofit sport organizations should educate voting members about the board's needs and issues for the coming period so that they may vote for those individuals they feel possess the requisite skills and competencies to be board members. The ASC (2005) also suggested that board member succession planning ought to be used increasingly by boards to facilitate appropriate board composition. SPARC (2004: 108) highlighted some of the vagaries of the board member election and selection processes that exist within most nonprofit sport organizations:

> Getting the right people on the boards of sport and recreation organizations is a common challenge. Many board members feel obliged to volunteer for duty. Others have been loyal workers in the organization and their election to national office is a way of recognising their service. Other members have their achievements on the sporting field recognised with a board appointment.

1. The ability to think strategically
2. Oral communication skills, including listening and the ability to present points of view coherently and persuasively
3. Financial literacy and financial analysis skills
4. The ability to understand and relate to stakeholders
5. Analytical and critical reasoning skills
6. Being a team player
7. Being ethical, honest, open and trustworthy, a high level of personal integrity
8. Independence and inquisitiveness
9. The willingness to commit the time and effort required to do the job properly
10. The courage of convictions coupled with a willingness to listen to other perspectives
11. The ability to establish quality peer relationships
12. A stewardship orientation (i.e. protecting and maintaining order for the benefit of current and future generations of participants)
13. Broad business experience
14. Understanding and experience in the sport
15. Community/stakeholder connections and influence

Figure 5.1 Board member skills and competencies. (*Source*: ASC (2005: 6–7); reproduced with permission of the Australian Sports Commission)

The nature of governance challenges are not always apparent to those outside the board so 'most boards need to proactively communicate those challenges to those who influence board selection … otherwise, a board position may owe more to personal popularity and profile than to an ability to contribute effectively to the board's work' (SPARC, 2004: 109). Nonprofit sport organizations have also been prone to recruiting individuals with specialist skills such as lawyers, accountants, marketing experts or human resource managers, which can provide a board with functional skills but may not necessarily ensure board members possess the requisite governance skills or attributes of 'independence, integrity and emotional intelligence' (SPARC, 2004: 110).

The SPARC (2004) governance guidelines are more prescriptive than those of the ASC (2005) and UK Sport (2004) in detailing the processes that nonprofit sport organizations should use to select board members. The 11 key steps in the SPARC (2004) guidelines are:

1. Confirmation of the number of board member positions to be filled.
2. Confirmation of the role of the board, its structure and how it operates. The board should identify the key challenges for the organization over the next 5 years and other governance matters such as contingent liabilities that potential new board members need to be aware.

3. Existing board members should develop a list of the skills, experience and attributes the board requires to deal with the challenges identified in Step 2 and then assess the current board membership against the list in order to identify the requirements for new board members.
4. The board should then develop a recruitment profile for new board members. If the board is directly elected by the members then the board should communicate the desired attributes of new board members so that voting members can make informed choices.
5. If board members are not elected then the board should identify suitable candidates from whom they can make a selection.
6. Candidates are assessed against the recruitment profile developed in Step 3 and discussions held with each and their referees if appropriate.
7. The board selection panel interviews a final group to select new board members.
8. New board members are provided with a clear role description, a set of performance expectations and their terms of appointment.
9. The board and individual board members' performance is evaluated to ensure the right mix of skills, attributes and experiences are delivering effective board performance.
10. The list of required board skills, experiences and attributes should be developed and maintained after board performance reviews.
11. The board should maintain a list of potential board members for future appointment.

Arguably, these guidelines can be utilized in practice only by nonprofit sport organizations that are well resourced and have a high level of understanding of the governance function and the role of the board. In a study of board member selection in nonprofit sport organizations, Hoye and Cuskelly (2004) explored the relationship between board performance and the use of a range of recommended board member selection, orientation and evaluation processes. Despite a small sample size they found evidence that the use of a higher number of such processes was related to higher levels of board performance.

Utilization of a greater number of processes recommended by agencies such as the ASC and SPARC was a distinguishing feature that differentiated effective boards from ineffective boards (Hoye & Cuskelly, 2004). These processes included the ability to co-opt members from outside the organization, using the board profile to recruit new members and interviewing nominees for board positions. None of the sport organizations in the study, either effective or ineffective boards, used a nominating or board development committee to recruit new members nor did they use written selection criteria for board members. The study confirmed the concerns expressed by SPARC (2004) that elections favour board candidates who are popular or have higher profiles. Board members and staff that were interviewed as part of the Hoye and Cuskelly (2004) study expressed some concern over the efficacy of election processes to select board members on the basis of ability to actively contribute to the board rather than just their popularity or profile.

Hoye and Cuskelly (2004) also found that interviewees from both effective and ineffective boards supported the idea of having board members appointed from outside the membership of the organization. However, two of the effective boards used their existing profile of board member skills to identify new board members who could bring certain skills to the board and used this as a basis to interview potential board members. A board chair of an effective board considered such a process to be akin to the senior board members 'anointing' new board members on the basis of their 'qualifications and their networking ability' (Hoye & Cuskelly, 2004: 92). The absence of formal selection criteria for board members is arguably due to the traditional nature of sport organizations electing individuals on the basis of representing a particular discipline, stakeholder group or geographic area of the sport. The collective skills of a board are therefore more a function of a ballot process conforming to an organization's constitution than of careful planning and selection to enhance the ability of the board to perform optimally. Few boards actually appoint people on the basis of skill requirements or a board profile which is most likely due to a reluctance to diminish the extent of direct membership representation on the board and the potential for disenfranchising the organization's membership.

In summary, the study by Hoye and Cuskelly (2004) demonstrated that actual board selection processes are far removed from those suggested by government agencies, although there was evidence of the adoption of some of the processes by some of the more effective boards. In order to illustrate the variation in board selection processes used by nonprofit sport organizations at national, state/provincial and local level, a number of examples from Australia, Canada and the UK are now presented.

Football Association

The Football Association (FA) is the governing body for the sport of football (soccer) in the UK. The FA operates one of the most financially significant sport leagues in the world, the English Premier League. The FA Council comprises 92 elected representatives from the various stakeholders, including the Premier League, the Football League, County Associations and other sport organizations. The FA Council meets six times per year and appoints a Board to govern the FA on its behalf. The membership of the Board comprises six representatives from the professional game and six from the national game, as well as the FA Chief Executive and FA Chairman (FA, 2006). The FA recently undertook a review of its governance structure, including a comparison with other national sport governing

81

bodies around the world (FA, 2005). It concluded (in part) that 'the FA is arguably the largest and most complex sporting organization in the world (and that) there has been little fundamental change from the historical model' (FA, 2005: 8) of how the sport is governed. The review made a number of recommendations for improving the decision-making structures and representative system for member organizations to more closely align the governance practices of the FA with contemporary governance practices. An important element of the review was an analysis of the role of independent board members in other similar sport governing bodies. The review concluded that independent board members are best used on a management board. Independent board members provide boards with challenging points of view, objectivity, and that the organizations that have them value their contributions. However, independent board members are only valuable when they understand the 'specificity of sport' (FA, 2005: 9). In other words, board members, irrespective of their level of independence require some working knowledge of the culture and programme and service delivery aspects of the sport. In addition, the review found that the use of independent board members by UK based sport governing bodies was increasing as 'an integral part of modernization' (FA, 2005: 10).

Canadian Olympic Committee

As early as 1997 the Canadian Olympic Committee (COC) addressed a wide range of governance issues in their *White Paper on Governance* (COC, 1997). The paper identified that the governance of sport in Canada had evolved through four stages (COC, 1997: 1):

> In the *early 60s–70s* it was volunteer driven. The volunteers planned, designed and implemented. They set policy and operated within that framework they set for themselves. There was little or no paid administrative support. In the *70s and early 80s* a new level of support was introduced. The sports were offered opportunities to hire staff to assist in the implementation of programmes and to improve communications and efficiency. There continued to be heavy volunteer involvement with an injection of paid continuity in the management. In the *late 80s and early 90s* the involvement of the professional staff increased. In addition, the number of professional staff increased. There was a growing involvement of the staff in the decision-making, the planning, the implementation and the policy setting. In certain organizations there was almost a transfer of policy and executive authority

from the volunteers to the staff. The *late 90s* and next millennium provide an opportunity to review the balance and develop a new model. The trend to decentralization, greater accountability, fiscal reality, and the determined vision, mission and values of the COC should be the forces which influence the final choice of the governance model.

In light of these changes in the way sport was governed in Canada, the paper articulated the COC's philosophy on maintaining a governance structure that 'ensures the majority of the decision-makers are elected by the Members of the COC' (COC, 1997: 2). The COC is a complex organization with many member organizations whose collective wisdom was considered essential to the success of the Olympic movement. Therefore, the system of governance adopted by the COC 'should encourage this collective wisdom to flourish and still ensure the ability of the COC to meet its mandates and objects' (COC, 1997: 2).

The COC has a three-tier governance structure. The first tier comprises the General Membership of the COC, made up of 446 individuals who represent the various stakeholders in the Canadian Olympic movement and meet annually. The COC has a complex array of membership categorizes which are specified in Figure 5.2. At the annual general meeting the General Membership assesses

> all aspects of the COC's business, including: reviewing the annual report and all financial statements, electing Class B members and directors at each quadrennial meeting, electing the executive members at each quadrennial, approving the COC vision and mission statements and reviewing by-law changes for approval' (COC, 2006).

The second tier of the COC governance structure is its 78 member Board of Directors, The Board is composed of 'a representative of each National Sport Federation governing a sport on the official programmes of the Olympic, Olympic Winter or Pan American Games; the IOC Members in Canada; the members of the Athletes Council Executive; a Coaches representative; the International Federation Presidents resident in Canada; 12 Directors-at-large; and the CEO' (COC, 2006). The Board of Directors meets and is responsible for managing the affairs of the COC including establishing the COC's vision, mission, values and direction, monitoring the progress of the COC towards its stated goals, and setting the overall policy and strategic objectives. Within these areas of responsibilities the Board 'approves the Strategic and Financial Plan for each quadrennium, the annual plan and budget, the COC financial statements and the Auditors' report, and selects Bid Cities to go forward on behalf of the COC' (COC, 2006).

A sub-committee of the Board of Directors known as the Executive Committee forms the third tier of the COC governance structure and operates more like a governing board as conceptualized in this book. The Executive Committee meets four times a year in between the Board of

Membership category	Membership description
Class A	*Appointed* representatives from each of the Pan American or Olympic National Sport Federations.
Class B	*Elected* members at-large who are admitted to membership at each quadrennial meeting of the members to a maximum of 125 members.
Class C	*Ex officio* current and honorary members of the International Olympic Committee (IOC) that reside in Canada.
Class D	*Non-voting*, honorary members recommended by the Board and Executive Committee.
Class E	*Appointed* representatives of National Sport Federations that are neither a Pan American Sport nor an Olympic Sport but are still recognized by the COC.
Class F	Chair of the Athletes Council (*Ex officio*).
Class G	*Non-voting* members who have requested COC membership. (Usually a nonprofit sporting entity whose primary purpose is compatible with the COC's objectives.)
Class H	*Appointed* coaches representatives designated jointly by the Coaching Associations (CAC & CPCA).
Class K	*Ex officio* Presidents of International Federations (IF) resident in Canada.

Figure 5.2 Membership categories of the COC (*Source*: COC (2006); reprinted with permission of the Canadian Olympic Committee)

Directors meetings and is responsible for 'approving the appointment of the CEO, providing direction to the CEO, identifying areas that may require policy and presenting a range of options to the Board for debate and approval, determining the size and composition of each Canadian Pan American and Olympic Team, and approving all award recipients' (COC, 2006).

The members at each tier of the complex COC governance structure obtain their positions through one of four channels that are prescribed under the COC General By-Laws. Fifty pages of by-laws detail the various rules and procedures for election, selection or appointment for each membership category and for each of the three tiers of governance (COC, 2005). Council, board or committee members are either appointed, elected or are ex officio (i.e. having the right to membership on the basis of a formal position they may hold elsewhere within an organization) or, depending on their class of membership, are designated in a non-voting capacity. Elected members hold their positions for a term of 4 years. In contrast, appointed representatives retain their membership until their appointing organization designates another representative or until the appointing organization ceases to be recognized by the COC. Ex officio members retain their membership for the duration of their term in office. Non-voting members are present only within the General Membership and comprise Class D and G members with the exception of the COC's Chief Executive Officer, who participates in all three tiers of governance but as a non-voting, ex officio member (COC, 2006).

Football Federation Australia

The Football Federation Australia (FFA) was the subject of a governance review in late 2002 and early 2003. The then Soccer Australia (SA) agreed to a major review of the structure, governance and management of soccer in Australia and that the review be managed by the ASC. In mid-2002, it was evident that SA was AUS $2.6 million in debt, had reduced staffing levels at the national office, was racked by political infighting, had a lack of strategic direction and had experienced mixed results in international competition. The review found that many of the state, territory and regional governing bodies suffered similar financial difficulties, political infighting and inappropriate governance systems. These problems lead to mistrust and disharmony within the sport, a lack of national strategic direction, inappropriate behaviour by representatives of member organizations, and factionalism that hampered national decision-making (ASC, 2003). The major finding of the review was that changes were required in four key areas:

1. Ensuring independence of the governing bodies;
2. Separating governance from day-to-day management;
3. Change the membership and voting structures for the national and state organizations
4. The relationship between SA and the National Soccer League (NSL).

Several issues were at the heart of the governance problems facing SA at the time. Amongst these issues were inequitable representation and voting structures for member organizations, a need to restructure the composition of the national board along with the nomination and election processes used to appoint national board members. For example, the membership of SA comprised 12 state and territory-based associations, the Australian Soccer Referees Association and the 12 Australian clubs participating in the NSL. The number of votes allocated to each state and territory varied for no logical reason. The review cited the example that Soccer Canberra, despite having more registered players than Soccer Tasmania, exercised three votes against Tasmania's five votes (ASC, 2003). A number of junior or amateur associations with large registration numbers exercised one vote, compared with other state bodies with fewer registration numbers or financial contributions that exercised four or more votes. The voting structures employed within state federations and associations also lacked consistency. For example, some federations and associations adopted a district basis as their voting structure. Others gave preference to premier and state league clubs while others excluded, or heavily weighted their voting structures against, amateurs, women, Futsal and school groups (ASC, 2003). There was also no consistent treatment of individual registrants within this complex array of voting structures. The review concluded that there was no genuine commonality of the membership representation and voting structures amongst SA's member organizations.

The review made 53 recommendations aimed at improving the structure, governance and management of SA. In terms of board composition the report recommended that the membership of SA be changed to recognize key interest groups and to reduce the power of larger states and the NSL. It was recommended that SA adopt a new constitution, and that each state and territory affiliate adopt a model constitution and membership agreements. The review also made a number of recommendations aimed at improving the electoral process for appointing board members. These included that the National Council of SA (comprising representatives of state and territory affiliates, standing committees representing specific interest groups and the NSL) elect independent board members of SA at the annual general meeting.

Victorian golf challenges

A review of the issues and challenges for golf clubs commissioned by the Victorian Golf Association (VGA) in 2004 included an examination of golf club governance. As the governing body for golf in the state of Victoria, Australia, the VGA represents the interests of approximately 125,000 amateur golfers and more than 350 golf clubs, the majority of which are membership based. The review revealed that more than half of Victoria's golf clubs found it difficult to fill board positions, particularly the core board member roles within golf clubs of President, Treasurer and Secretary. In addition, the review cited anecdotal evidence that:

> not only are recruits to the board hard to secure, but the quality of these recruits has generally declined in recent years in terms of their experience and know-how. The difficulty is generally greater at clubs with lower annual fee levels, as these clubs have fewer staff to

support board responsibilities and less funds to spend in areas that satisfy governance requirements and responsibilities (VGA, 2004: 112).

The review also found that approximately 60% of clubs had limits on the number of consecutive terms a general committee member could serve. These limits compounded the problem of recruiting and retaining sufficiently skilled and qualified people for board positions. Approximately 20% of clubs also imposed limits on the length of terms for general committee members. A particular quirk in the governance structures of some clubs was the impost of minimum periods of time general committee members were required to serve before being eligible for the role of President, Treasurer or Secretary. The review concluded that the problems of board member recruitment were partly the result of the constitutions of clubs that 'were written decades ago' (VGA, 2004: 119). Commenting on the need for constitutions to be reviewed frequently to ensure the continued relevance of governance practices, the review found that constitutional change or renewal is difficult because most clubs required 65% of the member vote to make amendments to this important instrument of governance.

These examples of board composition and selection processes within sport organizations at local and national levels in the UK, Canada and Australia highlight the dependence of most nonprofit sport organizations on delegate or member representation models for recruiting board members. They have also illustrated the convoluted processes in place to recruit board members, especially at the national levels.

Conclusion

This chapter has explored a number of issues regarding board composition, selection and recruitment of board members and board chairs. The right to govern nonprofit sport organizations rests with those individual and member associations with a stake in the way the organization is governed. A fundamental issue within nonprofit sport organizations is the requirement to maintain adequate member and stakeholder representation systems whilst ensuring the individuals elected, selected, invited or appointed to fulfil board roles are appropriately skilled and experienced. A review of the governance guidelines developed by agencies of the likes of the ASC and SPARC discussed the implications of moving sport organizations away from the traditional delegate or representative model towards the appointment of independent board members. The examples of board composition and selection processes that exist within sport organizations at local and national levels illustrated some of the convoluted processes used to recruit board members in nonprofit sport organizations. There are several challenges for nonprofit sport organizations in relation to board composition, recruitment and selection. These include the appointment of appropriately skilled board members, something that smaller organizations are finding increasingly difficult. Regardless of the electoral or appointment process in place for board members within nonprofit sport organizations there is clearly a need to develop better recruitment, selection and induction processes so that they can perform their individual roles to the best of their ability and work as part of a team, which is the focus of the next chapter.

6

Teamwork: board behaviour and culture

Overview

The earlier chapters in this book outlined the structural elements of governance within nonprofit sport organizations, the positions that fit within the structures and how individuals are selected for those positions. The efficacy of governance structural arrangements and the division of roles and responsibilities among volunteer board members and paid staff is affected by the nature and extent of the working relationships of individuals involved in those positions. This chapter describes and analyses guidelines concerned with how boards should work together, within and outside the board meeting room. A model of board behaviour is presented along with a detailed discussion of the dynamics of board culture. Utilizing principles from organizational theory, the issues of board culture manifestation, its impact on board behaviour, and how board culture might be managed are explored in detail. The impact of board culture and other governance elements on board member commitment are also explored through an examination of the research that has been conducted within nonprofit organizations and nonprofit sport organizations.

Teamwork guidelines

The governance guidelines developed by the UK National Council for Voluntary Organizations (NCVO, 2005), UK Sport (2004) and Sport and Recreation New Zealand (SPARC, 2004) are quite prescriptive in the roles and responsibilities nonprofit boards should fulfil. They set out a number of principles for board members to follow in the carriage of their duties, but the guidelines are largely silent on the topic of how board members can work effectively together. This paucity of detail is also evident in the relatively small amount of research that has been conducted into the culture and behaviour of nonprofit boards. This is surprising, given the fact that the Australian Sports Commission (ASC, 2005: 17) identified that 'one of the greatest challenges facing boards is the ability to achieve consensus and cohesion while at the same time encouraging diversity and legitimate dissent'. In trying to assist nonprofit sport organizations to address this issue, the ASC (2005) outlined a range of factors that contribute to the development of an effective board team (see Figure 6.1).

The majority of these suggestions relate to how the board conducts its business and how the individuals within boards interact with one another with respect to decision-making processes. The format and conduct of

- The skills mix of the board is appropriate to its role and tasks.
- There is agreement that the board will 'speak with one voice' about all policy matters when communicating with the CEO and the outside world.
- There is a robust and productive partnership with the CEO in which both good and bad news is shared openly and in a timely fashion.
- There is a positive and constructive boardroom culture in which all directors know that their contribution is valued.
- There is a good balance between talking and listening. Board members are willing to suspend judgement until an issue is fully canvassed and all perspectives are aired.
- The chairperson manages the meeting processes so that issues before the board are adequately addressed. Agenda and time management facilitate appropriate attention to board issues.
- Legitimate dissent and diversity are viewed as healthy components in boardroom dialogue and encouraged so that the full range of views, opinions and experience are available to support board decisions.
- The views of management are sought and valued.
- Board members can ask tough questions without management becoming defensive.

Figure 6.1 Factors that contribute to an effective board team (*Source*: ASC (2005: 17); reprinted with permission of the Australian Sports Commission)

board meetings, where the bulk of the board's work is done and decisions made, are therefore important elements that influence individual board member and collective board behaviour. The following section discusses recommended approaches to the conduct of board meetings and their implications for facilitating effective collective board behaviour.

The board meeting

Bieber (2003: 175) stated that 'board meetings in practice are the formal location for much of an organization's governance'. Indeed in state/ provincial, national and international nonprofit sport organizations, board members may only ever meet face to face within the context of board meetings. The importance of making board meetings focussed and productive and the influence of board meetings in shaping board member behaviour should not be underestimated. Fishel (2003: 141) argued that 'meetings can make or break a board'. Ill-directed or ill-prepared meetings can sap the energy and motivation of board members, whereas purposeful and well-organized meetings 'can build the organization's sense of direction and motivate the board members and staff involved' (Fishel, 2003: 141).

The ASC (2005: 20–21) addressed these issues in their guidelines for the conduct of board meetings which stated that:

- Board meetings should focus on governance matters affecting the control and direction of the organization, such as policy-making and review, financial health of the organization, strategic thinking and progress towards Key Result Areas, and legal compliance, rather than on administrative and operational matters.
- Board meetings should reflect an appropriate apportionment of focus between compliance with formal requirements, for example, monitoring financial performance, and monitoring overall achievement of Key Result Areas and engaging in strategic thinking.
- The board meeting is an ideal forum for the board to engage in strategic thinking in order to ensure the ongoing relevance and appropriateness of its strategic plan and Key Result Areas. The meeting should adopt a future focus building on past learning.
- Board meetings should be managed in a manner designed to encourage diversity of opinion, ensuring input from all board members as appropriate without prejudicing effective and efficient decision-making.

As discussed in Chapter 4, Inglis and Weaver (2000) argued that the traditional board agenda and meeting format adopted by boards fails to allocate sufficient time to the future of the organization. The ASC (2005) guidelines recommend a shift towards the board focussing on the strategic direction

- All board members have equal rights at the board meeting. This includes the right to:
  - have their questions, opinions and views heard;
  - question the CEO;
  - vote on an issue or refrain from voting;
  - have their vote recorded in the minutes or record of the meeting;
  - receive information relevant to the board meeting (agendas and papers) in time to prepare for the meeting.
- The board as a whole should develop an annual agenda at the commencement of the governance year, identifying key governance responsibilities and events and programming these into the year's board meetings. With the annual agenda as the basis for all board meetings, the chairperson, with input from other board members and the CEO as appropriate, should shape the agenda for each board meeting. Meeting agendas should include, as a regular item, the opportunity for individual board members to declare any existing or potential conflicts of interest regarding items on the agenda, before these items are discussed at the meeting.
- The board should meet as often as is required to carry out its governance duties. Typically, boards of sporting organizations meet monthly or every second month. Board meetings should take as long as is required to carry out the board's governance responsibilities.
- The board should ensure that appropriate records of board meetings are kept to provide an accurate account of decisions reached. Neither the CEO nor any board member should be required to take minutes at the board meeting, as this removes them from participating fully. Rather, the board should engage a meeting secretary or use a staff member to fulfil the role of minute taker.

Figure 6.2 Meeting procedures (*Source*: ASC (2005: 21–22); reprinted with permission of the Australian Sports Commission)

of the organization in order to shape the behaviour and thinking of board members. The guidelines also outline the rights of board members at board meetings, the benefits of setting an annual board agenda, the frequency and time for which boards should meet and the need for appropriate record keeping of board discussions and decisions (ASC, 2005) (see Figure 6.2).

The guidelines developed by SPARC (2004) are more prescriptive than those of the ASC, stating that board meetings 'should be stimulating, challenging and, ultimately, satisfying' and they should focus on:

> desired strategic achievements and understanding of the environment and issues impacting on the organization's ability to achieve its goals (and) the risk factors that could impede or disrupt the organization's ability to achieve the desired results (including the necessary monitoring of chief executive and organizational compliance with board expectations, policies and statutes, by-laws, etc.) (SPARC, 2004: 42).

SPARC (2004) also prescribed the order in which items should be considered during board meetings:

> The structure and sequence of items within a meeting is important. Many boards have benefited from an agenda that tackles more demanding strategic issues early in the meeting. Such boards leave monitoring and other compliance-type topics until later in their meeting. At that stage, it matters less if the board is tiring or some members have to leave before the agenda is completed. Another tactic is to schedule separate meetings for strategic thinking. Such retreat-style meetings can be worthwhile so long as it's not then assumed that strategic thinking is something to be undertaken periodically rather than as a matter of course (SPARC, 2004: 43–44).

SPARC (2004: 44) also recommend that in order for a board to become more focussed on discussing important rather than urgent matters, the following points should be considered:

- effective meeting planning and strong meeting management;
- appropriate, concise board papers which get to the heart of the matters on which the board must deliberate;
- prior exploration of the issues by board committees or taskforces helping to gather relevant information and to frame issues;
- good preparation by each board member;
- the ability of board members to ask probing questions;
- self-discipline and concentration by meeting participants;
- proactive policy that prevents the board from needing to consider everything in an ad hoc manner.

Aside from extensive guidelines for how board meeting agendas should be constructed and recommendations for the focus of board discussions, SPARC (2004) provided advice about facilitating greater participation from board members and ultimately increase their satisfaction. Echoing the sentiments expressed by Fishel (2003), the guidelines highlight that 'frustrated or disenchanted board members aren't likely to be constructive or effective contributors. At best, such members are likely to passively 'opt out'. At worst, they're likely to be disruptive' (SPARC, 2004: 44). The guidelines indicate that board member satisfaction with meetings is likely to be greatest when:

- meetings are well planned and support effective preparation;
- they are well chaired, balancing effectiveness and efficiency;
- board members work well together and the meeting process allows everyone to participate fully;
- board members are disciplined (e.g. they stick to the issue, they do not dominate discussion, they listen actively to others, they do not become parochial);

- respect is given to different points of view (and there is a diversity of viewpoints);
- the board's deliberations are based on dialogue (collaborative discourse) rather than debate (competitive discourse);
- there is a sense of having dealt deliberately and satisfactorily with important issues.

These recommendations highlight the fact that regardless of governance structural arrangements, the division of roles and responsibilities among volunteer board members, the processed used to recruit board members, and the behaviour of board members within the board is affected by how the board meetings are planned and facilitated and how the individuals work as a group. The following section outlines a model of board behaviour that attempts to explain the various influences on individual board member and collective board behaviour.

Board behaviour model

Miller-Millesen (2003) outlined a theoretical model of board behaviour based on the application of agency theory, resource dependence theory and institutional theory. Each of these theories provides an insight into certain aspects of board behaviour, or as Miller-Millesen (2003: 522) argued, 'each theory paints an incomplete picture of a highly complex phenomenon because each theory focusses on a different set of activities and functions'. Board behaviour is conceptualized as how a board performs, or in other words, the use of board process and structure in fulfilling its governance role. Agency theory is useful as it helps to explain the need to separate organizational ownership from managerial control, the need for boards to appoint appropriate staff and why they should monitor their actions to ensure they act in the best interests of the organization. The resource dependence view highlights that organizational survival is dependent on the ability of an organization to secure resources, something that board members play a key role in via their ability to facilitate exchanges with other organizations or individuals with whom they are connected. Resource dependence theory helps explain the role of board members acting as boundary spanners for their organization and the exercise of power and influence with others to assist the organization. Institutional theory helps to explain the external pressures that force organizations to adopt similar governance structures, processes and ultimately behaviours.

The model presented in Figure 6.3 is 'an integrative theoretical framework of board behaviour that identifies the conceptual links between environmental factors, organizational factors and board behaviour' (Miller-Millesen, 2003: 523). The model contends that board behaviour is subject to two environmental influences. The first of these is pressure from

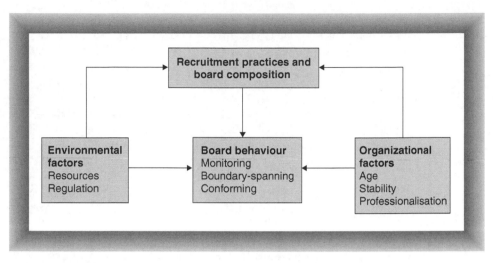

Figure 6.3 Model of board behaviour (*Source*: Adapted from Miller-Millesen (2003: 523)

the resource or funding environment in which an organization operates. Boards assist organizations learn how to cope with such pressures which, in turn, impact on the behaviour of the board in areas such as monitoring, boundary-spanning activities and ensuring the organization complies with funding requirements. The reporting and accountability requirements that federal agencies such as UK Sport impose on National Sport Organizations (NSOs) as part of funding or service agreements are illustrative of the pressures that force boards to adopt monitoring and compliance behaviours. The second environmental influence is pressure from institutions or regulatory agencies to adopt common practices which drive board behaviour. In the sport environment these pressures may, for example, take the form of the guidelines developed by the ASC or SPARC which NSOs are encouraged to adopt.

The Miller-Millesen model also posits that three organizational factors: age or life cycle stage; stability and professionalization can lead to variations in board behaviour. Miller-Millesen (2003) argued that board behaviour will change according to the life cycle or development stage of the board, whether the organization was in a state of crisis or radical change, and the extent of skills and expertise available within the board. Furthermore, the environmental and organizational influences have an impact on the recruitment practices and consequent composition of the board. Such influences may include the size of the board, the ideal mix of board members' age, gender, education, the skills boards should strive to achieve and how boards should go about future board member recruitment and selection.

Miller-Millesen (2003) argued that a range of prescriptive guides have characterized good governance (i.e. board behaviour) by outlining an ideal set of board roles and responsibilities. Some of these governance guidelines have been subject to empirical examination, albeit indirectly, by a number of researchers (cf. Provan, 1980; Jackson & Holland, 1998). The model presents a theory-based typology of board behaviour that links agency theory, resource dependence theory and institutional theory to various aspects of board behaviour. Agency theory helps to explain the monitoring behaviour of boards that manifests as the board controlling the mission and purpose of an organization, overseeing programmes and services, undertaking strategic planning, implementing fiscal control and evaluating the CEO. Resource dependence theory aids in understanding the boundary-spanning activities undertaken by boards including reducing environmental uncertainty, managing problematic interdependencies, raising money and enhancing organizational image. Finally, institutional theory helps to explain the behaviour of the board in ensuring the organization complies with its legal responsibilities, and in its implementation of mandates on behalf of organizational members or stakeholders.

The board behaviour model, however, also highlights how many board behaviours 'can be understood and interpreted from all three theoretical perspectives. For example, boards might engage in strategic planning because there are control issues (agency theory), or to manage resource dependencies (resource dependence), or because funders require it (institutional theory)' (Miller-Millesen, 2003: 539). The value of the model is that it highlights that best practice guidelines for board behaviour are based on three different theoretical perspectives. Miller-Millesen (2003: 543) concluded that 'until actual (board) behaviour is observed and explained, linking board activity to organizational performance will continue to yield ambiguous results'.

More empirical evidence of how nonprofit boards actually behave is needed in order to fully understand how they should behave in order to deliver better organizational outcomes. This is even more important for nonprofit sport boards. Doherty (1998: 18) observed that boards and 'committees are inevitable and instrumental to the management and delivery of sport'. However, research to date had not addressed areas such as 'group cohesion, or any other attitudes or behaviours of the work group (i.e. the board) or the individual's experience as a member' (Doherty, 1998: 18). The following sections explore the limited amount of research that has been conducted in these areas.

Board culture

Holland, Leslie and Holzhalb (1993: 142) suggested that the 'organizational culture perspective offers a promising framework for understanding and improving the performance of nonprofit boards'. However, authors such as Schein (1990) and Trice and Beyer (1993) argued that there is little agreement on what organizational culture means, how it should be measured and how it can be used to assist organizations. Despite these concerns, it is generally accepted that each organization has its own unique culture. That culture provides a sense of identity for organizational members, enhances the stability of the social system within organizations, facilitates the commitment of organizational members and guides the attitudes and behaviour of organizational members (Robbins, Millett, Cacioppe & Waters-Marsh, 2001).

Before exploring the value of this perspective in understanding board behaviour, it is necessary to first clarify the concept of organizational culture. Schein (1996: 229) defined organizational culture as the 'shared norms, values and assumptions' held by organizational members. These assumptions can be 'invented, discovered or developed by a given group' (Schein, 1990: 111). In turn, they are used to teach new group members how to perceive, think and feel in relation to operating within the group context. Organizational culture can be examined at three levels: (1) observable artefacts such as the physical layout of office space, annual reports, or specific language or jargon; (2) values which are apparent in charters, espoused philosophies, or norms and (3) basic underlying assumptions that determine group and organizational members 'perceptions, thought processes, feelings and behaviour' (Schein, 1990: 112).

It should not be assumed that within any organization there is a uniform understanding and adoption of a 'single' culture. Robbins et al. (2001) argued that large organizations have a dominant culture of core values that are generally accepted by all organizational members but separate groups within the organization can develop a distinct culture or subculture, comprising the core values of the dominant culture plus additional values unique to the smaller group. In this context the board can be considered as a unit of an organization that possesses its own subculture. In one of the earliest attempts to explore board culture Holland et al. (1993: 142) argued that 'the organizational culture perspective suggests that anyone seeking to help a board improve its performance must consider its underlying assumptions and beliefs, which are the foundations supporting its present customs'. At the heart of understanding board culture are the issues of 'how a board perceives and deals with its responsibilities, why it sustains its current habits of behaviour, and what it assumes and expects of its members' (Holland et al., 1993: 142).

In order to manage or change an organization's culture, Schein (1990) argued that it is important to understand how individuals learn the culture of an organization. This learning can occur in two ways. The first is through norm formation around critical incidents where a reaction by a group to an incident will become a norm, a belief and finally an assumption about how a group should behave in similar situations. The second is through group members modelling the behaviour of group leaders and internalizing their values and assumptions. Thus managers can influence the extent to which this individual learning of organizational culture takes place by utilizing primary embedding mechanisms. The include focussing their attention on: measuring and controlling certain organizational activities; their reactions to critical incidents and crises; deliberate role modelling and coaching; and, using deliberate criteria for allocating rewards and status in the recruitment, selection, promotion and retirement of group members. Managers can also utilize secondary mechanisms such as: the organization's structure; systems and procedures; design of physical space; stories, legends, myths and symbols; and formal statements of organizational philosophy creed and charter to educate individuals about an organization's culture (Schein, 1990). These same learning processes and mechanisms are evident in the activities of boards and the ways in which board members are orientated to their board's culture (Holland et al., 1993).

Maintaining organizational culture can be achieved through managing the way new organizational members are socialized. Schein (1990) argued that individuals respond differently to the socialization processes used by managers and organizations. The result is that they may adopt either: a custodial orientation where they totally conform to the organizational culture; the central culture elements with flexibility in how to act which is termed creative individualism or totally reject all norms and rebel. In order to achieve the ideal custodial orientation of a group culture, Schein (1990) suggested that managers need to provide formal induction and training, adopt a professional development approach to its provision, provide clear role models and provide a sequenced learning process. Holland et al. (1993: 144) argued that 'a board's culture is an essential element of its survival' and thus the maintenance of its culture is important for the stability of the board. Their view was that the culture of the board 'provides board members with a sense of order and purpose, identity, security, standards of expected behaviour, continuity and means of dealing with problems and controlling anxiety' (Holland et al., 1993: 144).

In one of few published studies of board culture within nonprofit sport organizations Doherty, Patterson and Van Bussel (2004) focussed on identifying the types and relative strength of perceived committee norms. They argued that norms had considerable influence on individual and group behaviour, and in the context of volunteer boards these may be important drivers of organizational behaviour, particularly in the absence of other behavioural control mechanisms such as remuneration. Norms were defined as unwritten rules of conduct for guiding behaviour that typically 'form with respect to behaviours that are most important to a particular group; for example, attendance, individual contribution, cooperation and/or group performance' (Doherty et al., 2004: 110). They noted also that groups only form norms 'around issues or circumstances that are important to the group, and help increase clarity and reduce uncertainty in group member behaviour' (Doherty et al., 2004: 111). The existence of strong norms would indicate consistent expectations amongst group members about specific behaviours while weak norms would indicate a lack of shared commitment to certain behaviours.

The Doherty et al. (2004) study investigated committee norms within community-based nonprofit amateur sport organizations in two categories: (1) performance or productivity norms such as expectations about group member attendance, punctuality, preparedness, contribution, cooperation, communication and task completion and (2) interpersonal or social norms such as expectations about how group members relate to each other, including mutual respect and group harmony, the degree of conflict tolerated by the group and an informal dress code. The study found that irrespective of length of tenure or committee role, committee members have the same understanding of each of the norms. The study also found that 'the perceived expectations of the group are apparently only a modest influence on an individual's effort on behalf of their committee' (Doherty et al., 2004: 128). They concluded that, contrary to their expectations, perceptions held by committee members of a range of performance and social norms may be less influential on individual behaviour than other forces such as intrinsic and extrinsic rewards, a personal sense of obligation to the board or a sense of altruism. In essence, they concluded that the 'group context may be less meaningful to individual behaviour in volunteer sport executive committees than other personal forces' (Doherty et al., 2004: 128). While board or committee members may share a common understanding of their expected behaviour, the study did not measure actual behavioural conformance with those norms, and was an area highlighted for further investigation.

The extent to which board members perceive their board acts as a cohesive group is another area of research related to board culture. Cohesion 'represents the unity, togetherness, concordance or harmony of a group' (Doherty & Carron, 2003: 117). Cohesion is a multi-dimensional construct, comprising: (1) an individual's attraction to the group-task or their feelings about their involvement in the group task; (2) an individual's attraction to the group-social or their feelings about their social interaction with the group; (3) group integration-task or an individual's perception of the similarity and unification of the group around its tasks and objectives and (4) group integration-social or an individual's perception of the similarity and unification of the group as a social unit (Doherty & Carron, 2003). The extent to which group members perceive their group is cohesive has been found to be associated positively with the degree to which individuals adhere to expected behaviour, lower levels of absenteeism, higher satisfaction and the amount of effort individuals are prepared to put into group activities. Doherty and Carron (2003) argued that committees and boards of nonprofit sport organizations are likely to perform more effectively if they are regarded as cohesive. In a study of sport volunteer committee members, Doherty and Carron (2003: 131) found that volunteer committee members 'perceived greater task cohesion than social cohesion in their committees'. They concluded that volunteers seek to become involved in committees to contribute to the tasks of the committee and to develop social relationships, and 'they perceive their committee to be integrated around those same aspects, but particularly the tasks of the group' (Doherty & Carron, 2003: 132). An important aspect of their study was to explore whether committee members' intention to quit as a volunteer committee member was related to their perception of group cohesion. They found that committee members were less likely to intend quitting if they perceived their committee to be united and cooperative regarding its objectives and tasks. Doherty and Carron (2003: 136) concluded that 'given the relative importance of task cohesion, team building should focus primarily on uniting committee members regarding group goals and tasks, and nurturing cooperation among members'.

In summary, board culture and specifically committee norms and group cohesion appear to be important influences on the behaviour of individual board members and the board as a group. It is generally accepted that organizational or board culture provides a sense of identity for board members, enhances the stability of the social system within the board and guides the attitudes and behaviour of board members. However, relatively little is known about the ways in which board members actually learn the culture of their board or how board members, board chairs or CEOs attempt to manage or influence that culture. Organizational culture is also linked to facilitating commitment of board members, which is the focus of the following section.

Board member commitment

The concept of organizational commitment has been shown to predict job performance, citizenship behaviour, absenteeism, intention to stay or leave and turnover behaviour in a variety of organizational settings (e.g. Meyer & Allen, 1997; Carbery, Garavan, O'Brien & McDonnell, 2003; Fuller, Barnett, Hester & Relyea, 2003). Meyer and Allen (1991) postulated that organizational commitment is made up of three components: (1) affective commitment where individuals become committed because they want to; (2) continuance commitment where individuals develop commitment because they have to as a result of a lack of alternatives or because to leave an organization would require them to sacrifice previous work efforts and (3) normative commitment where individuals feel they ought to be committed.

Organizational commitment has also been shown to predict intention to stay or leave for committee or board members of voluntary sport organizations. Cuskelly (1995: 259) argued that 'sporting organizations which develop and maintain a positive group environment through committee (group) processes which emphasis high levels of cohesion, support, trust, openness and participation in decision-making should be more likely to retain the services of volunteer administrators'. In a study to determine the relationship between committee functioning and organizational commitment within nonprofit sport organizations, Cuskelly (1995: 264) found that volunteer committee members 'who perceive their committee is cohesive, receptive to new ideas and uses open processes to make decisions and to handle conflict between members, are more likely to report higher levels of commitment'. The study concluded that the committees or boards of voluntary sport organizations should develop and maintain a welcoming environment through ensuring members 'have a clear understanding of the organization's goals, adequate opportunities to use their skills and experience, and equitable input to decision-making' (Cuskelly, 1995: 268). Adopting the teamwork guidelines developed by the ASC (2005) and discussed earlier in this chapter would appear to go some way to assisting sport organizations meet these aspirations. In a later study, Cuskelly, McIntyre and Boag (1998) reported that over time, perceptions of higher committee functioning were related to higher levels of reported commitment. This later study concluded that the development of organizational commitment amongst volunteers involved in sport committee or boards is a complex process requiring further investigation. Since this early work was completed, there have been no further reported studies of organizational commitment among sport committee or board members. There has however, been a number of reported studies investigating board member commitment within general nonprofit boards.

In a study of boards of nonprofit social service organizations, Preston and Brown (2004) found a positive relationship between affective commitment and board member performance. In other words, those board members that were more emotionally attached to the organization were more likely to engage in board member behaviours such as making larger financial contributions, donating more hours to the organization, attending more meetings and being involved in a wider cross section of board activities. The study also showed that board members experience an element of normative commitment, or a sense of obligation that they should remain committed to the organization and their role as a board member. There was, however, no relationship found between continuance commitment and board member performance.

A study of the relationship between organizational commitment and role fulfilment of chamber of commerce board members by Dawley, Stephens and Stephens (2005) concluded that higher levels of affective commitment, normative commitment and continuance commitment based on low alternatives were associated with desirable board member role fulfilment. They argued that in the volunteer context, the construct of continuance commitment based on personal sacrifice as measured by Meyer and Allen

(1997) may not be useful due to differences in the motivations of volunteers compared to paid staff. Stephens, Dawley and Stephens (2004a) also explored the relationship between four antecedents of commitment (board member tenure, leadership role, assessment of board performance and board size), the commitment variables (affective, normative, continuance (personal sacrifice) and continuance (low alternatives) and board member self-reported performance. They found positive relationships between tenure, affective commitment and board member performance, and that board members 'who have or are serving as leaders, perform better and have higher levels of affective commitment to the board' (Stephens et al., 2004a: 496). They concluded that nonprofit organizations would benefit from implementing strategies to nurture and retain board members as this leads to better commitment and performance.

In the third paper derived from their study, Stephens, Dawley and Stephens (2004b) explored the relationship between board members' potential to act in service, resource dependence or control roles and their associated levels of affective, normative and continuance commitment. The service role of a board member was defined as actions such as providing advice to senior management and participating in strategy development. The resource dependence role of a board member concerns the ability of the board member to bring resources to the organization. The control role of a board member was defined as the potential for a board member to invest time and effort into control functions if the performance of the CEO was deemed poor. Stephens et al. (2004b: 408) found that the:

> three corporate governance role potentials were strongly associated with normative and affective commitment ... (specifically) ... greater service and resource dependence role potential will lead to higher levels of affective and normative commitment, while higher levels of control role potential will lead to lower levels of affective and normative commitment.

The implications of their study were that boards should focus on recruiting board members that will be more likely to possess or develop higher levels of affective and normative commitment. In other words, boards should, for example, focus on recruiting board members who have high quality contacts that can be used to the organization's advantage as those board members will develop a heightened sense of commitment due to their personal contacts being utilized. Boards can also try and rotate people into leadership roles as this was found to foster a greater sense of commitment.

In summary, these studies have shown that board member commitment is driven by the degree to which boards are perceived to be functioning efficiently and effectively, the potential for board members to bring valuable resources to the board and the extent to which board members are involved in the development of organizational strategy. In turn, board member commitment is related to higher levels of individual board member and collective board performance.

Conclusion

The preceding chapters of this book outlined the governance structures of nonprofit sport organizations, the various positions that fit within these structures and how individuals are selected to governance roles. This chapter examined a number of guidelines outlining how boards should work together and the conduct of board meetings. Individual board member and collective board behaviour is influenced by two environmental factors, namely pressure from the resource or funding environment in which an organization operates, and pressure from institutions or regulatory agencies to adopt common practices which drive board behaviour. Boards adopt collective behaviours that assist organizations cope with such pressures by undertaking monitoring and boundary-spanning activities and ensuring the organization complies with funding requirements and associated reporting.

Board culture and specifically issues such as committee norms and group cohesion are important elements that affect individual and collective board behaviours. It is generally accepted that a positive board culture provides a sense of identity for board members, enhances the stability of the board and guides the attitudes and behaviour of board members. However, little is known about the processes affecting how board members learn or adopt board culture or how board culture can be managed or influenced. Research evidence suggests that board member commitment is affected by the degree to which boards are perceived to be functioning efficiently and effectively, as well as perceptions about their potential role as board members. Board member commitment is related to improved/higher levels of individual and collective board performance.

7

Offensive game plans: strategic governance

Overview

A fundamental aspect of the governance role is to determine the strategic direction of an organization and monitor performance toward desired outcomes. This chapter examines the role of the board in strategy formulation, implementation and monitoring as well as the processes that facilitate board involvement. The pressures on boards to engage with strategy are reviewed along with a number of prescribed guidelines on how boards should undertake their role in organizational strategy. The empirical evidence from both corporate and nonprofit sectors on the engagement of boards with strategy is reviewed. Finally, issues involved with enhancing the strategic contribution of the boards of nonprofit sport organizations are detailed.

Strategic contribution of the board

104

Much of the practitioner-oriented literature highlights the value of boards engaging in strategy as a way of focussing board activities and 'aligning the board, CEO and others with a common sense of direction' (Fishel, 2003: 105). According to Nadler (2004), there are a number of benefits for organizations that actively seek the involvement of board members in strategic activities. First, board members have an increased level of understanding of the environment in which their organization operates and the internal capabilities of their organization, thus enabling the board to make more meaningful contributions to strategic discussions. Second, by being involved, board members develop a sense of ownership and therefore commitment to organizational strategy. Third, board members bring differing perspectives to strategic issues facing their organization and can therefore improve the quality of decisions. Fourth, the processes involved in strategic thinking, debate over possible directions and strategies, and strategic planning force the board and senior staff to work closely with one another. Fifth, board members tend to feel more satisfied with their role when they believe that their skills and knowledge has been put to good use and they have contributed to the organization in some meaningful fashion. Finally, board members act as more informed and vocal advocates for their organization, when championing and defending organizational strategy.

The governance guidelines produced by Sport and Recreation New Zealand (SPARC, 2004) outlined the benefits of the boards of sport organizations engaging in strategic activities (see Figure 7.1).

The dilemma for boards that seek to contribute to the strategy of their organizations is to find an appropriate balance between organizational performance and conformance. Cornforth (2003a: 13–14) argued that:

> these contrasting roles require a very different orientation and behaviour on the part of board members. The conformance role demands careful monitoring and scrutiny of the organisation's past performance and is risk-averse. The performance role demands forward vision, an understanding of the organization and its environment and perhaps a greater willingness to take risks.

How then can boards make a meaningful contribution to organizational strategy while adequately monitoring conformance? As Edwards and Cornforth (2003) noted, empirical studies of the strategic role undertaken by nonprofit boards and how they meet the competing demands of performance and conformance roles are rare. As a starting point, it is necessary to define what is meant by the strategic contribution of the board. Edwards and Cornforth (2003) identified two principal problems in attempting such a definition. The first is the 'fuzziness of the boundary between operational detail and strategic focus' (Edwards & Cornforth, 2003: 78). Not only can board members find it difficult to distinguish between the two, they are often only made aware of strategic issues through examining operational details which raise questions for the future of the organization or the

- A process for ensuring the organization's purpose, desired strategic outcomes and values are constantly kept in the frame and relevant.
- A positive vision of the future which channels energy and resources and motivates directors and staff.
- A process which can engage all directors regardless of their level of experience or expertise in the organization's operational activities.
- An orientation towards the future that reduces commitment to the status quo and encourages a broader view.
- The commitment and confidence of key stakeholders on whom the organization depends, be they members, donors, funders or the like.
- A basis for effective governance by keeping both board and staff focussed on what's important.
- A process for identifying and reconciling conflicting expectations.
- A framework for monitoring and assuring performance accountability.

Figure 7.1 Benefits of sport boards engaging in strategic activities (*Source*: SPARC (2004: 56–57); reproduced with permission of Sport and Recreation New Zealand)

efficacy of current strategy. Board members are also reliant on their organization's CEO and staff to provide information on which to base their decisions. For board members to be able to focus solely on strategic issues require the CEO and staff to identify and present matters that are strategically significant as agreed by the board and management alike. In order that the right sort of reports are provided to the board 'requires time, skill, board input and a high degree of trust between board members and senior managers' (Edwards & Cornforth, 2003: 78).

The second problem is determining the difference between policy and strategy. Policy should be considered to be the values that drive board decisions while strategy should be seen as how an organization positions itself in the marketplace or relative to other similar organizations. In practice, however, board members may find it difficult to differentiate clearly between the policy and the strategy. Making a strategic decision usually involves the application of a policy framework or set of values. Edwards and Cornforth (2003) cautioned that the role of nonprofit boards in focussing on strategic contributions depends on how they perceive the overriding purpose of their organization. As a guide, strategic contributions of the board can be considered to be things such as the board commissioning papers and conducting discussions that incorporate assessments of organizational resources and capability, organizational performance, and options and priorities for the future (Edwards & Cornforth, 2003).

In their conceptualization of the strategic contribution of the board Edwards and Cornforth (2003) identified the relationship between organizational context, inputs and processes. The strategic contribution of the board is considered an outcome of their involvement in the organization. The inputs of board member skills, experiences, values and knowledge have an impact on the way in which the board receives and considers information and makes decisions. Both the inputs and the processes are affected by the environmental context in which the board and organization operate, such as the relationship between government and the non-profit sector, the regulatory environment, government policy, governance guidelines and the broader impact of globalization processes.

Nadler (2004) argued that engaging the board in strategy development is vital for boards and CEOs to maintain a healthy working relationship and for effective governance to occur. Organizations engage in four discrete types of strategic activity: strategic thinking, strategic decision-making, strategic planning and strategy execution. Strategic thinking 'involves the collection, analysis and discussion of information about the environment of the firm (or organization), the nature of competition, and business design alternatives' (Nadler, 2004: 26). This entails an analysis of what products or services to provide to the market, how an organization is going to compete with others and what shape the organization could take to facilitate its operations. Strategic decision-making involves making choices between alternatives in order to allocate organizational resources. Strategic planning identifies priorities for action, sets objectives and organizes the resources to enable the organization to execute its strategic decisions. Finally, strategic execution is where the organization 'focuses on implementation, monitoring results and appropriate corrective action' (Nadler, 2004: 26). The board's level of engagement with each of these four strategic activities needs to complement that of the CEO and paid staff. Figure 7.2 outlines an ideal balance for the role of board and senior management in each of the four strategic activities.

Nadler's (2004) model for how a board can make a strategic contribution to an organization is dependent on several conditions. First, the board must be balanced but diverse. In other words, the board should comprise independent members able to question and challenge decisions and strategies. Second, the board should possess some specific knowledge of the operating environment of the organization. The CEO and senior staff must decide to engage with the board and vice versa to ensure a complete understanding and personal commitment amongst the key decision-makers about the origins of the strategy and the merits of their decisions. Third, the CEO must be receptive to new ideas and open to strategic input. The culture of the board, within its accepted norms and standards of behaviour, must support 'constructive contention and the importance of different points of view' (Nadler, 2004: 32). Finally, the board must feel that it is accountable to its stakeholders as this will motivate them to be more engaged with important strategic decisions.

Description of task	Role of the board	Role of senior management
Strategic thinking Collecting, analysing and discussing information about the environment of the firm, the nature of the competition, and broad business design alternatives – different views of customer value proposition, scope competitive advantage and profit capture	▪ Be an active participant in the strategic thinking process ▪ Bring an outside perspective and accumulated wisdom ▪ Test the consistency of management's thinking ▪ Collaborate with management	▪ Initiate the process of strategic thinking ▪ Set the agenda, pose the questions and issues ▪ Provide rich and meaningful information ▪ Actively participate with the board in the discussions ▪ Summarize the output of board and management working together
Strategic decision-making Making the fundamental set of decisions about the business portfolio and business design	▪ Provide input for management's decision-making ▪ Provide ultimate review and approval on major decisions (resource allocation, initiatives, portfolio challenges, etc.)	▪ Make critical decisions ▪ Develop proposals to the board for critical directional decisions and major resource allocation ▪ Engage with the board in its review of decisions
Strategic planning Translating the critical strategic decisions into a set of priorities, objectives and resource allocation actions to execute the strategy	▪ Review core strategic plans presented by management ▪ Ensure understanding of the plans and their potential risks and consequences ▪ Comment and make suggestions on plans, as appropriate ▪ Approve plans	▪ Develop plans, working with staff support and operating management ▪ Review plans to ensure consistency with corporate objectives and strategy ▪ Present plans to the board for review
Strategic execution Undertaking the various initiatives and actions consistent with the strategic plan, including adjustments over time to account for environmental changes and different outcomes	▪ Review the process and progress of implementation of key initiatives vis-à-vis established milestones and objectives	▪ Ensure resources and leadership for execution are in place ▪ Monitor progress of execution ▪ Make changes in either the execution or the plan depending on outcomes

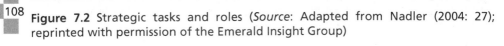

Figure 7.2 Strategic tasks and roles (*Source*: Adapted from Nadler (2004: 27); reprinted with permission of the Emerald Insight Group)

Pressures for boards to engage with strategy

The pressures for boards to engage more directly with strategic activities can come from stakeholders, regulatory agencies demanding higher standards of accountability, funding agencies determined to optimize their investments or from internal change agents such as CEOs, board chairs or new board members. In one of the first studies of the antecedents of board involvement in strategic decision-making in nonprofit organizations, Judge and Zeithaml (1992) found that active and involved boards were associated with higher levels of organizational performance. They found that board involvement increased as organizations aged, apparently because organizations encounter a 'wide range of circumstances over time and organization members develop a broad repertoire of skills' (Judge & Zeithaml, 1992: 784). Board involvement decreased as organizations diversified, possibly because the institutional pressures for board involvement in strategic decision-making are diluted as organizations diversify. The appointment of board members who are also in operational roles also leads to less board involvement in strategic decisions, possibly for fear of challenging authority (i.e. the board). The Judge and Zeithaml study also found that as board size increased, board involvement diminished, a phenomenon they attributed to group dynamics. When boards get too large, effective discussion and decision-making becomes difficult, leading to less involvement by individual board members.

Gopinath, Siciliano and Murray (1994) explored the reasons for boards to be involved in strategy. They used the model of the board role comprising control, service and strategy functions developed by Zahra and Pearce (1989) to argue the need for greater involvement by the board in strategy. Gopinath et al. argued that in profit-seeking corporations, majority shareholders may be seeking short-term gains from increased share value or dividend yields without regard to the long-term future of the corporation. In such cases the board has a major role to play in representing the interests of the corporation over the interests of its shareholders. In nonprofit organizations, similar pressures exist for boards to balance the interests of diverse stakeholders (e.g. government funding agencies) with the interests or preferences of major client groups to ensure the long-term future of the organization is secured.

The pressures for boards to be more involved with strategic activities were identified by Scherrer (2003) and conceptualized as comprising three institutional forces. The first is the legal system, where he identified a trend of increasing numbers of corporate boards being sued over the last four decades for failing to be more involved in strategic decision-making. The second is the increasing power of institutional investors that are majority shareholders in corporations. Institutions such as pension or superannuation funds are able to influence the involvement of boards in strategic oversight and involvement. Third, Scherrer (2003) identified the market for corporate control, comprising legislative bodies, lawyers, accountants, the public and stakeholders as placing pressure on corporate boards to be more involved in order to protect shareholder value and future growth.

Parallels can be found in the pressures facing nonprofit boards. These include: fear of litigation, the increasing power of government agencies who provide significant funding or contract the services of nonprofit groups and a similar market of external bodies striving to ensure that nonprofit organizations are well governed. These institutional forces have resulted in the development of prescriptive guidelines for how governance should be enacted within nonprofit organizations. The following section examines the guidelines for board involvement in strategic activities that have been developed by several government agencies responsible for the development, implementation and monitoring of sport policy.

Guidelines for the board's role in strategy development

UK Sport (2004: 22) states that 'effective strategic planning is critical to the success of governing bodies of sport' and that the board has a crucial role to play in the strategic planning process. UK Sport recommends that it is the role and responsibility of the board to articulate the wider strategic aims of the organization and thereafter delegate the task of developing strategic plans to the senior management team. The board's role is to 'oversee the development process and, eventually endorse or veto the final document' (UK Sport, 2004: 24). These guidelines also outline the importance of the board's monitoring function and the need to identify a number of key performance indicators within the plan. UK Sport (2004: 24) recommends that the strategic plan 'should be referred to regularly with access to most of it (though not commercially sensitive information) being made available to all stakeholders' and that the plan should be used to guide the development of the organization. This appears to be a far more 'hands-off' approach than that recommended in Nadler's (2004) model (see Figure 7.2) wherein the board is far more engaged with all four stages of strategic thinking, decision-making, planning and execution.

Guidelines developed by the Australian Sports Commission (ASC, 2005: 9–11) also recommend that it is the board's role to establish the organization's strategic direction. This direction should be reflected in the strategic plan, which should include:

- a mission statement or statement of purpose;
- the board's vision for the organization;
- a statement describing the organization's philosophy or values;
- a 'snapshot' or pre-plan position of the organization at the start of the period covered by the plan;
- an SWOT analysis of the internal (strengths and weaknesses) and external (opportunities and threats) operating environment;
- clearly stated organization-wide results or outcomes to be achieved, often referred to as Key Result Areas;
- each Key Result Area to have broadly stated objectives with related strategies and performance indicators (ASC, 2005: 9–10).

The ASC guidelines are more aligned with Nadler's (2004) model as they state 'the board develops the strategic direction and strategic plan in partnership with the chief executive officer and staff of the organization and the sport's key stakeholders' (ASC, 2005: 10). Only the board can change the strategic direction or alter the Key Result Areas within the plan. The guidelines also focus on the notion of setting aside time for the board to engage in strategic thinking, not just strategic planning:

> The process of developing the strategic direction and strategic plan and ensuring that they remain up to date and relevant is called 'strategic thinking'. Strategic thinking involves constant analysis and assessment of external and internal factors that might inhibit or help the organization to achieve its Key Result Areas, and results in decisions taken by the board and the chief executive officer to ensure sound, appropriate ongoing operations. Time should be set aside at every board meeting for strategic thinking (ASC, 2005: 10).

The ASC guidelines also make the distinction between strategic and operational plans, with operational plans being the purview of discrete operational areas of the organization and approved by the CEO rather than the board. Such operational plans should be consistent with the strategic direction and plan and 'generally speaking, the board should play no part in developing operational plans beyond setting the strategic direction and strategic plan' (ASC, 2005: 10). The resource constraints faced by smaller nonprofit sport organizations with limited staff impose some constraints on how such an ideal divide between strategy and operational planning occurs. Smaller organizations may require the practical involvement and support of board members in operational planning and execution. In these cases, the ASC (2005: 10) recommends that 'care must be taken to ensure that the chief executive officer leads the process so that the plans are grounded in reality and are achievable'.

111

Guidelines produced by SPARC (2004: 59) also seem to be aligned with the Nadler (2004) model by making a distinction between the roles of the board and senior staff in the four strategic activities. The SPARC guidelines recommend that 'the board's high-level purpose and outcome statements should generally have a longer-term focus, creating a framework within which the chief executive can prepare shorter-term (e.g. 1–3 years) business plans' (SPARC, 2004: 59). The guidelines also emphasize the point that strategic thinking comes before strategic planning. Due to the resource constraints faced by smaller nonprofit sport organizations the guidelines suggest that:

> The board should involve not only its chief executive and senior staff (in strategic thinking), but also key internal (e.g. regional sports organizations, clubs and individual members) and external stakeholders should also be engaged as appropriate. Given the relatively small size of most organizations, it is recommended that *all* staff be engaged in strategic thinking at some point. If these discussions are effective, they build commitment and ownership throughout the organization and lead to better decision-making (SPARC, 2004: 59).

A major focus of the guidelines from UK Sport, the ASC and SPARC is the emphasis on preparing and approving a strategic plan for the organization. SPARC (2004: 59–60) provide a generic framework for a strategic plan that can be adopted by most nonprofit sport organizations (see Figure 7.3).

How well do boards engage with strategy?

Despite the existence of a range of institutional pressures not all boards engage fully with strategic activities. This section explores the evidence for how well corporate and nonprofit boards engage with strategy. Scherrer (2003: 87) claimed that there was a distinct lack of involvement by corporate boards in meaningful strategic activities:

> The majority of corporations do not have their directors involved in the strategic decision making process; rather the directors review and approve the strategic decisions when they are presented to them. The board uses the milestones and goals set by the officers to determine the success of strategic decisions. This type of closed strategic decision-making process is self-serving and allows management to set the criterion by which their success in meeting goals of the process is determined.

This view is supported by Bart (2004: 112) who claimed that 'directors in recent years appear to have become largely disengaged from their

1. *Vision statement*: Much of the strategic management literature advocates the adoption of an inspirational vision of some Nirvana-like future. Can be useful as a statement of the ultimate that the board wishes the organization to achieve.
2. *Purpose statement*: The most powerful single statement a board can make. The purpose statement describes the organization's primary reason for being in terms of the benefit to be achieved and the beneficiary(s). A good starting question is, 'If this organization did not already exist why would we create it?'
3. *Values*: Cherished beliefs and principles that are intended to inspire effort, and guide behaviour, encouraging some actions and activities, and constraining others. There's an important ethical dimension to this. A good starting question for a discussion on values is to complete the sentence 'We believe in/that ...'
4. *Strategic outcomes*: The organization's high-level, longer-term deliverables. Stated as if they've been achieved, these allow you to understand the difference the organization will make to its world if it's successful.
5. *Key results*: The organization's short-term achievements on a year-to-year basis. Each key result is a subset of a larger strategic outcome.
6. *Performance measures*: Measurements or milestones that the board must monitor to be sure about achieving key results and ensuring the organization is on track. The chief executive should be invited to present these to the board. The onus should be on the chief executive to convince the board that key results are being achieved. In reality, many key performance indicators will be operational performance measures.
7. *Resource allocation*: Resources should be allocated for each of the key results. This ensures the results are achievable and that the strategic framework is realistic and the specified results achievable (rather than simply an inventory of wishful thinking).

Figure 7.3 Strategic plan content (*Source*: SPARC (2004: 59–60); reprinted with permission of Sport and Recreation New Zealand)

organization's corporate strategies, choosing instead to focus only on financial results and stock market performance'.

A number of authors have sought to explain the lack of board involvement in strategy as being due to lack of board power, inadequate board processes or the multiplicity of board appointments held by individual board members. In their study of corporate boards, Judge and Zeithaml (1992: 781) provided a description of the differences in the level of board involvement that exist within corporations:

> In a highly involved board, members worked in partnership with management to develop a strategic direction and then closely questioned top management about the progress of the strategic investments that had been made, trusting management to supply comprehensive and accurate evaluations. In contrast, a less involved board tended to rubber stamp management's strategic proposals and accept whatever evaluations top management gave it.

Carpenter and Westphal (2001: 653) found that the 'monitoring and advising behaviour of directors depends on the strategic perspective and base of expertise provided by their appointments to other boards'. In other words, the experience and expertise board members develop through their role as board members with other organizations impacts on their individual ability to contribute to strategic activities. Further, 'boards are less likely to be effective advisors and monitors when their members are appointed to the boards of other firms that are strategically irrelevant to the needs of the focal firm' (Carpenter & Westphal, 2001: 655). Thus, if board members are involved in disparate types of organizations, their ability to contribute to any particular organization is lessened, suggesting that in order to optimize board involvement in strategic activities, board members should be encouraged to be involved only in boards that are strategically relevant.

Research on the extent of nonprofit board involvement in strategy is scarce. In a major review of research on strategic management in nonprofit organizations, Stone, Bigelow and Crittenden (1999) concluded that many nonprofit organizations did not engage in formal strategic planning processes and that those that did were driven by the need to satisfy external funding requirements. Aside from the studies discussed in Chapter 4 dealing with the overall role of the board (e.g. Harris, 1993; Inglis, Alexander & Weaver, 1999; Inglis & Weaver, 2000), the strategic contribution of the board within nonprofit organizations has received little attention. Researchers of nonprofit organizations have explored the link between organizational structure and strategy (Brown & Iverson, 2004) and the relationship between planning and organizational performance (Crittenden, Crittenden, Stone & Robertson, 2004) but no studies have explored explicitly the nature or extent of board member involvement in strategic activities.

A recent study by Bart and Deal (2006) focussed on differences in the level of board involvement between corporate and nonprofit organizations. While not claiming that their study of Canadian corporate and nonprofit boards could be generalized to larger populations, Bart and Deal (2006) contend that their findings were interesting and worthy of commentary. They found that:

> of all the sources information received by both types of boards, the ones which were received in the least amounts concerned those items which make up the 'backbone' and 'guts' of any strategic plan, i.e. the external environmental analysis and the internal resource analysis (Bart & Deal, 2006: 17).

In addition, they noted that boards tended to receive and focus on a great deal of financial information which, they argued, was of little benefit to identifying the correct strategy for an organization. Board discussions also tended to focus on the quantity of information received. In other words, board members spend time discussing whatever information is placed before them, rather than discriminating between important and trivial issues. Boards of both types devoted, on average, three board meetings a year and only 2 hours per meeting discussing organizational strategy. Bart and Deal (2006: 18) argued that this was well short of what is required for boards and concluded that corporate and nonprofit organizations 'are just not receiving the kind of strategic attention that they need and deserve from their boards'.

Bart and Deal (2006) noted that there were some differences between corporate and nonprofit organizations in the level of board involvement in strategic activities. Compared to their corporate counterparts board members of nonprofit organizations were found to be giving more attention to each aspect of their organization's strategy. This included significantly higher levels of attention to overall strategy, as well as more attention to the mission statement and organizational values. Nonprofit board members were found to be more satisfied with their involvement in the strategic planning process of their organization. In summary, it would appear that boards of all types of organizations could be more fully involved in strategic activities. Despite the presence of a range of pressures to engage with strategy and clear guidelines for how they might be involved, research to date suggests there is much work to be done to improve our understanding of the current nature and extent of the strategic contribution of boards and what might be done to improve such contributions.

Enhancing the strategic contributions of sport boards

A study by Thibault, Slack and Hinings (1993) was the first to explore the nature of strategy within national sport organizations (NSOs). While the study did not specifically examine the role of the board in developing or monitoring strategy, the authors did note that 'like their counterparts in other countries, NSOs in Canada have, for much of their existence, placed little importance on the development of strategic plans' (Thibault et al., 1993: 27). With the expansion of government funding programs for sport in the 1990s and increased revenues from other sources such as broadcast rights, it could be argued that the imperatives for nonprofit sport organizations to undertake formal strategic planning have emerged only recently. Thus, the formal involvement of board members in strategic activities could be expected to be somewhat limited. Slack (1996) noted that the study of strategy within sport organizations was a neglected area of research. He noted that despite the central nature of strategy within all organizations, and its links to structure, culture and leadership, there had been very few studies of the topic within sport management.

- The board doesn't appreciate the importance of its leadership role and responsibilities – in particular its ultimate accountability for organizational performance.
- The board reacts in an ad hoc way to the immediate issues. It is diverted from the more important longer-term challenges.
- Setting a clear future direction for the organization would force the board to confront either fundamental philosophical differences between directors or to challenge one or more dominant individuals who are either anti-planning or who have 'bullied' the board into a particular stance with regard to the future.
- There is active resistance to looking forward because (of views such as) 'if it ain't broke don't fix it'; or 'survival is the name of the game'.
- The board does not know how to start.
- Individual directors are genuinely more interested in how the organization goes about its work (the means) rather than what it must achieve and why (the ends). They are more comfortable dealing with matters which are specific to their personal interests and experience.
- Directors have been disillusioned by the nature and results of past strategic planning in which they felt they were ignored.
- A critical mass of board members are task oriented and become impatient at having to deal with time-consuming discussion and analysis of issues, the answers to which they feel are obvious.
- The board is held back by the attitude and/or inexperience of its chief executive and staff.

Figure 7.4 Reasons sport boards are not effective in providing direction (*Source*: SPARC (2004: 56); reproduced with permission of Sport and Recreation New Zealand)

Ferkins, Shilbury and McDonald (2005: 219) highlighted the significant gap in the knowledge and understanding of the strategic function of non-profit sport boards:

> The small but growing body of knowledge on sport boards indicates that the evolutionary process of bureaucratisation and professionalization has resulted in changing board roles and relationships with paid executives. The contribution of the board in strategic activities such as developing the vision and mission, engaging in strategic planning including monitoring and responding to external environmental influences, and considering long-term, big picture issues as and when needed, is a topic superficially explored by sport management scholars. Understanding the factors that both constrain and enable sport boards to think and act strategically may provide an empirical basis for boards to build their strategic capabilities.

SPARC (2004) contends that most sport organization boards could do a better job in being involved in strategic activities and cited a number of reasons boards are not more effective in their direction-giving role (see Figure 7.4).

How then can the boards of nonprofit sport organizations seek to make more meaningful contributions to the strategy of their organizations? The guidelines from the ASC (2005) and SPARC (2004) provide a detailed rationale for why boards should be more involved along with steps as to what boards should do to be more involved in organizational strategy. The heart of the issue for sport organizations, however, seems to be clarifying the respective roles of the board and staff in all strategic activities. The four-part model developed by Nadler (2004) presented in Figure 7.2 may provide the necessary clarity. The model clearly outlines the role of the board and staff in each of the four discrete areas of strategic activity which are: strategic thinking, strategic decision-making, strategic planning and strategy execution. Nadler (2004) argued that adopting such a model yields clear benefits for organizations and their boards. First, adoption of the model delivers better strategic decisions and a more robust strategy than would otherwise have been developed. Second, by being more actively engaged, board members are more satisfied with their role. Third, the model acts as a way of educating board members about the internal and external operating environment of the organization, leading to better strategic discussions. Finally, the model assists with building ownership and commitment to organizational strategy amongst a key stakeholder, the board.

Conclusion

Determining the strategic direction of an organization and monitoring its performance toward desired outcomes is a fundamental aspect of the governance role that should be undertaken by the boards of nonprofit sport organizations. This chapter has outlined the role of the board in four strategic activities, namely, strategic thinking, strategic decision-making, strategic planning and strategy execution, and the processes that can facilitate the involvement of the board in these activities. Despite the many pressures on boards to be involved in strategy, and the development of a number of guidelines for how boards should be involved, it seems there is scope for improvement in how such involvement occurs within nonprofit sport organizations. There is clearly a need to gather more empirical evidence about the nature and extent of the current strategic contributions of boards and how they might improve their involvement across a range of strategic activities.

8

Defensive game plans: risks, compliance and conformance

Overview

The prescriptive literature on corporate governance is replete with recommendations for boards to focus on risk management and ensure their management teams operate in accordance with the operational objectives and standards set by the board. This chapter examines the role of the board in managing risks and ensuring compliance with legislative and other regulatory requirements. The pressures on boards to manage risks are reviewed along with a number of standards and prescribed guidelines on how boards should undertake the role of risk management. Two examples of compliance planning and risk management are discussed to illustrate the nature of the risk management challenges faced by the boards of sport organizations. Finally, some principles for enhancing the ability of boards to institute compliance monitoring procedures in meeting the requirements of a range of stakeholders are detailed.

Compliance and risk management roles of the board

As discussed in the previous chapter on the strategic contribution of the board, one of the more difficult challenges faced by nonprofit boards is to devote appropriate time and effort into optimizing organizational performance while closely monitoring the actions of staff and volunteers to ensure, at a minimum standard, compliance with the relevant laws. As Cornforth (2003a) noted, the contrasting roles of making strategic contributions and monitoring organizational activities and outcomes require very different orientation and behaviour by board members. McGregor-Lowndes (2003: 55) argued that the challenge was to

> implement legal compliance and risk management planning in order to protect the organization from adverse risk or breach of the law, but in a way that does not dampen the inspiration, enthusiasm or the vision brought by volunteers, staff or board.

Definitions of the monitoring role of the board tend to focus on risk management practices as well as the processes or internal controls boards utilize to ensure paid staff and other organizational members operate in accordance with the law and in line with the expectations of their stakeholders. McGregor-Lowndes (2003) described the differences between boards undertaking what he termed legal compliance planning versus engaging in risk management. He described legal compliance planning as an 'appropriate strategy for a nonprofit organization to manage the organization's, individual board member's and management's exposure to breaching the law' (McGregor-Lowndes, 2003: 56). In contrast, risk management is 'the process of managing an organization's potential exposure to liabilities, preventing them or providing funds to meet the liability if it occurs' (McGregor-Lowndes, 2003: 59). Boards should undertake legal compliance planning to prevent the organization or individuals being subject to legislative offences and possible penalties. In other words, the aim is to be fully compliant with the law and minimize any risks that the organization or individuals may breach the law. Boards should engage in risk management so that they can manage all risks and mitigate the impacts of risks on organizational performance and sustainability. The differences between these processes are further outlined in Figure 8.1.

UK Sport (2004: 24) identified that risk management has assumed higher importance within nonprofit sport organizations for a number of reasons. First, risk management assists the board in effective decision-making, and is complementary to the processes of strategic thinking, decision-making,

Focus	Legal compliance planning	Risk management
Treatment of risks	Seeks to eliminate or prevent them completely	Reduces and manages risks
Approach	Prevent a breach occurring regardless of the cost	Undertakes a cost/benefit approach (i.e. if costs exceed the benefits of controlling risks, then reduce level of control)
Benchmark for compliance standard	Set by the law	Set by the organization

Figure 8.1 Differences between legal compliance planning and risk management (*Source*: adapted from McGregor-Lowndes (2003: 60))

planning and execution as outlined in the previous chapter. In order for the board of an organization to identify strategic objectives and allocate resources to their achievement, the board needs to be cognizant of anything that could prevent those objectives being achieved, and implement strategies to overcome such impediments. UK Sport (2004: 24) highlighted that the 'governing board is responsible for ensuring that a risk assessment management policy is in place' that will assist the board in making decisions. Second, the nature of the physical activities that most nonprofit sport organizations facilitate present a number of risk management issues, including 'insurance for accidents and physical harm, vetting those working with young and vulnerable people, (and) maintaining the good reputation of the organization and all associated with it' (UK Sport, 2004: 24). Finally, other risks such as the potential loss of income streams or the sudden loss of organizational knowledge in the form of senior managers and other staff leaving should also be considered by the boards of nonprofit sport organizations.

SPARC (2004: 62) defines risks as 'uncertain future events that could impact on the organization's ability to achieve its objectives'. These events could be incidents that have the potential to negatively affect the organization, such as changes in government policy and funding conditions or alternatively, events that an organization fails to capitalize on such as failing to secure the rights to a major championship. While 'there is a natural tendency to think of risk as protecting the organization from something 'bad' – such as loss of reputation – a risk-averse board can damage an organization just as easily as a board that's over-lenient or reckless' (SPARC, 2004: 62). The Australian Sports Commission (ASC) (2005) identified a set of typical organizational risk categories as financial, human resource, reputation, client/athlete harm, governance, technology, stakeholder relations, strategic, occupational health and safety, and harm to or loss of physical assets.

A rationale for sport boards to engage in risk management is provided by SPARC (2004) who identified four reasons for such action: (1) to counter losses; (2) to reduce uncertainty; (3) to take advantage of opportunities; and (4) to fulfil a worthwhile purpose. Risk management can assist a board to reduce accidental losses of revenue or assets and 'typically involves reducing their probability, magnitude or unpredictability' by either avoiding or modifying activities that might lead to the losses (SPARC, 2004: 63). An effective risk management strategy can also reduce uncertainty by ensuring board members have all the required information to facilitate decisions, which in turn helps to remove 'doubts and makes boards and managers more confident in moving forward, and more optimistic in making needed changes' (SPARC, 2004: 63). Risk management can also help boards identify opportunities that might emerge in the future and thus help them prepare their organization to take advantage of such opportunities. Finally, boards that engage in risk management have a clearer understanding of their responsibilities for managing the various risks for their organization which, in turn, means that they are more effective in observing standards of corporate stewardship. Boards of nonprofit sport organizations have a duty to ensure they have sound internal management systems and controls, delivering value for the resources entrusted to them by organizational members and other stakeholders. Ultimately, the board is 'accountable for organizational performance, (so) it must be clear how much risk is acceptable in achieving its goals' (SPARC, 2004: 63).

The ASC (nd: 10–11) notes that the potential benefits that accrue to board members and their organizations for managing risks include:

1. More effective management of assets, events, programs and activities.
2. A safer environment for participants, officials, spectators and volunteers.
3. A broader thinking about business objectives and outcomes.
4. A greater ability to meet the needs of members and other stakeholders.
5. Flow-on benefits through the systematic identification of organizational deficiencies.
6. Improved communication, both internally and externally.
7. Improved compliance with the law, regulations and other formal requirements.
8. Lower costs and more budget certainty.
9. Enhanced image and reputation leading to increased interest in the sport and the organization, greater participation and more financial support.
10. Better sporting outcomes.
11. Higher morale, more commitment and accountability.
12. A better managed organization able to support Government objectives.
13. Better quality experiences for participants.

An approach advocated by UK Sport for dealing with various risks is to undertake a comprehensive risk assessment, conducted annually, with the results provided directly to the board. Based on the 'likelihood of the risk occurring and the level of potential risk the entity is exposed to, the board can decide to insure against it, implement measures to contain the risk, monitor it for significant changes or, if it is relatively insignificant, accept it' (UK Sport, 2004: 25).

In Chapter 7, the pressures for boards to engage more directly with strategic activities were identified as emanating from stakeholders, regulatory agencies demanding higher standards of accountability, funding agencies determined to optimize their investments or from internal change agents such as chief executive officers (CEOs), board chairs or new board members. While Scherrer (2003) identified the pressures for corporate boards to be more involved with strategic activities as comprising three institutional forces (i.e. the legal system, power of institutional investors and the market), these same forces also force boards to adopt better legal compliance planning and risk management strategies. Nonprofit organizations are also fearful of litigation and are subject to the increasing power of government agencies who provide significant funding or contracted revenue sources; and, operate within a market that seeks to ensure nonprofit organizations are well governed. These forces have led to the development by several government sport agencies of prescriptive guidelines for board involvement in legal compliance planning and risk management. At the same time the prescriptive literature has focussed on the need to develop board competencies in risk management and associated guidelines for implementing risk management within nonprofit organizations. The guidelines for legal compliance planning and risk management that have been developed by government agencies, together with industry standards, are the focus of the following sections.

Legal compliance and risk management standards

Organizations such as Standards Australia have developed a number of standards to assist organizations improve their legal compliance and risk management. For example the *Australian Standard for Compliance programs (AS 3806-2006)* provides guidance on the principles of effective management of an organization's compliance with its legal obligations, as well as any other relevant obligations such as industry and organizational standards, principles of good governance and accepted community and ethical norms. The principles cover commitment to achieving compliance, implementation of a compliance programme, monitoring and measuring compliance, as well as continual improvement. The standards are designed to assist organizations implement a legal compliance process that McGregor-Lowndes (2003: 56-57) outlined as involving four basic steps:

1. identify the offences to which the organization and its officers are exposed;
2. determine how the organization could breach the provisions and the likelihood of a breach;
3. design a programme to eliminate the risk of breaches;
4. ensure that the programme is implemented, is working and regularly revised.

McGregor-Lowndes (2003) also summarized the structural, operational and maintenance elements that comprise the Australian Standard for compliance which is outlined in Figure 8.2.

Standards have also been developed for risk management. The *Australian/New Zealand Standard for Risk Management AS/NZS 4360-1999* was the world's first risk management standard and was updated in 2004. The Standard provides a generic framework for establishing a risk management process. Standards Australia also produced a handbook for sport and recreation organizations, *Guidelines for Managing Risk in Sport and Recreation* that was produced with the endorsement of the Standing Committee on Sport and Recreation (SCORS). Based on these guidelines, the ASC developed a specific training programme on risk management for directors and board members of national sport organizations (ASC, nd). Based on the Australian New Zealand Standard for Risk Management, this training programme provides a useful model that boards can utilize in their approach to risk management (see Figure 8.3).

Guidelines for risk management

The governance guidelines produced by SPARC (2004) recommend that boards regularly review the main strategic and operational risks facing the organization. The guidelines emphasize the danger of boards focussing solely on the financial position of their organization, and suggest that 'this is a "cart before the horse" approach as an organization's financial position is often a consequence of more fundamental performance-related issues' (SPARC, 2004: 62). In order for boards to adequately fulfil their risk management role, SPARC (2004) recommended that the board focus on six dimensions: (1) characterize risks, (2) influence the risk management culture within the organization, (3) participate in major decisions relating to risk management, (4) monitor the management of significant risks, (5) suggest a wider use of strategies for less significant risks and

Structural elements
- *Commitment*: There needs to be dedication to effective compliance with the legislative requirements at all levels of the organization. This is led by the full commitment of the board and senior management.
- *Compliance policy*: A clear written policy that includes a statement of the organization's commitment to compliance with legislation.
- *Managerial responsibility*: All managers need to understand, promote and be responsible for compliance with the relevant laws within their day-to-day responsibilities.
- *Resources*: Adequate resources are necessary to implement the compliance policy.
- *Continuous improvement*: A philosophy of continuous improvement in compliance performance should be adopted.

Operational elements
- *Identification of compliance issues*: The compliance requirements of the organization need to be specifically identified and managed.
- *Operating procedures for compliance*: The legal requirements need to be integrated into the organization's day-to-day operating procedures and systems.
- *Implementation*: The compliance programme needs to be consistently enforced and provided with remedial measures and continuous training.
- *Complaints and failures handling system*: There needs to be a clearly defined system for capturing and recording compliance failures of the organization.
- *Record-keeping*: The components and applications of the compliance programme need to be systematically recorded.
- *Identification and rectification*: All compliance failures need to be classified and investigated to determine their cause and enable their rectification, particularly systemic and recurring problems.
- *Reporting*: Internal reporting arrangements are needed to ensure that all breaches are reported in an appropriate way to those with sufficient authority to correct them.
- *Management supervision*: The compliance programme should include appropriate supervision at all levels to ensure compliance with the organization's policy and operating procedures.

Maintenance elements
- *Education and training*: Appropriate induction and ongoing training is necessary about the compliance plan.
- *Visibility and communication*: The organization's commitment to compliance needs to be well publicized to staff, volunteers, stakeholders and other third parties.
- *Monitoring and assessment*: Compliance can be promoted and maintained, and compliance failures identified, by appropriate monitoring and assessment.
- *Review*: The compliance programme needs to be regularly reviewed to ensure its effectiveness.
- *Liaison*: Ongoing liaison with the regulatory authorities is necessary so that the organization is aware of current compliance issues and practices.
- *Accountability*: There needs to be appropriate reporting on the operation of the compliance programme against documented performance standards.

Figure 8.2 Elements of the Australian Standard for compliance programmes (*Source*: McGregor-Lowndes (2003: 57–58); reprinted with permission of Professor Myles McGregor-Lowndes, Centre of Philanthropy and Nonprofit Studies, University of Queensland, in David Fishel's the Book of the Board: Effective Governance of Nonprofit Organizations, Federation Press, Sydney, 2003)

Stage	Actions
1. Establish the context	■ Objectives ■ Stakeholders ■ Criteria ■ Define the key elements
2. Identify the risks	■ What can happen? ■ How can it happen?
3. Analyse the risks	■ Review controls ■ Likelihoods ■ Consequences ■ Level of risk
4. Evaluate the risks	■ Evaluate risks ■ Rank risks
5. Treat the risks	■ Identify options ■ Select the best responses develop risk treatment plans ■ Implement

Figure 8.3 Risk management process (*Source*: adapted from ASC (nd: 15))

(6) report to stakeholders on the risk management strategies employed by the organization. These dimensions are detailed in Figure 8.4.

The ASC (2005) also makes recommendations about the role boards of sport organizations play in risk management. They emphasize that risk management 'involves not only taking protective measures but also evaluating opportunities and, where appropriate, taking considered risks designed to facilitate the growth and development of the organization' (ASC, 2005: 14). The ASC (2005) defines two specific roles for boards in relation to risk management. The first is to develop a broad appreciation of the risks facing the organization and the likelihood of occurrence together with the potential impact should these risks occur. The second is to ensure that a risk management plan for the organization is developed. This process involves 'identifying the risks facing the organization, assessing the level of threat each presents, deciding what action to take in response to each risk and ensuring effective CEO response to the risks through regular monitoring and review' (ASC, 2005: 14). The ASC recommended that after the board has established the level of acceptable risk and developed an appropriate plan, responsibility for implementing the plan should fall to the CEO to take the 'actions necessary to minimize the negative impact and maximize the positive opportunities arising from risk-taking' (ASC, 2005: 14).

1. Characterize risk – ensuring it knows the key risks facing the organization and that it has a good understanding of their probability and potential impact.
2. Set the tone and influence the risk management culture within the organization. The challenge has been neatly summed up in the following quotation: *The board's key role is to ensure that corporate management is continuously and effectively striving for above average performance, taking account of risks.* For example, is it a risk-taking or a risk-averse organization? Which types of risk are acceptable and which are not? What are the board's expectations of staff with respect to conduct and probity? Is there a clear policy that describes the desired risk culture, defines scope and responsibilities for managing risk, assesses resources and defines performance measures?
3. Participate in major decisions affecting the organization's risk profile or exposure, ensuring that important questions such as, 'Should the risk be spread by working with another organization or transferred through the use of funder/sponsor under-writing or insurance?' are addressed.
4. Monitor the management of significant risks to reduce the likelihood of unwelcome surprises by, for example, receiving regular reports from management focusing on key performance and risk indicators, supplemented by audit and other internal and external reports.
5. Satisfy itself that less significant risks are being actively managed, possibly by encouraging a wider adoption of risk management processes and techniques.
6. Report annually to key stakeholders on the organization's approach to risk management, with a description of the key elements of its processes and procedures. The board's expectations regarding risk management and the delegation of its authority to management should be formally documented in policy. This creates accountability and an explicit framework for performance monitoring.

Figure 8.4 Risk management roles of the board (*Source*: adapted from SPARC (2004: 63–64); reprinted with permission of Sport and Recreation New Zealand)

These guidelines are based on the standard for risk management reviewed in the previous section. However, the boards of sport organizations are not legally bound to follow them or ensure that their organization implements the strategies. This raises the issue of how well the boards of nonprofit and sport organizations fulfil their monitoring role. The following section reviews the limited empirical evidence available in this area.

How well do nonprofit boards manage risks?

Despite widespread recognition of the importance of boards fulfilling a monitoring role, Miller (2002: 430) identified that 'scholars know little about the monitoring behaviour of nonprofit boards of directors'. As discussed in Chapter 1, agency theory has been used extensively in the study of corporate boards and predicts that 'shareholder wealth and organizational performance will be maximized when an independent board of directors monitors the chief executive's propensity to behave with self-interest' (Miller, 2002: 430). Agency theory highlights the value in separating organizational ownership and control whereby the board of directors takes responsibility for monitoring decisions and actions of staff. Such a separation contributes to assuring stakeholders that organizational resources are well utilized for intended or planned outcomes.

Agency theory is well suited for the examination of board behaviour within the corporate sector, where the board is clearly the principal and management the agent. However, its utility for analysing board behaviour within nonprofit organizations is diminished for two reasons. First, it may be difficult to identify the principal within nonprofit organizations as they often have complex governance structures and no clear sense of who 'owns' the organization. As a consequence, it may be hard to determine whether the principals and agents have conflicting goals, therefore making it difficult to assess the extent to which management is compliant with the directives of the board. Second, organizational performance is inherently more difficult to measure for nonprofit organizations and 'further complicates the board's monitoring responsibilities' (Miller, 2002: 432). As Chait, Holland and Taylor (1996) found, in the absence of clear performance indicators, nonprofit board members tend to focus on monitoring financial data rather than utilizing measures that may indicate progress toward strategic objectives or programme outcomes.

Despite theoretical shortcomings, Miller (2002) applied agency theory to an examination of the monitoring behaviour of nonprofit boards. Agency theory assumes that conflict will exist between principals and agents and that principals need to 'invest in some sort of incentive scheme or information system to assure that the agent will not behave opportunistically' (Miller, 2002: 446). However, within nonprofit organizations, Miller (2002: 446) found that:

> board members do not expect conflict between the executive director and the purpose for which the organization was created. The board believes that the executive management will not act opportunistically and that what management actually does is ensure goal alignment and convergence in its relationship with principals.

In addition, Miller (2002) found that even after a board might uncover inappropriate administrative behaviour on the part of its paid staff, board members still tend to turn to the executive director for advice and guidance.

The monitoring challenges in the nonprofit sector are further complicated by the presence of multiple stakeholders, which for sport organizations encompass members (individual and other organizations), funding agencies, sponsors, suppliers and higher order governing bodies. As Miller (2002: 447) highlighted, these organizations expect their 'boards to be accountable to the competing interests of multiple stakeholders with no clear indication of how performance will be assessed and no agreement as to who owns (the organization)'. In order for boards to successfully implement their monitoring functions, they must develop a clear understanding of ownership of the organization and specify the performance expectations for each ownership group (i.e. members, funding agencies, sponsors). These expectations can be incorporated into the organizational performance assessment process, thereby enabling the board to 'effectively monitor executive action to assure that managerial behaviour is consistent with owner expectations' (Miller, 2002: 447). Failing to do so results in the board members not paying attention to measures and information related to progress toward strategic outcomes. Miller (2002) found that board members subsequently tend to monitor organizational performance and managerial actions based on their professional and personal experiences and backgrounds, and such behaviour should not be considered as monitoring at all.

Balser and McClusky (2005) studied how nonprofit organizations identify stakeholders and their expectations. They argued that nonprofit organizations are accountable in terms of fiduciary responsibilities, legal requirements, professional standards and an obligation to serve the public good. As a result they are subject to both formal and informal expectations from government agencies, organizational members, the public, the media and organizations with whom they cooperate for service and programme delivery. The boards of these organizations must interpret the expectations of these various stakeholders and evaluate the 'appropriateness of the expectations against the values and mission of the organization, the executives' professional norms, and the organization's own interpretation of the public good' (Balser & McClusky, 2005: 296). The board must then implement a process to monitor the actions of staff and the organization in meeting these expectations. In summary, there has been little empirical research into the monitoring role of nonprofit boards, how boards monitor executive actions and how boards identify the information needs of their stakeholder groups. There have been no specific studies of the monitoring roles undertaken by the boards of sport organizations, and this is clearly an area where much research remains to be done.

In order to illustrate the extent to which the boards of sport organizations involve themselves in monitoring roles such as legal compliance planning and risk management, the following sections provide two practical examples of legal compliance planning and risk management within a state/provincial sport organization and professional football clubs. These examples also illustrate the nature of the risk management challenges faced by the boards of sport organizations.

The Basketball Association of South Australia

The Basketball Association of South Australia Incorporated (BASA) is a nonprofit state/provincial governing body of which the membership comprises nine metropolitan basketball clubs from Adelaide, the capital city of the state of South Australia. BASA is the registered proprietor of Findon Basketball Stadium, the premier basketball stadium in South Australia, owns the licence for the Adelaide 36ers (a franchise team in the National Basketball League (NBL)). It also owns the licence for the Adelaide Quit Lightning (a franchise team of the Women's National Basketball League (WNBL)). BASA had received substantial amounts of funding from the South Australian Government to support its operations and was also heavily in debt to the government for the cost of building the Findon Basketball Stadium.

In 2002, BASA was struggling to meet debt repayments and sought a review of its financial relationship arrangements with the South Australian Government. The Government agreed to provide further support, subject to BASA preparing long term budget and planning documents. At the same time the South Australian Government requested that its Auditor-General investigate the affairs of the BASA. In 2004, the Auditor-General concluded that in general the affairs of the BASA were conducted with due regard to economy and efficiency, but the Government should consider extinguishing some of its debt (AUD11M in 2002) as it was unrealistic to expect that BASA could meet its financial obligations in the foreseeable future.

A major cause of the failure of the BASA to meet its financial obligations was their ownership of the NBL and WNBL franchises. At the time, no other nonprofit basketball governing body in Australia owned a franchise. The Auditors'-General report cited a previous review of the BASA which highlighted that:

> BASA is heavily reliant on the success of the Adelaide 36ers to provide monies to meet administration costs and debt funding obligations. The Adelaide 36ers earns the majority of its revenue through ticket sales, sponsorship and sale of corporate entertainment facilities. The future profitability of the Adelaide 36ers will depend on the success of the NBL in general. Adelaide Quit Lightning has enjoyed enormous on-field success since joining the WNBL. Consistent with other teams in the WNBL, Adelaide Quit Lightning has found it difficult to attract sponsorship and attendances. Adelaide Quit Lightning has consistently made operating losses in the range of approximately $100,000 to $180,000 which have been funded by BASA. (Auditor General South Australia, 2004: 31–32).

The BASA claimed other issues such as a general downturn in the economy, increased competition for sponsorship revenue from other professional sport teams in the State, and competition from other large venues for major events affected its ability to meet its financial obligations. However, these were considered secondary issues to the fundamental risks of continued ownership of the national league franchises. The BASA case highlights the significant risk management issues faced by the volunteer board members of nonprofit sport organizations, even at the state/provincial level. Board members need to be cognizant of how existing and future arrangements impact on their organization and engage in continuous risk management practices.

English professional football clubs

The corporate governance performance of English professional football clubs has been researched extensively over the last 5 years. Hamil, Holt, Michie, Oughton and Shailer (2004) noted that increased television broadcast right revenues had meant the turnover of Premier and Football Association leagues increased more than 170% between 1994/1995 and 2001/2002. At the same time the ability of the clubs involved in these leagues to generate a profit declined considerably, with operating profits declining by 332% (Hamil et al., 2004). Hamil and his colleagues noted that the 'paradox of rising revenue and declining profitability distinguishes football from most other lines of business where increases in revenue streams are usually translated into increased profitability' (Hamil et al., 2004: 45). The reasons for this are threefold. First, football clubs are considered as community assets that have nonprofit objectives, and do not exist exclusively to generate profits for owners. Second, football consumers (fans) are intimately involved in the running of the clubs unlike other consumers who are removed from the supplier. Third, football leagues operate on a cooperative basis by sharing revenue between member clubs who jointly produce league products. The quality of corporate governance of football clubs is a key determinant of success. However, as Hamil et al. (2004: 45) point out, 'all the evidence suggests that general standards of corporate governance in football are poor with a lack of adequate internal and external control mechanisms'.

The Football Governance Research Centre (FGRC) undertakes an annual survey of corporate governance of English football clubs. These surveys have shown that the corporate governance of football needs to improve, among other things, the level of compliance with company law and codes of corporate governance. Hamil et al. (2004: 46) noted that some clubs do not meet 'the basic requirements of running a business as laid out by company law' and that other clubs do not meet best practice guidelines for corporate governance as laid out by the Organisation for Economic Co-operation and Development (OECD) or the Combined Code of the London Stock Exchange. For example, the Combined Code stipulates that there should be an audit committee with at least three non-executive directors, organizations should regularly review their internal control measures, and that organizations provide a clear and accurate statement of their financial position. Hamil et al. (2004: 48) noted that 'only 87.5% of quoted clubs had an audit committee and only one third of quoted clubs met the requirement that this committee should have at least three non-executive directors'.

The results of the FGRC surveys revealed also that the overall quality of risk management by English football clubs was poor. For example, a third of clubs did not have a process for evaluating the nature and extent of risks facing their club, and only 41% of clubs undertook an assessment of the likelihood of risks occurring. The FGRC (2005: 33) stated that 'risk has increased in the football industry over the past decade making it all the more essential for clubs to have sound procedures for risk assessment and internal control'. The highly competitive market in which football clubs operate demands that they utilize appropriate risk management strategies. The implementation of risk management must start with their governing boards making the decision to invest the requisite time, resources and effort.

Implementation issues

There are a number of resources that nonprofit sport organizations can turn to for assistance with the implementation of monitoring systems for legal compliance planning and risk management. These include industry standards, guidelines produced by government sport agencies, and in some cases voluntary codes of conduct for best practice in corporate governance several of which have been discussed in this chapter. Regardless of the framework adopted or the type of sport organization and market in which they operate, there are some common principles that boards should follow. Amundson (2004) argued that nonprofit boards have a tendency to implement their monitoring role either by being dependent largely on staff reports or they micro-manage because that is what they think the monitoring function is all about. Amundson (2004) suggested that boards need to implement six processes for achieving better monitoring (see Figure 8.5). Amundson (2004) argued that the focus of monitoring is not to assist boards make decisions or to satisfy the curiosity of individual board members. Rather monitoring processes should be implemented to assist

1. *The financial audit:* Boards generally put too much faith in this function as a monitoring tool. Often it is because they misunderstand what they are getting with an audit. In addition, to be effective as a tool for monitoring the CEO, the auditor should report to an audit committee rather than staff, and the audit committee needs to understand what they need from the auditor. Nevertheless, if properly used, the financial audit can be very useful tool in the board's monitoring toolkit.
2. *The statutory compliance audit:* Associations typically have a variety of statutory responsibilities, and boards often do not understand the scope and the degree of compliance with these obligations. In our experience, staff and advisors may also not be aware of the full extent of the obligations. The organization's compliance with its own bylaws should be included within the scope of a statutory compliance audit.
3. *Policy compliance audit:* To effectively oversee the management of the organization, boards require well-defined and complete policies. However, the existence of the policies is not enough. If the Boards depend solely on reports by the CEO that there is compliance with those policies, they are falling short in their monitoring responsibilities. A good practice is to undertake annual policy compliance audits that focus on selected policies each year.
4. *Internal controls review:* There is no excuse for the ongoing incidents of volunteer and employee malfeasance. If associations and charities ensured that internal controls met common standards, the risk of fraud or theft would be reduced considerably. If a review of internal controls is not included in the financial audit, then a separate internal controls review should be undertaken periodically.
5. *Legal review:* If an association accesses legal advice infrequently and with respect to specific purposes, then a legal review of the organization may be warranted. However, the scope of the review should be very clearly defined to limit the cost, and avoid duplication of work undertaken in other monitoring functions (such as a statutory compliance audit or a privacy audit). Examples of areas examined in a legal review could, for example, include copyright/trademark issues, competition law issues, and human resource management issues.
6. *Privacy audit:* It is practically impossible for the board to determine that the organization is in compliance with applicable privacy laws without undertaking a privacy audit. The audit should address the privacy measures in place, as well as the implementation of those measures.

Figure 8.5 Implementing the board's monitoring role (*Source*: adapted from Amundson (2004); reprinted with permission of Association Xpertise Inc)

boards in their assessment of the performance of the CEO and the extent to which they are meeting their governance and oversight responsibilities.

Conclusion

As it is in the corporate sector, risk management and compliance with legislative and regulatory requirements are fundamental roles for the boards of nonprofit sport organizations. The pressures on boards to fulfil these roles come from stakeholders, the accountability demands of regulatory agencies, funding agencies seeking optimal returns for their investments, and from internal change agents such as CEOs, board chairs and new board members. A range of resources, including industry standards, guidelines from government sport agencies, and voluntary codes of conduct for best practice in corporate governance have been developed to assist boards with improving their monitoring role. Despite an array of prescriptive guidelines and frameworks there has been little empirical research into the monitoring role of nonprofit boards, and a dearth of published studies on the monitoring roles of nonprofit sport organization boards in particular. This is an important area for further research in order to improve our understanding of how boards undertake their monitoring role and how boards can be more effective and efficient in activities such as legal compliance planning and risk management.

9

Team leadership: dual leadership challenges

Overview

The challenges of dual leadership that exist within nonprofit sport organizations are the focus of this chapter. The increasing professionalization of the sports industry has led to a reduction in volunteer control of many nonprofit sport organizations and has challenged decision-making processes within these organizations. This chapter discusses the effects of professionalization on leadership within nonprofit sport organizations and the nature of the relationship between boards and staff, in particular the chief executive officer (CEO). The distribution of power within boards and who has influence over decision-making within boards is also explored. Finally, the duality of leadership within nonprofit sport organizations is discussed through an examination of prescribed governance guidelines and the findings of an increasing body of research.

The effects of professionalization

As discussed in Chapter 3, Thibault, Slack and Hinings (1991) investigated structural changes in Canadian NSOs that occurred as a result of the introduction of paid professional staff (generally referred to as professionalization). Thibault and her colleagues found that as a consequence of hiring professional staff, the pattern of centralization increased initially and then decreased, often to a point lower than before the appointment of the professional staff member. This phenomenon was attributed to volunteers initially fearing the 'challenge that professionals pose to the culture of voluntary sport organizations' (Thibault et al., 1991: 93) and after a period of time becoming more comfortable with the notion of professionals' involvement. Thibault et al. (1991: 95) was the first study to draw attention to 'a particular difficulty over control which could be a specific consequence of volunteer – professional relations'.

Subsequently, a number of studies have focussed on the professionalization and bureaucratization processes that have occurred within nonprofit sport organizations since the early 1990s (Slack & Hinings, 1992; 1994; Amis, Slack & Berrett, 1995; Kikulis, Slack & Hinings, 1995a, 1995b, 1995c). Recent work carried out by Hoye and Cuskelly (2003a, 2003b) has established that in some cases, professionalization has led to executives assuming a far more central role in the governance of nonprofit sport organizations. The increasing body of research in this area has explored the nature and effects of change instigated by professionalization, as well as the sources of commitment and resistance to professionalization processes in nonprofit organizations.

The effects of professionalization can be conceptualized in three ways. First, the introduction of paid staff into senior management roles within nonprofit sport organizations has altered the nature of the role of volunteer board members and in particular that of the board chair. As a consequence the relationship between volunteers and paid staff has evolved in recent years and often involves negotiations to define the boundaries of their respective responsibilities in working together to govern and manage the organization. Second, professionalization has increased the potential for conflict over who has real power and influence in decision-making within these organizations. Finally, professionalization has created the conditions for dual leadership with board chairs and executives assuming various elements of the leadership role within nonprofit sport organizations. How this dual leadership role is negotiated, defined and executed in the context of governance and management requirements presents individuals in those roles and the board as a whole with a number of challenges. The remaining sections of this chapter explore the prescriptive guidelines and the empirical research evidence into the changing nature of the board–executive relationship, power and influence in decision-making and dual leadership within nonprofit sport organizations.

Board–staff relations

The nature of board–executive relationships within nonprofit sport organizations has the potential to impact on the quality of the decision-making processes within boards, and ultimately on the effectiveness of the board. The relationship between boards and executives is particularly important for the governance of nonprofit sport organizations in light of increasing professionalization within these organizations in recent years. The potential for conflict between executives and volunteers over the control of decision-making processes within nonprofit sport boards is well documented (Amis et al., 1995; Kikulis et al., 1995a; Auld, 1997).

Nonprofit governance models such as those developed by Carver (1997) and Houle (1997) define the nature of the board–executive relationship as hierarchical with the executive being subservient to the board. Middleton (1987: 152) argued that the perception of the board–executive relationship as 'a partnership built on mutual trust and effective communication' does not accurately depict practice. Middleton (1987) also asserted that the board–executive relationship is paradoxical. While the board has ultimate responsibility for decisions, the basis for making these decisions depends on the information provided by the executive, who in turn is employed by the board. The relationship between the board and executive might be more appropriately defined as a dynamic interaction subject to ongoing negotiation of their respective responsibilities rather than a partnership in the true sense of the word.

The well-published governance consultant, John Carver (1997) argued that even though the relationship between the board and executive is crucial for effective board performance, it is the least understood aspect of nonprofit governance. Houle (1997: 97) stated 'the relationship between the board and executive is a subtle one, usually built up over a long time … (and that any change involves) … a great deal of interplay'. There has been little research on board–executive relationships, hence little is known about how this interplay occurs, or how executives and board members might approach and negotiate the development of their inter-relationship. Research efforts have focussed on the central role the executive plays in the organizational governance, the varying levels of influence that board members and executives might exert in organizational leadership or decision-making, and the distribution and use of power within boards (Harris, 1989; Herman & Tulipana, 1989; Heimovics & Herman, 1990; Murray, Bradshaw & Wolpin, 1992; Golensky, 1993; Heimovics, Herman & Jurkiewicz, 1995).

Harris (1989) argued that self-fulfilling cycles of expectations between the board and staff impacted on their relationship. In particular, Harris (1989: 327) found that staff may not share 'professional and administrative information, decisions and problems' with their board for a variety of reasons. These include: attempting to retain power by limiting board access to information; to save board members time, assuming that a board may not be interested; or, having a perception that these things are not relevant to the work of a board. The existence of such poor working relationships between the board and executives meant that board members are denied opportunities to participate fully and gain a complete understanding of the issues facing the executive and other paid staff. This can result in board members being unable to develop a complete understanding of key issues and consequently making decisions without being fully informed about the issues. Such circumstances can give rise to staff considering board members as 'remote' or disinterested, and perpetuate the cycle of withholding information and not fully involving board members in the work of the organization. Harris (1989) concluded that executives might be a key determinant of the success of any particular governance structure based on their attitudes about access to and control of information flowing to both staff and the board.

Herman and Tulipana (1989: 50) defined board–executive relations as 'multi-faceted and could be characterized on many dimensions (e.g. frequency, status differentials, trust and communication patterns)'. Heimovics and Herman (1990: 68) focused on critical incidents faced by the organizations and found the overwhelming view of staff, executives and board members was that 'the chief executive, not the board president, is assigned predominant responsibility (for dealing with critical incidents)'. Their research challenged the 'prescriptive, taken-for-granted role and interpret ation of final responsibility of boards for outcomes in the nonprofit organization' (Heimovics & Herman, 1990: 70). They highlighted the idea that the executive may be more important to board performance than had been previously thought. A later study by Heimovics et al. (1995: 234) explored the political dimensions of leadership in nonprofit organizations and found the widely held view that 'effective chief executives understand the centrality of their leadership role and accept responsibility as initiators of action, with their boards, to find resources and revitalize the missions of their organizations'. They defined this view as the 'psychological centrality of the chief executive role in a hierarchy of responsibility for organizational outcomes … and explains the reason … nonprofit chief executives are expected (by others and themselves) to take substantial responsibility for organizational outcomes' (Heimovics et al., 1995: 235). The results of their study again highlighted that the notion of the board–executive relationship being a conceptualized as a partnership is overly simplistic. The partnership conceptualization fails to adequately reflect the socially constructed nature of the board–executive relationship.

In light of the evidence on board–executive relationships within non-profit organizations, two government sport agencies developed guidelines for the creation, development and maintenance of board-executive relationships within nonprofit sport organizations (ASC, 2005; SPARC, 2004). The ASC (2005) recommended that the board must assume the CEO is competent and should therefore be delegated maximum authority to manage the operational issues of the organization. They also specified a number of principles for an effective board–executive relationship which are outlined in Figure 9.1.

The ASC (2005) also recommended that if executives are given the authority to manage the organization, it is important that board members do not meddle in the operational affairs unless requested to do so by the executives. For example, 'board members, on the invitation of the CEO, might participate in the recruitment and selection of senior operational staff' (ASC, 2005: 22). At the same time, board members should be able to liaise with staff, taking care to ensure that they do not instruct staff or

An effective and productive board–chief executive officer relationship is built around:

- Mutual respect for their separate but mutually interdependent roles and responsibilities.
- A clearly defined and documented delegation, including the authority to appoint and manage personnel.
- A clear expectation that the chief executive officer will be held accountable for the performance of the organization within the bounds of the delegation.
- Mutual agreement about the limits to the freedom granted to the chief executive officer in order to carry out his or her role and tasks.
- Clearly defined, unambiguous results to be achieved.
- A fair and ethical process for evaluating chief executive officer effectiveness.
- An expectation that the expertise and experience of individual board members will be available to the chief executive officer as advice, not as instruction.
- A commitment for the board to 'speak with one voice' on all matters relating to the chief executive officer, such as policy, strategic direction and performance expectations.
- Regular and objective feedback and two-way dialogue about important performance matters.

Figure 9.1 ASC principles for an effective board–executive relationship (*Source*: ASC (2005: 21–22); reprinted with the permission of the Australian Sports Commission)

undermine the CEOs' position and legitimate authority. Finally, 'board members should know the key staff and their roles, and staff members should know who is on the board' (ASC, 2005: 22).

The Sport and Recreation New Zealand (SPARC, 2004: 68) guidelines follow the prescribed model discussed earlier in recommending that the 'relationship between a board and chief executive should be approached as a partnership in which each respects the other's roles, responsibilities and prerogatives'. They also make the point that nonprofit sport organizations are generally small, with little likelihood of developing chief executive candidates from within their membership or small staff pool. As a consequence, CEOs therefore are frequently recruited from outside the organ-ization. CEOs may not have a great deal of experience in working with governing boards and so 'to ensure there is an effective partnership between boards and chief executives requires considerable support and professional development' (SPARC, 2004: 68). SPARC also note that the board–executive relationship is full of contradictions. First, the executive is usually a full-time appointment who is employed by part-time volunteer board members. The executive has operational control over the organiza-tion, including the information the board requires to make decisions, 'yet the board carries ultimate accountability for these decisions' (SPARC, 2004: 73). Second, the executives' role is to lead the organization and at times provide leadership to the board, even though legally the board is the ultimate lead-ership entity. SPARC (2004) speculate that these contradictions can only be resolved by the board and executive developing an effective working rela-tionship. As a result they specify a number of elements that nonprofit sport organizations should consider in seeking to develop an effective board–executive relationship which are outlined in Figure 9.2.

The relationship between the board and executive has clearly received a great deal of attention in the governance guidelines developed by the ASC (2005) and SPARC (2004). The nature and effectiveness of the relationship has also been the subject of a number of studies in sport (Amis et al., 1995; Auld, 1997; Inglis, 1997b; Auld & Godbey, 1998; Koski & Heikkala, 1998; Shilbury, 2001; Hoye & Cuskelly, 2003b). Of these studies, the work by Hoye and Cuskelly (2003b) focussed on the elements of the board–executive rela-tionship that were related to more effective board performance. Their research revealed that effective board–executive relationships were based on the existence of mutual trust that manifests as the board trusting their CEO to properly and fully implement board decisions, CEOs feeling able to speak freely at board meetings, and the board trusting in the quality and accuracy of the information provided to it by their CEO. They also found that board members were heavily dependent on CEOs for informa-tion to make decisions. Finally, Hoye and Cuskelly (2003b: 71) noted that because the membership of the board often changes on a regular basis, the 'relationship between the executive and board members tends to be a con-tinual cycle of negotiation and re-negotiation'.

1. Role clarity

Role clarity is an essential starting point for an effective organizational relationship. It is vital that the directors and chief executive understand and respect each other's role and responsibilities, that they understand the difference between governing and managing, and support each other.

2. Mutual expectations must be explicit and realistic

Undeclared expectations and untested assumptions will impede any relationship personal or organizational. The board should detail what it expects of its chief executive and the chief executive should make clear what they expect of their board. Ideally, these should be documented, and reviewed regularly.

A list of director expectations of the chief executive would likely include:

- the achievement of desired results;
- loyalty;
- respect for the experience, independence and wisdom of directors;
- honesty and openness;
- assistance with strategic and other board-level thinking;
- to be treated as a collective group, not singled out and set against each other;
- to be told what a governing board requires to know in order to meet its duty of care obligations;
- to be kept abreast of critical strategic issues and events that could impact on the organization's ability to achieve its desired results and
- to feel proud of their association with the board and the organization.

A list of chief executive expectations of their board would likely include:

- clearly stated outcomes to be delivered;
- clearly defined boundaries of authority;
- that the board speak with one consistent voice;
- to be allowed to manage, free from interference by the board or individual directors;
- to be given support for worthy effort;
- recognition for achievement and the occasional thank you;
- honesty and openness;
- the availability of directors' wisdom and advice, and a sounding board when requested;
- a genuine commitment to the organization and an honest effort to understand the business and its issues;
- thorough pre-meeting preparation and attendance at meetings and workshops;
- regular honest performance feedback and
- teamwork, partnership and a sense of common purpose.

3. Reporting and information requirements

Directors need to clarify exactly what information they require, in what form, about which issues and when. No chief executive should be left to guess their board's information needs. Provided the board's interests, requirements and

Figure 9.2 SPARC elements to consider in developing an effective board–executive relationship (*Source*: SPARC (2004: 73–75); reprinted with the permission of Sport and Recreation New Zealand)

strategic priorities are clear, a smart chief executive can anticipate the need for certain information and provide this without needing to be asked.

4. A fair and ethical process for chief executive performance management
The chief executive has a right to expect the board to provide regular performance feedback against agreed performance expectations.

5. The chief executive/chair relationship
Most directors and chief executives benefit from the chief executive having a sound working relationship with the chair.

6. The chief executive's role at board meetings
Chief executives must be clear that board meetings are for board business, not a management forum. Chief executives commonly stack the agenda with matters of importance to them, rather than focusing on what the board needs to do its job.
   The chief executive has two primary roles at board meetings:

- helping the board understand and address the future – providing advice and support to the board's dialogue and decision-making and
- helping the board analyse and understand the past and providing evidence that the organization is doing what it should.

7. Helping the board understand the risks faced by the organization
The board needs to be regularly appraised about the nature of organizational risks and the planned response. A chief executive can help the board fulfil its duty of care by developing risk mitigation strategies and promptly reporting key issues.

Figure 9.2 (Continued)

Power and influence in decision-making within boards

House (1991: 29) noted that power is used within organizations to influence important decisions, outcomes and processes such as 'goals, strategies, significant policies, decisions' premises, distribution of resources, allocation of important prerequisites, distribution of authority, organizational arrangements and the motivations of others'. As governance involves the use of power in all of these facets of organizational life it is important to understand the dynamics of the use of power within boards and its implications

141

for how boards and executives work together. The majority of research concerning power in organizations has focused on identifying the sources of power held by individuals, categorized as legitimate, reward, coercive, referent and expert power (French & Raven, 1959; Pfeffer, 1992).

Much of the literature regarding power within nonprofit boards has focused on exploring what should be the ideal balance of power between the board and the CEO (Murray et al., 1992). However, there have been attempts to explore other patterns of board power such as the work by Murray et al. (1992) who identified five patterns of board power relations within Canadian nonprofit voluntary organizations: (1) executive dominated board; (2) chair dominated board; (3) fragmented power board; (4) power sharing board and (5) the powerless board. An executive-dominated board tends to rely on guidance from the executive and makes decisions with little argument or debate and does not devote significant time to developing plans. The executive and paid staff are trusted by the board on the basis of their perceived 'expertise, experience and track record of successfully managing the organization' (Murray et al., 1992: 167). Chair-dominated boards are controlled by the chair who drives the development of strategy and wields power over the selection of board members on the basis of their links with the board chair or their support of the chair. A fragmented power board is subject to constant conflict and factions making effective governance and decision-making difficult. The divisive nature of the board precludes most strategic planning activities and major decisions are not made without 'considerable politicking' (Murray et al., 1992: 168). In direct contrast to the fragmented board, the power sharing board operates on the basis of equality and democracy, making it 'difficult to achieve major changes or launch big projects because it takes so much time to work through the consultative, consensus-based form of decision-making' (Murray et al., 1992: 168). Finally, the powerless board is beset with uncertainty, suffers from an absence of leadership, holds disorganized meetings and demonstrates a total lack of planning. Murray et al. (1992: 169) noted that 'apathetic and aimless are two adjectives that sum up the climate of such a board'.

These five patterns of board power were confirmed by Golensky (1993), and Hoye and Cuskelly (2003a) in studies of board–executive relationships within nonprofit organizations and nonprofit sport organizations, respectively. Golensky (1993: 188) noted that 'under one set of conditions, the board and executive may constitute a partnership (but) the same individuals could become locked in a power struggle in other circumstances'. This was the first study to argue that conceptualizing the board–executive relationship as a simple partnership was misleading and that the five patterns of power within boards developed by Murray et al. (1992) were probably closer to describing the reality of board–executive relationships over time.

In the context of nonprofit sport organizations, Doherty (1998) noted that the use of power may be unique to a particular group within the organization such as a governing board but there were a limited number of studies exploring the use of power within the boards of sport organizations. In one of the first studies that attempted to explore the distribution of power and influence in decision-making between volunteer board members and CEOs, Chelladurai and Haggerty (1991) found that the CEOs had the most amount of influence in the majority of decision-making areas. In contrast, Kikulis et al. (1995a) found that while the majority of Canadian NSOs had been professionalized, the organizations maintained a volunteer controlled and professionally supported decision-making structure. This finding was supported in a study of Finnish NSOs by Koski and Heikkala (1998) who concluded that volunteer board members had maintained a certain level of control over decision-making, but the power of CEOs had increased in recent years.

In a widely cited work in this area, Inglis (1997b) found that the amount of influence exerted by board members and CEOs varied according to the nature of the decisions being made. In addition, volunteers and CEOs are involved in and prefer to remain involved in certain types of decision-making within boards. She found that the influence of volunteers and CEOs varied in the following decision-making areas: fundraising, setting financial policy, advocacy roles, hiring decisions, strategic planning, programme delivery, representing specific interest groups, policy development and budget allocations. Auld (1997) also found that certain decisions were perceived to be the responsibility of volunteer board members over the executive and vice versa. He also found that both volunteers and professionals perceived that professionals had the most overall influence in decision-making within the board. The perception that there were some areas of decision-making that were more the domain of volunteers than CEOs and vice versa was also confirmed by Auld and Godbey (1998). Shilbury (2001: 276) also noted the increasing influence of paid staff in decision-making within nonprofit sport organizations and stated 'that influence and by implication control, may have been ceded to executive directors'. Research conducted by Hoye and Cuskelly (2003a) supported the argument that the distribution of decision-making power and influence within nonprofit sport organizations is not based on a simple divide between volunteers and CEOs.

Dual leadership

The introduction of professional staff into nonprofit sport organizations has led to the creation of dual leadership positions (i.e. Board Chair and CEO). Inglis (1997b: 17) highlighted that:

> Leadership is one of the critical areas emerging from the changing structures and processes of amateur sport organizations. The uniqueness

of the dual leadership between volunteers and paid staff in nonprofit amateur sport poses additional complexities given the sharing of roles and the dynamics associated with the sharing of responsibilities.

This section briefly discusses selected research on the topic of leadership within general nonprofit organizations and then explores the small number of studies that have focused on leadership in nonprofit sport organizations with particular reference to dual leadership.

The first thing to note for nonprofit organizations is the work by Herman and Tulipana (1989) who found that board members' perceptions of their influence varied (in part) due to the existence of a dominant coalition – the group of individuals who truly controlled an organization. This dominant coalition often includes senior staff, the executive, some board members and 'representatives of major funders, regulatory and licensing agencies, and sometimes regional or national bodies in the same domain' (Herman & Tulipana, 1989: 58). The existence of a dominant coalition means that while there might well be only two formal leadership positions in the governance structure of these organizations, there are in reality many individuals contributing to organizational leadership. Nevertheless, Herman and Tulipana (1989: 58) concluded 'executive directors are frequently a very important part of the dominant coalition, and thus they are centrally involved in decisions about who to include on the board, as well as in training new board members and setting expectations'. Heimovics and Herman (1990: 68) reinforced the importance of the CEO in leading nonprofit organizations when they stated 'the chief executive, not the board president, is assigned predominant responsibility (for dealing with critical incidents which organizations had to face)'. Their work questioned the 'prescriptive, taken-for-granted role and interpretation of final responsibility of boards for outcomes in the nonprofit organization' (Heimovics & Herman, 1990: 70). The central leadership role adopted by some CEOs in nonprofit organizations was also supported by Heimovics, Herman and Jurkiewicz (1995: 234) who concluded that 'effective chief executives understand the centrality of their leadership role and accept responsibility as initiators of action, with their boards, to find resources and revitalize the missions of their organizations'.

Leadership is one of the most studied topics in management and organizational theory. A myriad of theories have been developed to explain leadership within organizations (Kent & Chelladurai, 2001; Northouse, 2001). Leader–member exchange (LMX) theory focuses on explaining the relationships that evolve between leaders and followers and has been used increasingly in the governance literature in recent years (Gomez & Rosen, 2001; Northouse, 2001; Graen & Uhl-Bien, 1995). In light of the previous discussions of board–executive relations and power and influence in decision-making, LMX theory offers a useful heuristic to explore the

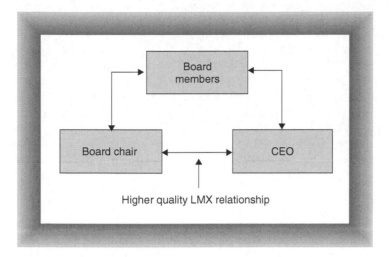

Figure 9.3 LMX relationships within a board

dynamics of leadership within the context of nonprofit sport organization boards. These relationships are depicted in Figure 9.3.

The genesis of LMX theory can be found in the work of Dansereau, Graen and Haga (1975) who recognized that many managerial processes in organizations occur on a dyadic basis. In essence, leaders and followers develop exclusive exchange relationships (dyads), some of which are high quality, and others of low quality. High-quality exchange relationships are based on the presence of high mutual trust, respect and obligation between leaders and followers. Low-quality exchange relationships are characterized by low levels of mutual trust, respect and obligation. Because leaders treat individuals differently (Duchon, Green & Taber, 1986), they tend to develop different dyadic relationships. High-quality LMX exchanges have been found to be related to a number of positive organizational outcomes such as 'less employee turnover, more positive performance evaluations, higher frequency of promotions, greater organizational commitment, more desirable work assignments, better job attitudes, more attention and support from the leader, greater participation and faster career progress' (Northouse, 2001: 115).

Effective leadership is more likely when leaders and followers are able to develop mature leadership relationships. The ability to develop such relationships is 'influenced by characteristics and behaviours of leaders and members and occurs through a role-making process' (Graen & Uhl-Bien, 1995: 229). The establishment of mature LMX relationships can occur only if three conditions are met: '(1) mutual respect for the capabilities of the other, (2) the anticipation of deepening reciprocal trust with the other and (3) the expectation that interacting obligation will grow over time as career-oriented social exchanges blossom into a partnership' (Graen & Uhl-Bien, 1995: 237). In other words, volunteer and CEOs will not develop mature LMX

145

relationships with other individuals in governance roles without first evaluating the potential dyadic relationship using these criteria.

The initiation of mature LMX relationships rests on the assumption that they are more likely to be made by leaders than by followers. In the context of the governance structures of nonprofit sport organizations LMX relationships are more likely to be initiated by board chairs, CEOs, or perhaps by senior board members. Northouse (2001) explained that followers who accept offers to develop a mature LMX relationship with their leader become part of an 'in-group' or part of a trusted inner circle. As a result they may work harder at fulfilling their role and display higher levels of loyalty. In return they may receive or expect to receive more responsibility and opportunity for career advancement. In contrast, followers who do not accept these offers will find themselves in an 'out-group' where they simply do the minimum work required in their job, but generally no more and are given no special treatment by their leader. Duchon et al. (1986) noted that the process in which these dyadic exchange relationships develop is observable to other members of the group. This means that within 'discrete work environments, such as a board, all members are potentially aware of the existence of an 'in-group' and an 'out-group' depending on their ability to interpret the quality of the exchange relationships that exist between the various dyads' (Hoye, 2006b: 299).

The first reported attempt to apply LMX theory to the study of sport organizations was carried out by Kent and Chelladurai (2001). They focused on testing the relationships between LMX, transformational leadership behaviours, organizational commitment and organizational citizenship behaviour amongst university athletic department employees. Kent and Chelladurai (2001: 154) found that transformational leadership assisted in 'the cultivation of high-quality LMX between middle-level managers and the third-tier employees'. Later studies by Hoye (2004; 2006b) applied LMX theory specifically to the dynamics of leadership within the boards of nonprofit sport organizations. Hoye (2004: 66) found that executives and board chairs 'perceived the quality of LMX relationships between themselves as significantly higher than their respective LMX relationships with board members'. In other words, executives and board chairs recognized that they enjoyed a more mature working relationship (dyad) with each other than with other members of the board. This was perhaps due to the nature of their roles which requires executives and board chairs to work closely together, so 'offers from either executives or board chairs to create mature working relationships would therefore be more likely to occur' (Hoye, 2004: 66).

In a further study Hoye (2006b: 309) argued that 'board leadership is perceived to be shared between board chairs and executives with the majority of board members following'. Hoye (2006b: 310) also confirmed that 'the creation and development of mature working relationships takes a significant amount of time and is undertaken through a process of negotiation

Is there over-reliance on the chair?

While it is important that the chair and chief executive have an effective working relationship, this should not be at the expense of the wider board/chief executive relationship.

Should there be a special relationship?

Board members often claim the chief executive should communicate with the board via the chair, however it can be argued there should be no independent relationship between these two key figures. The latter view holds that the chief executive Is employed by the board as a whole, not by the chair alone, and therefore accountability should be expressed to the entire body.

For what purpose?

Chairs and chief executives often meet outside the boardroom to keep the former up to-date with key issues in the organization. Many boards expect their chair to be more familiar with details of the organization's strategic actions and activities than other board members. While this expectation is common it is not a maxim to be applied to all boards under normal circumstances. There may be abnormal circumstances that require the chair and chief executive to 'sing the same song' in public. Then, it is essential that the two leaders be consistent. It is common for a chair and the chief executive to meet prior to a board meeting to coordinate and discuss the agenda. This is an ideal time to share perspectives, discuss issues and for the chief executive to sound out any issues.

How often?

It is common for chief executives and their chairs to meet weekly or more. Under *normal* circumstances, however, this should not be necessary. A competent chief executive, properly empowered via sound delegation policies, should not need to meet with any member of the board on a regular basis in order to carry out their role. There is no rule applying to the frequency of chief executive/chair meetings. Circumstances and common-sense should prevail. Care should be taken to ensure that these meetings do not become mini-board meetings. A chief executive must not assume that telling the chair about a board issue means the board has automatically been advised. In turn, the chair must ensure they do not become a filter or gatekeeper for information that should be received by the full board.

Document the desired relationship

Where there is board agreement that the chief executive and chair should meet outside of scheduled board meetings, there is value in having a written protocol that governs this relationship. Boards with such a charter could consider including a provision as follows:

- With the approval of the board the chair may establish a regular communication arrangement with the chief executive in which there is an exchange of information for various purposes related to the more effective functioning of

Figure 9.4 The board and CEO relationship (*Source*: Adapted from SPARC (2004: 80–81); reprinted with the permission of Sport and Recreation New Zealand)

> the board and to enhance the board/chief executive partnership. This might include an opportunity for the chief executive to use such sessions as a sounding board for proposed actions or to check interpretations of board policy. However:
> - The chair will recognize that such sessions are not to be used to 'personally' supervise or direct the chief executive.
> - The chair will not inhibit the free flow of information to the board necessary for sound governance. Therefore the chair will never come between the board and its formal links with the chief executive.

Figure 9.4 (Continued)

or role making'. He concluded that board chairs tended 'to focus on developing their relationship with the executive over board members, perhaps because the potential for a heightened sense of mutual obligation exists in this dyadic relationship than others' (Hoye, 2006b: 310).

In light of these research findings, the guidelines developed by SPARC (2004: 80–81) do not seem to offer much clarity for how the relationship between the board chair and CEO should operate. The guidelines focus on defining how often and for what purpose the board chair and CEO should meet and communicate outside formal board meetings (see Figure 9.4). However, the SPARC guidelines make no mention of how the board chair and CEO might develop and maintain their relationship, nor do the guidelines acknowledge the probability of a dominant coalition in the governance of the organization.

Conclusion

This chapter has explored the leadership challenges that exist within nonprofit sport organizations which have come about through the increasing professionalization of the sports industry. The diminution of volunteer control in many nonprofit sport organizations has challenged decision-making and leadership processes in the governance of these organizations. The effects of professionalization have altered the role of volunteer board members and in particular the role of the board chair. Subsequently, the relationship between volunteers and paid executives has evolved and now involves negotiating the boundaries of their respective responsibilities and how they work together in organizational governance and management. The professionalization of nonprofit sport organizations has also heightened the potential for conflict over who has real power and influence in decision-making and has created conditions which have led to the development of dual leadership between board chairs and executives. There is an increasing body of research evidence about the changing nature of leadership which has been paralleled by the development of guidelines about how relationships between CEOs and board members ought to be initiated, developed and maintained. However, there is scope for improvement in how these relationships should be managed. There is a need to gather more empirical evidence about the nature and extent of the important relationships between volunteers and professional staff in leadership roles and how the qualities of these relationships impact on board performance and the effectiveness of organizational governance.

10

Team performance: board, board member and CEO performance

Overview

The underlying premise of much of the prescriptive literature and the majority of the research reported in this book is that better performing boards will result in better organizational outcomes. The notion that there is a positive relationship between board and organizational performance has remained virtually unchallenged yet there is very little supporting evidence in the research literature. The concept of board performance naturally leads to a discussion of how board performance is measured, the criteria applied and who conducts the evaluation. Allied to the notion of board performance are questions of how to evaluate the performance of individual board members and chief executive officers (CEOs) and whether individual performance is a precursor to overall board performance.

This chapter explores these issues and questions and is structured in five parts. First, the empirical evidence on board performance evaluation is presented along with examples from nonprofit and sport industry guidelines. Second, the empirical evidence on the correlates of board performance is reviewed. Third, is a brief discussion on organizational performance and a review of the debate surrounding the relationship between board and organizational performance. Fourth, guidelines for conducting individual board member performance evaluations are reviewed along with a discussion of the research on individual and board performance. Finally, the chapter reviews the recommended guidelines for conducting CEO performance evaluations.

Evaluating board performance

The nonprofit literature abounds with prescriptive guidelines for evaluating board performance and there have been numerous attempts to develop empirically driven measures of board performance. This section reviews some of the more widely cited guidelines for evaluating board performance. These guidelines have been developed either by nonprofit and sport agencies or from published research on board performance measurement. The National Council for Voluntary Organizations (NCVO) (2005: 20) outlined a set of principles for the evaluation processes that ought to be utilized by nonprofit boards:

1. The Board should ensure that:
   - at least every 2 years, it sets aside time to reflect on its own performance and functioning as a team;
   - the performance of individual trustees is regularly assessed and appraised, either by the chair or another trustee, or by using external assistance;
   - the performance of the chair is likewise assessed and appraised, either by another trustee, the Board as a whole, or using external assistance;
   - the performance of sub-committees, standing groups and other bodies is similarly appraised and reviewed.
2. The results of these appraisals should be used to make necessary changes and improvements, to inform the creation of appropriate training programmes and to guide trustee renewal and recruitment.

While these guidelines do not articulate exactly how such performance evaluations should be conducted they do highlight that performance evaluations should be conducted for the board as a group, for individual board members including the board chair and for any sub-committees of the board. Further, the results of these evaluations should be used for performance improvement initiatives and as an aid in the recruitment of future board members.

The guidelines developed by the Australian Sports Commission (ASC) (2005: 25) are more specific and emphasize the board's role in conducting its own evaluation:

1. The board should evaluate its own effectiveness annually.
2. The board should explicitly set standards and performance expectations to provide a basis for a formal annual evaluation of its governance effectiveness. The board should assess its performance according to pre-agreed objective criteria, preferably derived from its own governance policies and processes.
3. Best practice approaches to board evaluation include:
   – setting time aside, at least annually, for the board explicitly to address its collective and individual member performance;
   – using an independent facilitator or consultant to help the board design a suitable evaluation process and to ensure that this is carried out independently and confidentially;
   – conducting peer and self-appraisal of all board members, and the chairperson.
4. The outcome of the evaluation process should be used as the basis for board and individual board member development goals, leading to an improvement in board performance over time.

The guidelines developed by Sport and Recreation New Zealand (SPARC) (2004) are more detailed and highlight the benefits of boards conducting self-assessments of their performance across a range of criteria. These include: identification of board-wide performance improvements; succession planning; assistance to individual board members and identification of areas where the personal contribution of board members could be enhanced. The SPARC (2004) guidelines are reflective of most board evaluation processes. They rely on board members making judgements about the collective performance of the board and having the information collated by an independent facilitator who, in turn, provides feedback to board in order to drive a discussion about improving performance. SPARC (2004) also highlight a number of reasons boards may resist performance evaluation (see Figure 10.1).

Prescriptive guidelines for board performance evaluation have focussed generally on self-assessment processes which is reflected in research attempts to develop board evaluation instruments. It is somewhat surprising that there have been few documented attempts to empirically develop board evaluation tools given the focus on performance improvement in much of the literature on nonprofit boards. Research efforts in this area have focussed

1. We are subject to re-election. In other words, members will determine whether a board is doing a good job. In a broad sense this is true, however, members are not inside the boardroom and cannot typically provide the performance feedback a self-assessment would generate.
2. We have our hands full just surviving. Boards of struggling organizations often find themselves continually under pressure because of ineffective governance and leadership. A review process would allow them to step back and reflect.
3. It will undermine teamwork. Asking directors to review their performance introduces an element of competition that could undermine efforts to build cooperation and collaboration among directors. Similarly, the process will invite critical comments that will create tension. As any sports team knows, however, ignoring performance shortcomings is far more divisive.
4. An evaluation process is not appropriate for volunteers. Because they are volunteers, giving freely of their time, directors should not be expected to perform to the same standards as paid counterparts in other types of organizations. In other words, given theirs is a voluntary contribution it should be accepted without judgement or assessment. To accept this contention is to undermine the board's position of trust.
5. Performance evaluation is not appropriate for 'eminent' directors. A board comprising eminent sports, professional and business people should not be subject to review because it implies they could be doing a better job. The mere suggestion of a review is somewhat insulting and disrespectful.

Figure 10.1 Reasons for resisting attempts to evaluate board performance (*Source*: Adapted from SPARC (2004: 98); reprinted with permission of Sport and Recreation New Zealand)

predominantly on two board performance measurement scales: the Board Self Assessment Questionnaire (BSAQ) developed by Jackson and Holland (1998); and, the Self Assessment for Nonprofit Governing Boards Scale (SANGBS) developed by Slesinger (1991).

Holland (1991: 26) noted that ideas for improving board performance were 'based almost entirely on individual experience and opinion, tends to be exhortative rather than empirical, is more anecdotal than systematic and provides a limited basis for understanding the problems or improving the practices of governance'. On making this assessment, Holland (1991) sought to explore whether it was possible for a board to measure its own performance and whether an appropriate scale could be developed for assessing board performance. His initial attempt yielded a 69 item scale (the BSAQ) with items covering six board competencies: (a) understands institutional context, (b) builds capacity for learning, (c) nurtures the development of the board as a group, (d) recognizes complexities and nuances, (e) respects and guards the integrity of the governance process and (f) envisions and shapes institutional direction. Seven years later, Holland and Jackson (1998) revised the BSAQ by using data from four separate studies to examine the reliability, validity and sensitivity of the scale. The final version of the BSAQ was made up of 65 items that Holland and Jackson (1998: 177) reported as providing a reliable, valid and sensitive measurement of board performance that was a 'useful tool for guiding efforts to understand and strengthen the governance of nonprofit organizations'.

In contrast, Herman and Renz (1997, 1998, 2000) have argued consistently for the adoption of a social constructionist approach to measure board performance. The social constructionist approach maintains that individuals gain knowledge through their social interactions with others and the world around them and that the meanings people ascribe to things are based on their own individual social construction of reality (Berger & Luckmann, 1967). Not inconsistent with the SPARC (2004) guidelines discussed earlier, the social constructionist perspective considers effectiveness to be the collective judgements of individuals directly involved with the object being judged. The social constructionist perspective notes that these judgements may change over time according to the interactions or impressions collected by the individuals making the judgement. Further, the individuals making the judgements may not be consciously aware of the criteria or information they use to form such judgements. Herman and Renz (1997, 1998, 2000) adopted the social constructionist perspective through their use of the SANGBS to explore the relationship between board performance and organizational effectiveness in nonprofit organizations.

There has been no research published by sport management scholars which aims to develop board performance measures specifically for sport organizations. One of the first reported studies of board performance in sport was conducted by Papadimitriou (1999) who researched Greek National Sport Organizations (NSOs). Papadimitriou (1999) found that different external constituent groups (e.g. athletes, coaches, scientific staff, funding agency staff, sponsors) used different criteria to conceptualize and judge effective board performance. Later research efforts related to sport board performance have followed the work of Herman and Renz (1997, 1998, 2000) in adapting the SANGBS for the context of nonprofit sport organizations (cf. Hoye, 2004, 2006b; Hoye & Auld, 2001; Hoye & Cuskelly, 2003a, 2003b).

Correlates of board performance

Research into the correlates of nonprofit board performance have focussed on exploring: the personal motivations of board members (Taylor, Chait & Holland, 1991); the influence of a cyclical pattern in the life cycle of boards

(Wood, 1992; Dart, Bradshaw, Murray & Wolpin, 1996); appropriate structures, processes and planning (Bradshaw, Murray & Wolpin, 1992;
Herman, Renz & Heimovics, 1997; Herman & Renz, 2000; Cornforth,
2001) and undertaking board development activities (Fletcher, 1992;
Holland & Jackson, 1998). Taylor et al. (1991) found that more effective
boards had members whose motivations were based on their individual
connections or empathy with the cause of the organization. They argued
that boards could foster this connection by orienting board members
to the organization, utilizing individual members' skills and involving
board members in social events with the rest of the organization.

In the context of crises situations, Wood (1992) discovered the presence
of a cyclical pattern in the operation of boards and their ability to perform
effectively. She found that boards typically cycled through four stages:
(1) a founding stage with high levels of input from board members and a
collegiate atmosphere within the board; (2) super-managing, with board
members recognizing the need to implement more organized systems and
processes and an accompanying high level of involvement in operational
matters by the board; (3) a corporate stage, with the board attempting to
mirror the way corporate boards operate, emphasizing processes rather
than the mission of the organization and (4) ratifying, with board members more interested in the prestige of their position than the mission of
the agency, generally lower levels of interest or commitment in the business of the agency, with the result that the board is unable to respond to
crises. Wood (1992) concluded that boards move through these stages
over a period of years until a crisis situation forces the board to re-evaluate
its role and board processes.

Dart et al. (1996) offered a contrary view to Wood (1992) and
suggested that board life-cycle models can be interpreted as a set of
general statements that describe the elements of a nonprofit board that
evolve over time. They suggested that the life-cycle models espoused by
Wood (1992) and Mathiasen (1990) could be reduced to the following
points. As an organization ages: (1) board members will be recruited
with more managerial and professional skills, (2) the board will have
less involvement with volunteers and/or operational roles, (3) the board
will have more involvement with governance roles (policy development
and planning) (4) fundraising activity by the board will increase, (5) the
board will become more formally organized, (6) the board will have a
more elaborate committee structure, (7) the board will be larger in size
and (8) the community profile of board members will increase so that they
will be selected in part for their prestige in the community (Dart et al.,
1996: 370).

In contrast to these statements, Dart et al. (1996: 376) concluded that
'boards only partially behave in a manner described by life-cycle models'.
However, three elements of the life-cycle model were supported by their
study: (1) as nonprofit organizations develop, the board will become more

formally organized, (2) the board will have a more elaborate committee structure and (3) the board will be larger in size.

Bradshaw et al. (1992) found that board structure and board practices contribute to overall board performance. The adoption of prescribed board practices was found to contribute to more effective board performance as reported by Herman and Renz (2000) and Herman et al. (1997). These practices covered areas such as using the existing profile of the board to recruit new board members, having a board manual to assist with the induction of new board members, following standard meeting procedures, conducting board evaluations and specifying the powers of the CEO. Cornforth (2001) examined the influence board inputs, structures and processes have on board effectiveness. He concluded that boards perform better if board members have the time, skills and experience to fulfil their duties and if boards utilize three processes: (1) develop clear board roles and responsibilities,(2) establish a common vision for the board and management of organizational goals and (3) ensure the board and management periodically review how they work together.

Holland and Jackson (1998: 133) investigated the impact of board development work on board performance and found that 'boards of a variety of nonprofit organizations can take intentional steps that improve board effectiveness'. The value of undertaking board development work for improving board performance was recognized in earlier work by Fletcher (1992). She concluded that the work of the CEO in developing the board was crucial to improving board performance. Useful CEO board development activities identified by Fletcher (1992) were:

- Being actively involved in recruiting new board members;
- Undertaking the primary role to orient and train the new board members in the workings of the board;
- Setting the agenda for board meetings in conjunction with the chair of the board;
- Supporting the work of the board's committees;
- Assisting the board in policy development but not taking a leading role;
- Getting the board involved in public relations and fundraising;
- Supporting but not leading the board's strategic planning function;
- Supporting the board's financial oversight function;
- Helping the board chair do their job and moulding their own role to suit each new incoming board chair;
- Cultivating individual board members and discovering their motivations for becoming a board member.

Efforts to explore the correlates of board performance in the context of sport organizations have focussed on group cohesion (Doherty & Carron, 2003); the strength of committee norms (Doherty, Patterson & Van Bussel, 2004); patterns of board power (Hoye & Cuskelly, 2003a); the quality of board-executive relations (Hoye & Cuskelly, 2003b) and the quality of leader–member exchange relationships (Hoye, 2004, 2006b). The work of Doherty and Carron (2003) and Doherty et al. (2004) was discussed in detail in Chapter 6. They stressed that group context had little influence on the individual behaviour of board members but that board members were more likely to remain committed if they perceived their board to be acting cohesively as a group. The findings of Hoye and Cuskelly (2003a, 2003b) and Hoye (2004, 2006b) were discussed in detail in the previous chapter. Their studies demonstrated that positive board-executive relations, shared leadership between the chair and executive as well as the sharing of power and influence within the board were important factors in relation to effective board performance.

In summary, research evidence suggests that a variety of factors influence board performance. These factors include adopting appropriate structures and prescribed board practices, motivating individual board members, conducting regular board review and development processes, developing group cohesion, fostering positive relations between boards and executives and establishing shared leadership between volunteers and paid staff. Whether effective board performance is a precursor to better organizational outcomes is the focus of the next section.

Organizational and board performance

In a comprehensive review of nonprofit organizational effectiveness studies over two decades, Forbes (1998) highlighted the difficulty of conducting organizational effectiveness studies for nonprofit organizations. The majority of studies in this area have focussed on: (1) outright assessment of organizational effectiveness, (2) searching for correlates of effectiveness or (3) exploring the effectiveness of assessment processes (Forbes, 1998). It is beyond the scope of this book to present a comprehensive overview of all of these studies, rather the following section focuses on the relationship between organizational and board performance.

A system resource approach was used by Provan (1980) to assess the contribution of boards to organizational effectiveness. The systems resource approach considers the ability to acquire scarce resources as an important requirement for organizational effectiveness. While Provan recognized the shortcomings of the approach as it did not measure the ability of the organization to achieve stated goals, he utilized it because he was researching 'the contribution to agency effectiveness of one particular organizational unit; namely, a powerful board of directors whose primary purpose is to facilitate the acquisition of scarce resources from the agency's external environment' (Provan, 1980: 224). He found that boards were able to positively influence the amount of funding received by an agency if the agency was already receiving large amounts of funding. However, he concluded that in terms of 'enabling an agency to be effective in its efforts to acquire funding, the results of this study strongly suggest that a powerful board of directors may be less important than previously believed' (Provan, 1980: 234).

The work by Bradshaw et al. (1992) discussed earlier found that certain aspects of board activities were correlated with organizational effectiveness, namely: strategic planning, good meeting management, sharing of a common vision, involving themselves in the operations of the organization and avoiding conflicts with staff. Green and Griesinger (1996) found evidence of a significant relationship between board performance and organizational effectiveness for the first time. They found that boards of effective organizations were more involved in activities such as 'policy formulation, strategic planning, programme review, board development, resource development, financial planning and control and dispute resolution than were boards of less effective organizations' (Green & Griesinger, 1996: 398).

Herman and Renz (1997, 1998, 2000) used a social constructionist perspective, explained earlier in this chapter, and a multiple constituency model to investigate stakeholder judgements of nonprofit organizational effectiveness. The value of the multiple constituency model is that it 'recognizes that organizations have (or comprise) multiple stakeholders or constituents who are likely to differ in the criteria they use to evaluate the effectiveness of an organization' (Herman & Renz, 1997: 187). They concluded that practitioners and experts used adherence by the board to correct procedures to judge effectiveness whereas other stakeholders, such as board members, preferred different criteria such as financial data. They concluded that the 'idea that there is a single objective organizational effectiveness independent of the judgements of various stakeholders is no longer tenable or useful' (Herman & Renz, 1997: 202). In subsequent studies, Herman and Renz (1998, 2000) found that, while not claiming to have established a causal connection, using correct procedures by the board was related to greater performance at both board and organizational levels.

In a recent attempt to explore the relationship between board performance and organizational performance, Brown (2005: 317) noted that 'existing research has found significant relationships between board and organizational effectiveness, but much work remained to be done to establish the nature and causal direction of these relationships'. Brown (2005) developed a model (see Figure 10.2) that outlined the theoretical relationships between the three major theories of nonprofit governance, the dimensions of six board competencies developed by Chait, Holland and Taylor (1996) and organizational effectiveness. He suggested that the contextual dimension of board competency 'reflects one aspect of the monitoring functions

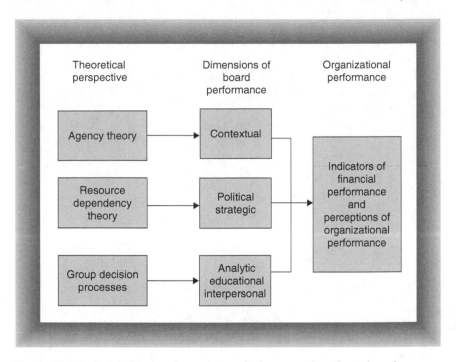

Figure 10.2 Relationship between theoretical perspectives, board performance and organizational performance (*Source*: Adapted from Brown (2005: 320))

proposed by agency theory and a unique function for nonprofits' (Brown, 2005: 322). The political dimension highlights the boards' role in maintaining their connection with their respective community and drawing resources to the organization. The strategic dimension of board competencies has been well established in the literature and also relates to the resource dependency perspective. The final three board competencies: analytic, educational and interpersonal dimensions relate to group and decision theories about how information is managed and used for decision-making. The analytic dimension suggests that a board's capacity to apply multiple perspectives to addressing and solving problems is related to board performance. Similarly the educational dimension of board competency suggests that boards that are well placed to educate their board members about board processes and performance expectations will perform at a higher level. Finally, the interpersonal dynamics of board meetings and board member interactions impact on board behaviour and so adopting formal processes for managing these interactions should impact on board performance. Brown (2005: 333) found support for 'all three theoretical perspectives, with a consistent theme that strategic contributions of the board are identified as one of the most salient features associated with organizational performance'. He also claimed that the interpersonal

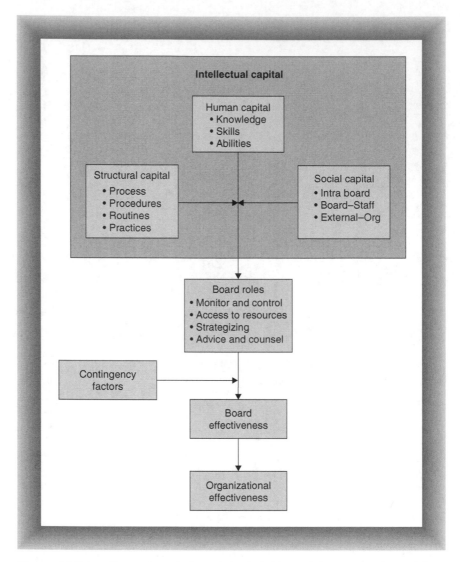

Figure 10.3 Intellectual capital model of the board (*Source*: Adapted from Nicholson and Kiel (2004: 12))

dimensions of board competency are a potentially significant driver of board performance and worthy of future research attention.

An intellectual capital model of the board and its relationship to corporate board performance was developed by Nicholson and Kiel (2004). While this model has been created for profit-seeking firms, the principles that underpin its development are relevant to nonprofit board and organizational performance. The model, presented in Figure 10.3, suggests that firm or organizational performance will be positively impact by board effectiveness and that board effectiveness, in turn, is dependent on the successful execution of four board roles, namely 'monitoring and controlling, strategizing, providing advice and counsel and providing access to resources' (Nicholson & Kiel, 2004: 8). Contingency factors such as organizational size and management competency will have an impact on how well these board roles are carried out which, in turn moderates 'the relationship between board effectiveness and firm performance' (Nicholson & Kiel, 2004: 8). The attributes of the board that enable it to perform its roles are considered to be its intellectual capital, comprised of three elements: (1) human capital, or intelligence of individuals, (2) structural capital that consists of the organizational routines used to facilitate group interactions and (3) social capital, or the relationships that exist between board members, between the board and staff and between the board and external constituencies. The model provides a comprehensive assessment of the many variables that impact board performance and ultimately impacts on organizational outcomes. As such it offers both researchers and practitioners a clear conceptual framework for exploring how boards can improve their contributions to organizational performance.

In summary, the studies reported here have attempted to establish a link between board and organizational performance. They have highlighted that the 'empirical assessment of both board and organizational performance has been challenging, making accurate understanding of these concepts difficult' (Brown, 2005: 317). The studies have demonstrated the value of researching board performance from social constructivist perspective, and the need to gather perceptions of board performance from those individuals directly involved with the board. The models developed by Brown (2005) and Nicholson and Kiel (2004), respectively, offer insights to this important link and contribute to furthering our understanding of how the boards of nonprofit sport organizations can influence organizational outcomes.

Board member performance

Given the attention devoted to board performance in nonprofit organizations it is somewhat surprising that there is a dearth of literature on the performance evaluation of individual board members. This may be explained in part by the inherent difficulties of conducting performance evaluations of individuals who are acting in a voluntary capacity. Evaluating individual board member performance raises questions about the relevance of evaluation criteria, the evaluation processes utilized, to whom the results of individual evaluations should be reported and what, if any, action ought to be undertaken as a result of an evaluation.

Hoye and Cuskelly (2004: 96–97) found that nonprofit sport organizations struggled with the 'questions of how to conduct such evaluations, what criteria to use and who should perform board and board member evaluations'. They concluded that 'evaluating the performance of board members who are elected by their general membership, in addition to subjecting them to regular re-elections, may deter many members from standing for election to the board' (Hoye & Cuskelly, 2004: 97).

It is clear that board member evaluation is recognized as an important part of improving governance practices and board performance within nonprofit organizations. The NCVO (2005: 20) guidelines stipulate that boards should ensure that 'the performance of individual trustees (board members) is regularly assessed and appraised, either by the chair or another trustee or by using external assistance' but provide no criteria on which to base such evaluations. Similarly, the ASC (2005) and SPARC (2004) governance guidelines recommend that individual board member performance evaluations should be conducted but offer no guidance about criteria or processes to use in undertaking such evaluations. In the corporate sector, The London Stock Exchange (LSE) (2004) recommends that corporate board members be subject to individual performance evaluations on an annual basis. They propose the following set of questions as the basis for conducting such evaluations:

1. How well prepared and informed are the non-executive directors for board meetings? Is their meeting attendance satisfactory?
2. Do they demonstrate a willingness to devote time and effort to understanding the company and its business? Do they have a readiness to participate in events outside of the boardroom such as site visits?
3. What has been the quality and value of their contributions at board meetings?
4. How successfully have they contributed to strategy development and risk management?
5. How effectively have they tested the information and assumptions with which they are provided? How resolute are they in maintaining their own views and resisting pressure from others?
6. How effectively and proactively have they followed up on any areas of concern?
7. Does their performance and behaviour engender mutual trust and respect within the board?
8. How actively and successfully do they refresh their knowledge and skills? Are they up to date with market and regulatory developments?
9. Are they able to present their views convincingly yet diplomatically? Do they listen and take on board the views of others? (LSE, 2004: 12).

For the most part, these questions appear to be applicable to nonprofit sport organizations and could form the basis for developing a set of questions specifically designed to evaluate the performance of individual board members.

CEO performance

The performance evaluation of the CEO has attracted far greater attention than board member performance in the governance guidelines developed by sport agencies. The ASC (2005: 24) states that the board is responsible for evaluating the CEO's performance and that such an evaluation should only be done in relation to 'objective criteria for which he or she has been delegated full operational authority'. The criteria should be based on organizational objectives, the extent of compliance with board directions provided to the CEO and the appropriate use of the authority the board has delegated to the CEO. In addition, the evaluation of the CEO should not be carried out by the board chair but by a sub-committee of the board (ASC, 2005).

The SPARC (2004) governance guidelines recommend similar processes, in particular that the CEO should only be evaluated against objective and agreed criteria in areas under their direct operational control. It is also important that the board is able to distinguish between the performance of the CEO and the performance of the organization. SPARC (2004: 82) also highlighted that in the context of membership based organizations such as nonprofit sport organizations:

> It is inevitable that stakeholders (including staff) will offer opinions about their chief executive's performance. Often such opinions will have little to do with the board's expressed expectations. They may relate, for example, to the chief executive's personality rather than to whether or not they have achieved the results expected, within the boundaries set. These opinions shouldn't influence an evaluation unless they accurately reflect actual performance or relate to valid criteria for evaluating the chief executive's effectiveness.

SPARC also highlighted the importance of the board being responsible for the CEOs performance evaluation rather than leaving it to the board chair. Finally, SPARC (2004) provided a useful checklist for conducting the performance evaluation of a CEO which is outlined in Figure 10.4.

Conclusion

The chapter has explored the concepts of performance evaluation at the level of the board, individual board members and the CEO and has highlighted the conceptual, measurement and practical difficulties of incorporating such evaluations into the governance practices of sport organizations.

1. Planning

There is no substitute for effective advance planning in relation to the board's responsibilities. The following principles and questions should assist:

- Keep it simple – the board should clearly express the desired and unambiguous results for the year and nominate priorities and (if necessary) weightings. Measurements should be tied to the desired outcome, not to the input or activity.
- What is to be achieved? – Results, like profitability or return on capital, can be clearer and more coherent and easily measured in a commercial environment. Behaviour (or processes) like stakeholder management may, in non-commercial environments, be just as important.
- Base document – the board should draw up an annual statement of performance expectations that states succinctly the key results the board wants the chief executive to focus on achieving during the year. This should be derived from the existing plans and include strategic outcomes and key performance indicators (KPIs).

2. Performance monitoring

The board should avoid rushed, and late, annual reviews. These are heavily influenced by recency. Continuous informal feedback is best. It should be affirmative as well as identifying any concerns. The chief executive's regular reporting to the board is also part of the performance review process. When the chief executive reports to the board on organizational achievement the whole board can be involved in a timely review process. Such reports should be in accordance with a board-approved monitoring schedule. Additionally, more formal 'stocktakes' should take place every 3–4 months. These focus more particularly on the chief executive's performance. They also provide a chance to reset expectations before it is too late. There should also be a final, formal, end-of-year 'wrap-up' review.

3. Who should do it?

The board should not leave the chief executive's performance review solely to the chair because the chief executive is accountable to the whole board. The board should adopt a process whereby all members contribute to reviewing the chief executive's performance. The chief executive can help trigger the board's thinking by preparing a self-assessment. Staff and stakeholders will provide useful feedback for the board and chief executive. Some chief executives worry that staff feedback is risky because they may not be popular, however anecdotal evidence, as opposed to formal feedback, is arguably more damaging. The use of 360° surveys should be considered.

4. Reset expectations

Performance expectations should remain as current as possible. Formal statements of performance expectations should be changed as and when necessary.

Figure 10.4 A checklist of key elements in chief executive performance management (*Source*: SPARC (2004: 82–84); reprinted with permission of Sport and Recreation New Zealand)

5. Review remuneration

Depending on the nature of the chief executive's employment contract there may be two key elements in a remuneration review: market relativity and recognition of performance. The 'relativity' consideration is whether or not – over time – the chief executive's remuneration is kept similar to those in comparable positions. To the extent that the remuneration is inconsistent with acceptable benchmarks the board will either have a dissatisfied chief executive (below the market rate) or dissatisfied stakeholders (above market). While superficially attractive to both parties, many approaches to rewarding performance are fundamentally flawed and encourage inappropriate behaviour. Any performance-related remuneration component should be measurable. Remuneration reviews should focus on ensuring the board has relevant information available to it, allowing it to make sound judgements about market rates and its position relative to that rate. There are various proprietary salary surveys available to this end.

Figure 10.4 (Continued)

Improvements in board performance appear to be driven by a number of factors. Amongst these are the adoption of appropriate structures and prescribed governance practices within the board, the motivation of individual board members, developing the skills of board members, the development of group cohesion within the board, fostering positive relations between board members and executives and establishing shared leadership between volunteers and paid staff. While there have been many attempts to establish a casual link between board performance and organizational effectiveness, the empirical evidence and measurement techniques are weak. Recent work from the corporate and nonprofit literatures has advanced several models of how this relationship might work, yet much remains to be done in order to further understand board performance and the processes by which nonprofit sport organization boards influence organizational effectiveness.

11

Team rules: ethics and principles of good governance

Overview

The behaviour of non-executive directors within corporate boards and board members within nonprofit organizations has come under increasing scrutiny in recent years. A series of reviews of corporate and nonprofit governance legislation and regulatory systems in countries such as Australia, Canada, the USA and the UK have drawn attention for the need for tighter regulation of boards and a need for higher standards of ethical behaviour from board members. Sport organizations at the community and professional levels are not immune to such calls from their members, funding agencies and stakeholders for better governance standards.

This chapter explores the ethical dimensions of governance, the pressures to improve the ethical behaviour of boards and board members and the variety of mechanisms for delivering such improvements. The chapter is presented in six parts. First, the concept of ethical governance is reviewed along with the implications of poor ethical behaviour and the pressures from government, the market and organizational stakeholders to improve ethical standards of governance. Second, the statutory obligations of board members in relation to their governance role are reviewed. Third, the development of various corporate governance codes of practice, standards and guidelines are examined. Fourth, recent developments such as codes practice and guidelines in the nonprofit sector are analysed. Fifth, specific sport governance guidelines developed by national sport agencies and other bodies are outlined. Finally, other influences on ethical governance in sport organizations are discussed and some examples of codes of conduct for sport organizations are reviewed.

Ethical governance

Farrar (2005) argued that in recent times there has been a resurgence in the idea that corporate entities exist not only for shareholders but for a wider group of stakeholders. This concept is not new for nonprofit organizations. Nonprofit sport organizations that primarily service the interests of members do so in the context of having to meet the needs of a diverse group of stakeholders. These may include government agencies, employees, volunteers, sponsors, consumers, contractors and other affiliated organizations. The ethical dilemma this presents is that members of nonprofit sport organizations (i.e. the 'owners') are able to directly influence the way in which their organization is governed through exercising their power to vote for the election of individuals to the board to represent their interests. In contrast, most other stakeholders rarely have enforceable rights. The employees and volunteers of sport organizations have their rights 'determined by contract and employment law' (Farrar, 2005: 451). Consumers also have their rights enshrined in the contract established through the sale of goods and services and via consumer protection legislation. Moving beyond consideration of the rights of these two discrete groups to how other stakeholders might influence governance standards requires the application of ethics and moral rights (Farrar, 2005).

There are four levels of expectations or duties that can be imposed on organizations in relation to the application of ethics and moral rights. According to du Plessis, McConvill and Bagaric (2005: 352) it can be expected of any organization that it will:

1. not directly harm people,
2. not engage in activities that are socially or environmentally unsustainable,

167

3. not lie or otherwise misrepresent the activities of the corporation,
4. engage in activities that are socially desirable.

The first three expectations are generally unspoken. Although there are numerous examples of inappropriate corporate behaviour that has affected the health of individuals, produced environmental problems, or has clearly been dishonest. Nevertheless 'the first three duties are not highly controversial ... and there is no tenable argument for carving out a business exemption in relation to them' (du Plessis et al., 2005: 353). There is also, arguably, very little resistance in the community to the ideal that organizations should fulfil a duty of benevolence that is exhibited by engaging in good corporate citizenship behaviours or following guidelines for Corporate Social Responsibility (CSR).

The need for all types of organizations to demonstrate ethical governance behaviours is based on demonstrating accountability to stakeholders, promoting confidence in the individuals charged with governance responsibilities, demonstrating commitment to ethical principles, and highlighting how organizations deal with conflicts of interest and probity issues. Standards Australia (2003) argued that organizations that define a set of ethical principles for governance will benefit by: (1) helping to foster a climate for ethical behaviour amongst the board and senior management, (2) having a set of principles to refer to in decision-making in areas the organizations may not have encountered previously and (3) clearly articulating the values that underpin their governance practices. Standards Australia (2003) outline a set of seven ethical principles that underpin corporate governance:

1. Accountability – to shareholders and stakeholders.
2. Transparency – the provision of information to interested parties, excluding that which would infringe the privacy or intellectual property of individuals or is not in the national interest.
3. Fairness and balance – in the use of organizational power.
4. Honesty – in the provision of information to internal and external stakeholders.
5. Dignity – upholding the right to human dignity in all dealings.
6. Legal – exhibit full compliance with the law and adhere to conventional codes of behaviour.
7. Goodwill – in the conduct of all organizational activities.

There are many pressures for nonprofit sport organizations and their boards to adhere to governance behaviour standards and ethical principles whether externally imposed or developed specifically for the organization and its board. These pressures arguably stem from eight sources (see Figure 11.1). First, all organizations irrespective of organizational form are subject to a range of legislative and statutory requirements imposed by the state. Second, each of the leading stock exchanges in Western economies have developed standards of corporate governance (cf ASX, 2003; LSE, 2004;

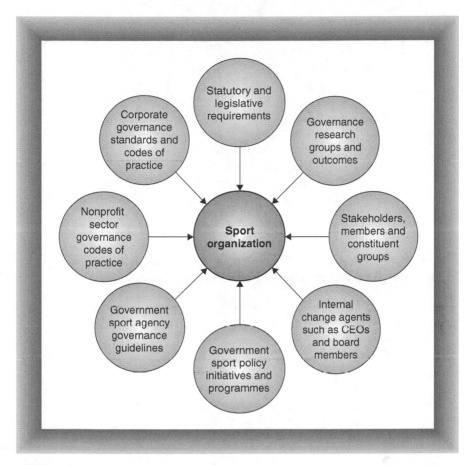

Figure 11.1 Sources of regulatory and compliance pressure for ethical governance behaviour

New York Stock Exchange, 2004) that listed sport organizations such as professional football clubs and other sport franchises must comply. These standards also put compliance pressure non-listed sport organizations in order that they may be seen as equal to their listed rivals. Third, the non-profit sector has developed voluntary codes of conduct for governance (cf NCVO, 2005) that offer clear guidance for how nonprofit sport organizations might improve their ethical governance performance. Fourth, major government sport agencies have developed and promulgate governance guidelines for sport organizations (e.g. SPARC, 2004; UK Sport, 2004; ASC, 2005). Fifth, specific government sport policy initiatives such as the ASC GMIP, discussed in Chapter 2, are directly targeted towards improving the ethical standards of governance in sport organizations. Sixth, internal change agents such as CEOs, board chairs and other individuals may champion change in the ethical standards of governance of their organization. Seventh, other organizational stakeholders such as the European Olympic Committee (EOC) or International Sport Federations (ISFs) may issue directives to member organizations to improve governance standards or members themselves may agitate for change. Finally, specific governance research groups such as the UK-based FGRC or groups such as the Canadian Centre for Sport Law may indirectly influence the adoption of higher ethical standards amongst sport organizations.

In a review of corporate governance regulation, Farrar (2005: 348) noted that 'legal regulation represents the core of corporate governance but that core is surrounded by a penumbra of systems of self-regulation' that offer differing degrees of enforceability. He suggested that after legal regulation, rules for listing companies enforced by stock exchanges and statements of accounting practice were the next layer of regulation. Sitting outside these rules were voluntary codes of practice for corporate governance where the system relies on organizations to comply or explain their reasons for non-compliance. The final layer of self-regulation consisted of codes of ethics developed by industry associations or organizations themselves. Farrar (2005) outlined the arguments for and against self-regulation which are set out in Figure 11.2.

Adopting a framework similar to Farrar (2005), the degree to which the various pressures on sport organizations to adopt good governance behaviours are able to be enforced can be represented by a continuum (see Figure 11.3). At the highest level, statutory obligations are enforceable by law with either non-discretionary or discretionary punishment. In the absence of any sport industry specific code of practice, sport organizations that are listed companies are likely to adopt corporate governance codes of practice. Nonprofit sport organizations might adopt the principles espoused by nonprofit codes of governance practice or standards. Governance guidelines developed by government sport agencies are just that – guidelines. Without formal enforcement, the adoption of such guidelines might be strongly encouraged but difficult to enforce through protocols such as funding and service agreements. Arguably the next most likely pressure for sport organizations to adopt ethical governance behaviour comes from internal change agents and stakeholders agitating for better performance and increased accountability. While not strictly an enforcement mechanism, such pressure might result in the adoption of better governance behaviour. At the lower end of the enforcement continuum are pressures from government policy and programmes which target governance improvement specifically. Such policies and programmes tend not to be enforced. They are provided more as a resource that organizations can access if they choose or if they are facing a crisis in governance. Finally, pressures from research groups may find evidence of governance performance issues. Such evidence might lead to action by sport organizations or government agencies which is clearly not enforceable.

Arguments for self-regulation	Arguments against self-regulation
▪ The persons enforcing the regulations are experts in the field. ▪ It is not expensive.	▪ Self-regulators can appear to be acting as both judge and jury. ▪ Imposes a burden on staff to ensure compliance and deal with resolving conflicts.
▪ It is faster and more flexible than legal enforcement. ▪ The rules are easily updated to keep pace with market changes. ▪ The emphasis is on the spirit of compliance and discouraging evasion. ▪ Participation generates greater professional integrity and discipline. ▪ Operates at a higher level than simple rule enforcement. ▪ Avoids the establishment of a potential combatant situation between government regulators and those being regulated. ▪ More informal and therefore scope for intervention for non-compliance before punitive action is taken. ▪ Sanctions of disapproval and loss of reputation are stronger. ▪ Avoids unnecessary litigation.	▪ The sanctions are either excessive or ineffective. ▪ Lack of investigative powers. ▪ Relies on organizations consenting to be involved and has no effect on those who fail to consent. ▪ Vague jurisdictional basis if sanctions are subject to legal challenge. ▪ Uncertainty if agencies are protected from defamation. ▪ Can result in unnecessary duplication. ▪ Lack of public accountability. ▪ Likely to be gaps in the regulatory framework. ▪ Less certain and predictable outcomes.

Figure 11.2 Arguments for and against self-regulation (*Source*: Adapted from Farrar, (2005: 350–351))

The remainder of this chapter focuses on discussing the content of the various codes, standards and guidelines for ethical governance behaviour and their impact on the governance practices of contemporary sport organizations.

Statutory requirements

Common law requires board members to exercise reasonable skill and diligence in the carriage of their duties. They must fulfil their fiduciary

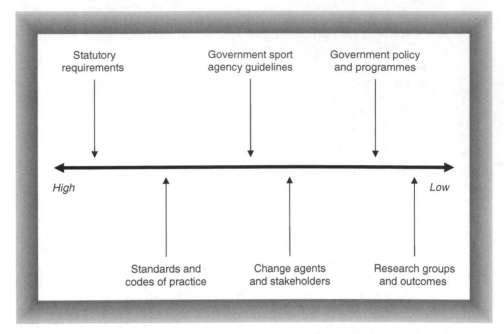

Figure 11.3 Enforcement continuum for ethical governance behaviour

duty that 'arises from the existence of what the law calls a fiduciary relationship, which exists whenever one party has duties or obligations imposed on it because it has been entrusted with powers that may be exercised for the benefit of another' (Healey, 2005: 30). In the case of board members, their positions exist for the good of the organization so they are obligated to exercise power only for the benefit of the organization.

The statutory requirements for governance behaviour differ between federal and state/provincial jurisdictions and on the basis of organizational form. In the Australian context, Farrar (2005: 417) noted that nonprofit sport organizations will generally be either 'incorporated associations under state legislation, usually one of the Associations Incorporations Acts, or companies limited by guarantee under the federal Corporations Act'. Similar arrangements exist in Canada. The statutory requirements of the relevant legislation differs markedly and 'there is a real need for harmonization of the legislation and for the expression of provisions equivalent to the basic fiduciary duties for the committee and officials of such bodies in all the states' (Farrar, 2005: 417). This lack of harmonization between state legislation, combined with 'the lack of clear norms of behaviour in incorporated associations' (Farrar, 2005: 425) makes it difficult to monitor standards of governance behaviour in nonprofit sport organizations.

In relation to the specific legal obligations of nonprofit board members, Volunteer Canada (2002: 5) stated that board members 'have a relationship of trust with the members of the organization, and it is from this trust relationship that certain important legal duties arise'. The fundamental responsibility of board members is to 'represent the interest of the members in the directing the affairs of the organization, and to do so within the law' (Volunteer Canada, 2002: 5). In the Canadian context, these legal duties are prescribed in federal legislation and in provincial legislation for incorporation of both business and nonprofit organizations. This representative role requires board members to fulfil three basic duties:

1. The duty of *diligence*: this is the duty to act reasonably, prudently, in good faith and with a view to the best interests of the organization and its members.
2. The duty of *loyalty*: this is the duty to place the interests of the organization first, and to not use ones' position as a director to further private interests.
3. The duty of *obedience*: this is the duty to act within the scope of the governing policies of the organization and within the scope of other laws, rules and regulations that apply to the organization (Volunteer Canada, 2002: 5).

Board members who fail to fulfil these duties can be found liable. This generally occurs in three different circumstances: (1) when the law (i.e. an Act or statute) is broken with the resultant penalty of a fine or imprisonment, (2) when a contract is breached which may result in financial compensation being owed or some form of remedial action taken to correct the breach or (3) by an act or failure to act that leads to injury or damage to another person with a resultant penalty of financial compensation (Volunteer Canada, 2002: 7).

In summary, board members of sport organizations, whether listed companies or nonprofit incorporated associations, must fulfil certain obligations under common law and the specific requirements of the legislation under which their particular organization operates. However, statutory requirements specify only the minimum standards for behaviour. The following sections outline the influence of the various other pressures and the obligations on board members to act ethically in the performance of their governance duties.

Corporate sector governance codes, principles, guides and standards

As discussed previously, there has been a proliferation of codes, guides and standards of corporate governance produced for the majority of

Western economies. These have usually been developed in response to failures in governance performance by high profile corporations and by regulatory bodies or stock exchanges with the aim of protecting the interests of investors. The ASX's (2003) governance principles include:

1. Lay solid foundations for management and oversight by recognizing and publishing the respective roles and responsibilities of board and management.
2. Structure the board to add value through having a board of an effective composition, size and commitment to adequately discharge its responsibilities and duties.
3. Promote ethical and responsible decision-making.
4. Safeguard integrity in financial reporting by having a structure to independently verify and safeguard the integrity of the company's financial reporting.
5. Make timely and balanced disclosure.
6. Respect the rights of shareholders and facilitate the effective exercise of those rights.
7. Recognize and manage risks.
8. Encourage enhanced performance of the organization, management and board.
9. Remunerate fairly and responsibly and in relation to corporate and individual performance.
10. Recognize the legitimate interests of stakeholders.

The ASX's (2003) set of principles is one of the few governance codes that explicitly mention the value of promoting ethical and responsible decision-making. The New Zealand Securities Commission (NZSC) (2004) also stipulates that directors should observe and foster high ethical standards. They recommend that boards should develop a written code of ethics that detail explicit expectations for ethical decision-making and personal behaviour of directors in respect of:

■ conflicts of interest, including any circumstances where a director may participate in board discussion and voting on matters in which he or she has a personal interest;
■ proper use of an entity's property and/or information; including safeguards against insider trading in the entity's securities;
■ fair dealing with customers, clients, employees, suppliers, competitors and other stakeholders;
■ giving and receiving gifts, facilitation payments, and bribes;
■ compliance with laws and regulations and
■ reporting of unethical decision-making and/or behaviour (NZSC, 2004: 7).

The NZSC (2004) also recommend that the code of ethics should include measures for dealing with breaches, that the code should be communicated to employees, and that employee training in ethical behaviour should be provided. The code of ethics should also be regularly reviewed and the 'board should monitor adherence to the code and hold directors, executives and other personnel accountable for unethical behaviour' (NZSC, 2004: 7). The code of ethics should also be published and information about implementing the code and monitoring employee and director compliance with the code should be provided in annual reports.

The value of developing a written code of ethics and putting in place mechanisms to review the code, monitor compliance and report breaches is also supported by Standards Australia (2003). The Australian Standard 8000-2003 stipulates that corporate boards should approve a written code of conduct that should 'set out ethical and behavioural expectations for both directors and employees' (Standards Australia, 2003: 16). By the board and senior management team demonstrating absolute commitment to a code, 'a culture of good governance (can) be established' (Standards Australia, 2003: 16). Farrar (2005) argued that the adoption of such codes is to some extent a self-serving exercise to avoid further externally imposed regulation. He suggested also that self-regulation in the form of codes and standards are 'often expressly encouraged by government' (Farrar, 2005: 452) as a way of avoiding further government investment in regulatory mechanisms.

Nonprofit sector governance codes of practice

As with the corporate sector there have been many attempts to develop codes of practice for nonprofit organizations including ethical behaviour guidelines for board members. The need for improvement in the governance practices of nonprofit organizations was highlighted by the Canadian Panel on Accountability and Governance in the Voluntary Sector (1999). Their report highlighted the need for a sector-wide code of ethics to guide the behaviour of individuals acting as board members and to improve levels of accountability within the sector. The more recent code of governance developed by the UK-based NCVO (2005: 4) also highlighted that 'good governance is a vital part of how voluntary and community organizations operate and are held accountable'.

The NCVO (2005: 4) noted that their code was developed in response to needs expressed within the sector for 'guidance to clarify the main principles of governance and to help them in decision-making, accountability and the work of their boards'. Part of the code emphasized the need for board and board member integrity, specifically that the board and individual

175

trustees (board members) act in accordance with high ethical standards, and ensure that conflicts of interest are dealt with properly (NCVO, 2005: 26). The code outlines three supporting principles and associated guidelines, not detailed here, for board and organizational action to ensure high standards of ethical behaviour are maintained:

1. No personal benefit – trustees must not benefit from their position beyond what is allowed by the law and is in the interests of the organization.
2. Conflicts of interest – trustees should identify and promptly declare any actual or potential conflicts of interest affecting them.
3. Probity – there should be clear guidelines for receipt of gifts or hospitality by trustees (NCVO, 2005).

Dawson and Dunn (2006) examined the appropriateness of codes of conduct as a regulatory tool for governance behaviour of nonprofit organizations. They argued that the voluntary nature of such codes meant that 'parties sign up to them because they want to, and as such are more likely to put the code into practice as a matter of choice' (Dawson & Dunn, 2006: 35). However, they also highlighted that such voluntary codes have 'some significant regulatory shortcomings, particularly in terms of compliance and enforcement' (Dawson & Dunn, 2006: 36). These shortcomings were identified as the lack of pressure voluntary codes apply to the organizations most in need of guidance, the potential for them to be simply a badge of credibility with little substantive change in behaviours, and the danger that they reinforce behaviours based on an organizations' concern with 'stakeholder perceptions rather than behaviour more specifically directed to the organization's mission' (Dawson & Dunn, 2006: 36).

Dawson and Dunn also identified several potential shortcomings of the NCVO (2005) code. First, the code did not clearly define the sector for which it was designed or the categories of organizations which may apply the code. Second, the code may not suit all types of organizational structures within the nonprofit sector, in particular, the commonly used federated structure. Third, nonprofit organizations may struggle to identify stakeholders with a legitimate interest in the governance of the organization. Thus, 'the diffuseness of stakeholders and the diversity of their interests away from purely economic concerns make fashioning a governance code for not-for-profit organizations somewhat more complex' (Dawson & Dunn, 2006: 38). Finally, they argued that the voluntary nature of the code may mean that the organizations for which the code was designed may be the least likely to adopt the code in the absence of a sector-wide regulatory body. Despite these shortcomings, they concluded that the code had much to offer nonprofit organizations in assisting them to improve governance standards.

In the UK the sport sector seems to be aware that the wider nonprofit sector may be of some use in assisting them to improve their governance practices. In a report on the progress of the UK Sport Modernisation Program, it was noted that 'there was a specific need for a model governance best practice guide to be developed for NGBs (UK Sport, 2003: 60). Further, the report identified that the resources developed by organizations such as the NCVO could provide a useful basis for developing a guide for NGBs.

Sport governance guidelines and principles

The major sport agencies from Australia, New Zealand and the UK have developed specific guidelines for nonprofit sport organization governance. As discussed in Chapter 2, these guidelines have generally been written with assistance from individuals and organizations with backgrounds in corporate governance. The governance guidelines produced by the ASC (2005: 13) highlight the fiduciary duty of board members, specifically the fact that they act as 'trustees on behalf of stakeholders for the achievement of appropriate outcomes, the financial security of the organization, and the expression of a moral and social responsibility to the members and the community at large'.

The ASC (2005: 13) also draw attention to two significant moral duties of board members. The first is their moral duty to the sport that 'involves keeping up to date with the sport they represent and sporting matters generally, and presenting their organization and the sport it represents in a positive manner'. The second is the moral duty to maintain an understanding of the concerns and expectations of stakeholders (i.e. organizational members, sponsors, funding agencies) and to ensure that the board and management of the organization affords them due consideration.

The ASC guidelines also articulate three moral obligations of the board as a whole. The first is an obligation to keep organizational members and appropriate stakeholders informed about current and future issues that may affect them or the future of the organization. The second is that the board has a responsibility to foster an effective working relationship with the CEO. This requires the board to carry out 'all employer-related duties consistent with the law and in a manner that creates an open, honest and productive working relationship leading to the achievement of board-established outcomes and, in general, an effective organization' (ASC, 2005: 13). The third of these obligations is to govern according to the principles of equity and transparency, considering the interests of the entire organization, without giving preference to any individual or group of stakeholders.

In addition to government sport agencies, sport organizations such as the EOC have sought to influence governance standards in sport organizations. In 2001, the EOC co-hosted a conference on sport governance with the Fédération Internationale de l'Automobile (FIA) that developed a statement of governance principles for sport. In the foreword to the conference report, Jacques Rogge, President of the IOC, argued that sport organizations must keep pace with the political, economic and legal environment in which they operate. He also stated that 'the autonomy of sports and the governing role of sports organizations have increasingly been challenged by various stakeholders, court decisions or legislation' (Governance in Sport Working Group, 2001: 2). The statement of governance principles that resulted from the conference was one means for sport organizations to demonstrate to public authorities and stakeholders that by pledging to respect the principles they were 'standing for certain fundamental standards in the running of their sport' (Governance in Sport Working Group, 2001: 2).

The nine governance principles developed by the Governance in Sport Working Group focused on the system of governance that sport organizations should adopt including the role of governing bodies, structures and accountability measures, and the distribution of revenue among affiliated organizations. The principles were not designed to act as a code of behaviour for board members, although they do stress the importance of sport organizations having democratic processes for the election and appointment of board members, ensuring transparency in communicating and dealing with stakeholders and having appropriate processes to deal with conflicts of interest. It was argued that sport organizations that adopted the principles for good governance would reap the following benefits:

- It will provide a useful 'check list' for sporting bodies to ensure that they are behaving responsibly with respect to their members and to third parties with a legitimate interest in their activities.
- It should go a long way to providing a solid defence to any litigation, serving to demonstrate that all actions and decisions are properly motivated and subject to appropriate checks and balances.
- By demonstrating the virtues of self-regulation, it should assist in persuading legislators that there is no need to interfere further in the running of sports (Governance in Sport Working Group, 2001: 3).

In summary, the statutory requirements, corporate and nonprofit governance codes and guides to principles and standards, including those specific to sport governance stipulate how sport organizations should determine their governance structures, systems and processes and what sort of behavioural standards are expected of those people fulfilling governance roles. In addition to these governance codes and guides, sport organizations are subject to a number of other pressures to develop and adapt their own codes of behaviour with a goal of improving governance standards. The remaining section of this chapter briefly reviews these pressures and provides some examples of codes of behaviour that have been developed by sport organizations.

Other pressures for ethical governance behaviour

As noted at the start of this chapter, there has been a number of specific government sport policy initiatives designed to improve governance practices within sport organizations. Elements of programmes like the UK Sport Modernisation Program and the ASC GMIP are targeted directly towards improving the ethical standards of governance of sport organizations and the associated governance structures, systems and processes used by these organizations. The impact of these programmes is not uniform, as there is a tendency for funding or service agreements to not enforce these guidelines.

The pressures faced by organizations to adopt codes of conduct or to take other steps to improve the ethical behaviour of board members can come from internal change agents such as CEOs, board chairs or other individuals who recognize deficiencies in governance standards and advocate the need for change. This is more likely to occur when an organization is faced with a crisis or with new appointments to the board particularly the CEO or board chair. Pressure for change may also come from external stakeholders such as ISFs that are seeking to improve governance standards within their respective organizational networks.

Sport organizations may also be pressured indirectly to improve standards of ethical governance behaviour through the dissemination of research findings from groups such as the UK-based FGRC or the Canadian Centre for Sport Law. In recent years, these organizations have published reviews of governance performance for sport organizations that have attracted significant media attention. Increasing awareness of ethical issues in sport may, in turn, influence sport organizations themselves or other stakeholders such as funding agencies to exert pressure on sport organizations to review their governance practices or the behaviour of their boards.

Irrespective of the source of pressure exerted on sport organizations to adopt ethical governance behaviour, there are many examples of principles of governance or codes of conduct being developed by specific sport organizations. At an international level, for example, the CGF (2006: 33–34) operates under a code of conduct that is applied to all member organizations and the people appointed to governance positions. The code

179

emphasizes that individuals should adhere to the following seven principles for behaviour:

1. *Selflessness*: The Federation, Affiliated (Commonwealth Games Associations) CGAs, and Executive Board Members shall take decisions solely in the Federation's interest. They shall not do so in order to gain benefits for themselves or their sport.
2. *Integrity*: The Federation, Affiliated CGAs and Executive Board Members shall not place themselves under any financial or other obligation to individuals or organizations that might influence them in the performance of their duties.
3. *Objectivity*: In carrying out the business of the Federation including appointing or electing officials, awarding contracts or recommending individuals for rewards or benefits, the Federation, Affiliated CGAs and Executive Board Members shall make choices on merit.
4. *Accountability*: The Federation, Affiliated CGAs and Executive Board Members are accountable for their decisions and actions to the Federation and shall submit themselves to whatever scrutiny is appropriate. The Executive Board Members and members of elected committees shall report regularly to and communicate with the Affiliated CGAs which elected them. Communication shall not be confined to meetings held during Annual General Assemblies of the Federation.
5. *Openness*: The Federation, Affiliated CGAs and Executive Board Members shall be as open as possible about all the decisions and actions that they take. They shall give reasons for their decisions and restrict information only when the wider interest clearly demands it.
6. *Honesty*: The Federation, Affiliated CGAs and Executive Board Members have a duty to declare any private interests relating to their duties and to take all steps to resolve any conflicts arising in a way that protects the interest of the Federation and sport in general.
7. *Non-Discrimination*: The Federation, Affiliated CGAs and Executive Board Members shall not discriminate against any country or person on any grounds whatsoever including race, colour, gender, religion or politics and shall adhere to the Gleneagles Declaration (CGF, 2006: 33–34).

The CGF operates an Ethics Commission that has powers to investigate allegations of misconduct or breaches of the code of conduct and report to the Executive Board with recommended action. In turn, the Executive Board reports to the General Assembly of the CGF on the proceedings of the Ethics Commission. The General Assembly may impose sanctions on those found guilty of breaching the code. Sanctions can include removing individuals from office, removing the voting rights of affiliated member organizations or even preventing CGAs from competing in the Commonwealth Games (CGF, 2006).

At a national level, the SLSA (2003) developed a code of conduct for national directors that includes the following set of behavioural expectations:

- Meet fiduciary responsibilities as required under all relevant Commonwealth and State legislation.
- Act within their duty of care to make decisions in the best interests of the Company.
- Develop strategic planning and direction of the Company including monitoring organizational performance and evaluating strategic results.
- Develop and implement policies.
- Interact with key stakeholders and members to inform them of achievements and to ensure that they have input into determination of strategic goals and direction.
- Report back to the stakeholders at the annual general meeting through the President and the CEO.
- Monitor CEO and organizational compliance with the relevant commonwealth and state legislation and with the Company's own policies.
- Evaluate its effectiveness as an Australian Council (SLSA, 2003: 7).

The code of conduct also stipulates a number of limitations for directors, including specifying that directors report to the President and are accountable for the performance of their duties, that directors must work in a spirit of cooperation with the CEO of SLSA, that they are not allowed to incur expenses or debts on behalf of SLSA, and that they are expected to abide by the organization's policies, regulations and directives.

The governing body for Canadian rowing, Rowing Canada Aviron (RCA), has a code of conduct for their board of directors that is much more extensive that the SLSA. The code specifies explicitly that directors are appointed on the basis of trust to govern the affairs of RCA on behalf of the membership. The code stipulates that directors:

(a) must be familiar with and comply with the Part II of The Canada Corporations Act under which RCA is constituted;
(b) must avoid any behaviour that would bring RCA into disrepute;
(c) has a duty to act with the utmost honesty and good faith and must always act in the best interests of RCA;
(d) must exercise the care, diligence and skill of a reasonably prudent and informed person under comparable circumstances;
(e) must act as his or her judgement dictates when issues arise on which an RCA decision of general application may not be in the interest of a director's rowing club or Provincial Rowing Association. The expectation is that a director would support the decision that benefits the sport of rowing as a whole;
(f) must not speak publicly on rowing matters when or in such a way that the comments could be perceived to be an official representation of RCA

unless authorized to do so by the Board or the President (but directors are otherwise encouraged to speak publicly on rowing matters);

(g) must be aware of the identity of RCA's sponsors, be supportive of their role as sponsors and refrain from displaying support for sponsors' competitors when involved in national rowing activities (RCA, 2004: 1).

The RCA code of conduct also stipulates how directors should behave in relation to the treatment of confidential information, conflicts of interest, the acceptance or offer of gifts and their outside interests. The RCA code of conduct, together with the CGF and SLSA examples, highlight the commitment of sport organizations to develop a culture of ethical behaviour amongst their board members and others involved in governance activities.

Conclusion

This chapter has explored the ethical dimensions of governance as well as the various pressures influencing sport organizations to monitor and improve standards of ethical behaviour at the board level. There has been limited empirical research into the ethical standards of behaviour of board members in the governance of sport organizations, or in the wider non-profit sector. Despite an array of resources being made available to sport organizations to assist with the development of their own codes of conduct and improvements to governance structures, systems and processes it is not clear the extent to which these resources influence the ethical behaviour of boards and board members or whether ethical standards in sport governance have improved with the passage of time.

PART THREE

Sport
Governance
Future

12

Team changes: surviving and managing governance change

Overview

Sport organizations are subject to a variety of external and internal pressures that often lead to change in their governance structures and systems. This chapter explores the drivers of governance change and the effects of change on boards and individuals in governance roles. This chapter is presented in three sections. The first section reviews the drivers of change for sport governance structures and systems. This is followed by a discussion of how changes in structures and systems are manifested within sport organizations. The final section discusses the approaches of sport organizations to managing the impacts of governance change. There is an emphasis on instituting governance reforms introduced by national sport agencies such as the processes involved with the amalgamation of formerly separate nonprofit sport entities.

Drivers of governance change

Before the specific drivers of governance change are explored it is worth briefly reflecting on the changing nature of the environment in which non-profit sport organizations operate. Bugg and Dallhoff (2006), as part of a national study of board governance practices amongst Canadian nonprofit organizations, identified a number of trends impacting on their governance. These included changing demographics of the population, specifically an ageing volunteer workforce, a generally ageing population base and increased diversity of the population. They also identified a changing funding environment with more targeted funding schemes and heightened reporting requirements, more complex inter-organizational relationships for service delivery, less people willing to take leadership roles, and a general decline in the level and quality of financial and human resources available to nonprofit organizations.

Bugg and Dallhoff (2006) also identified a number of elements that reflected the changing nature of governance within nonprofit organizations. These included:

- An increased focus on governance.
- Increased demand for a reduced supply of qualified board members.
- Rising expectations and requirements for directors.
- Increased demand for efficiency and effectiveness.
- More emphasis on the processes used by boards and their culture.
- Increased demand for transparency and accountability.
- Increased emphasis on performance measurement.
- Increased attention on risk management.

These trends are all evident in the changing nature of sport governance, particularly within the international and national levels of sport. In Chapter 2, six environmental influences on governance within nonprofit sport organizations were reviewed in detail. These included: (1) changes in the relationship between government and the nonprofit sector; (2) the regulatory environment in which nonprofit sport organizations operate; (3) the emergence of elite sport development as a priority in government sport policy; (4) governance guidelines developed by government for sport organizations; (5) the impact of globalization processes on sport and (6) the expectations of stakeholder groups (see Figure 12.1). These influences often place nonprofit sport organizations under considerable pressure to change their governance structures and systems. These changes are often brought about by the demands of statutory requirements from regulators, to meet grant funding conditions from government sport agencies, or to meet higher standards of transparency, accountability and performance

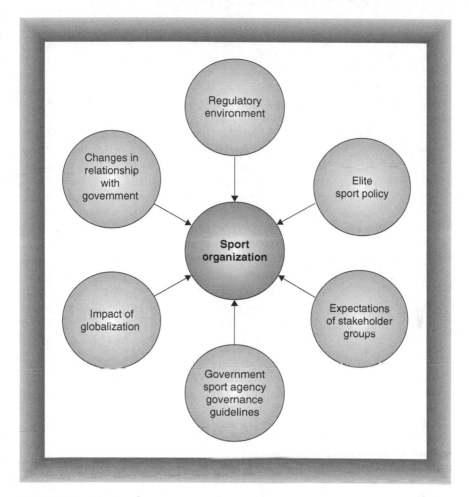

Figure 12.1 Drivers of governance change

from a variety of stakeholders. Changes are also made in response to market pressures, reviews of governance performance and organizational effectiveness. In some cases, significant governance reforms result from crisis events or reported corruption within sport organizations (Forster, 2006).

The emphasis of government sport policy on elite sport development in countries such as Australia, Canada, New Zealand and the UK has influenced the strategic focus of the boards of national governing bodies (NGBs), particularly those involved in Olympic or Commonwealth Games sports. As highlighted by Green (2004) such policy directions have led to boards focussing on elite sport development often at the expense of mass participation sport. This is not to say that these sports have blindly accepted this shift in policy. Indeed, Green (2005) argued that sport NGBs have lobbied for increased support for community and mass participation sport programmes with varying levels of success. Nevertheless, government sport policies have tended to maintain a resource dependent relationship wherein the decision-making and strategies of many sport NGBs prioritize support of their elite development over mass participation and community-based sport programmes.

An increasingly complex regulatory environment has also led nonprofit sport organizations to undertake significant governance reforms. Many nonprofit sport organizations have become incorporated bodies and in some cases, companies limited by guarantee. There are heightened expectations placed on nonprofit sport organizations to adopt prescribed guidelines for governance practice based on existing codes in the corporate and nonprofit sectors. As discussed in the previous chapter, pressures from a range of sources are also compelling sport organizations to adopt codes of ethics or codes of conduct for their board members. Furthermore, Cuskelly, Hoye and Auld (2006: 49) noted that nonprofit sport organizations were subject to an 'increased compliance burden of adopting new business practices and more stringent reporting requirements as a result of changes in government sport policy'.

A subtle but equally influential driver of governance change is the processes of globalization. Forster (2006) argued that governing bodies for sports such as football and athletics have increased their revenue and power as a result of globalization. He cites the global reach of the various World Cup tournaments and the Olympic Games that have evolved dramatically over the last 20 years as examples of how globalization has changed the governance of world sport. Organizations such as the International Olympic Committee (IOC) and the major International Sport Federations (ISFs) enjoy unprecedented status with governments for their ability to deliver major sporting events into national economies. These organizations have moved from an amateur base to becoming significant international nonprofit entities. Forster (2006: 78) argued that globalization has led to ISFs and other international sport organizations earning legitimacy and authority, and with it, a shift in their organizational objectives and 'underlying philosophies' as they have moved to adopt a highly commercialized orientation in their operations. As discussed in Chapter 2, the changes brought about as a result of globalization and the expanded commercial power of some international sport organizations has presented a number of governance challenges at both international and national levels. Nonprofit sport organizations are often faced with difficult strategic decisions and maintaining appropriate governance structures as they grapple with striking the right balance between commercial development and the maintenance of tradition and associated participation opportunities.

The weight of sometimes divergent expectations that stakeholders place on sport organizations was highlighted in Chapter 2. An example of how stakeholder expectations can impose change in the governance of sport organizations was provided by the Football Governance Research Centre (FGRC)

(2005) which highlighted the growing importance of supporters' trusts in the governance of UK football clubs. They argued there had been a 'significant shift in the way supporters' trusts are regarded' by the football community and that the number of trusts and level of trust representation on the boards of football clubs was increasing (FGRC, 2005: 50).

Finally, concerns over the performance of an organization, board or a critical event can be the catalyst for change within the governance of sport organizations. UK Sport (2003) identified a number of performance concerns for the more than 300 sport NGBs that exist within the UK sport system. They identified that the performance of sport NGBs could be adversely affected by external factors such as 'initiative-led rather than strategy-led funding; over reliance on grant funding and limited reserves, too many organizations setting strategy and not enough delivery; limited performance measures; and fragmented delivery of funding' (UK Sport, 2003: 3). At the same time sport NGBs were subject to a number of internal factors that had the potential to impact on their performance:

- Reticence of NGBs to invest in themselves.
- The struggle to recruit high quality staff.
- Too much time spent on firefighting.
- Difficulty in retaining and recruiting volunteers.
- Limited focus on member services.
- Ignoring basic business principles.
- Poor corporate governance and financial mismanagement (UK Sport, 2003: 3).

Poor organizational performance or failure to meet government funding conditions can lead to a governance review process being imposed upon or, in some cases requested by a sport organization. The Australian Sports Commission (ASC) has conducted many reviews of Australian national sport organizations (NSOs) including the high profile Crawford Report that led to the radical governance reform and organizational restructure of Soccer Australia into Football Federation Australia in 2003. The ASC has also facilitated reviews of other sports such the Equestrian Federation of Australia and Canoeing Australia. Governance reviews are also conducted at the state/provincial levels of sport, such as the review of the Edmonton Boxing and Wrestling Commission conducted in 2006 by the Edmonton Office of the City Auditor in Alberta, Canada. The outcomes of such reviews can encompass wholesale changes to governance structures, constitutions and voting systems or limited to minor improvements to governance practices.

Gill (2001: 18) listed a number of critical events in the life of nonprofit organizations that can be a prelude to governance change including:

> legal incorporation; recruitment of first staff; significant growth or downsizing in staff or budget; substantive change in mandate; prospective

merger with another organization; attempts to make significant shifts in organizational culture; loss of key board members; turnover of significant numbers of board members; turnover in the chief executive officer (CEO) position; major public controversy; major external or internal conflict; and, significant changes in the financial, political or policy environment.

Events such as these challenge the capacity of governing boards to react appropriately and in a timely manner, test the adequacy of their existing policy frameworks and sometimes bring into question existing governance structures and systems. Nevertheless, Gill (2001: 18) found that in a study of 20 nonprofit organizations:

> volunteer boards have remarkable resiliency and a tremendous capacity to respond creatively and constructively to crises and major transitional events. In most cases, this required some combination of the introduction of new board members, a shift in power to a 'new guard', commitment to improved governance practices, and a strengthened partnership with a new CEO.

In summary, the pressures for change in governance standards and performance come from a variety of sources and can present sport organizations with significant challenges. The following section outlines the type of governance reforms and related organizational changes that may result from these pressures.

Manifestation of governance change

Governance change generally manifests in one of three ways: (1) reform of existing systems and structures; (2) merger or amalgamation with another entity (3) a recommendation for closing down an organization. The most common form of governance change confronting sport organization boards is reform of governance systems and structures. A comprehensive reform programme devised for sport NGBs, the UK Sport Modernisation Program, identified seven elements that UK Sport believed would lead to better NGB performance. These included: developing the volunteer base; core staffing; executive and management capacity; having a clear vision and mission with associated values and strategies; modern information technology capabilities; good communication and improved governance and internal decision-making. In terms of improvements to governance, UK

Sport (2003) suggested that reforms should focus on developing systems and processes that adhere to best practice guidelines, the development of a long term strategic plan, developing a strategic review procedure, and clarifying the governance roles and responsibilities of the board and CEO.

Government sport agencies are increasingly compelling sports to have a single governing body at the national level which represents both genders and all disciplines within a particular sport. In Australia, for example, the ASC has applied pressure in the form of threatening to withdraw funding support to sports such as hockey and golf unless they merged the respective mens' and womens' governing bodies. Similarly, pressure has been applied to multi-discipline sports such as athletics, gymnastics, cycling, canoeing and equestrian at both national and state levels to amalgamate separate governing bodies representing specific disciplines within a sport.

Pressures for significant governance reforms can result from more distal societal or market forces. For example, it has been well documented that in rural and regional Australia, the decline in regional city and town populations has forced many small Australian Rules football clubs to merge with traditional rivals in order for the sport to survive. An enquiry into country football (Victorian Rural and Regional Services Development Committee, 2004: 75) found that between 1990 and 2003, a total of '36 clubs and six leagues disbanded, 66 clubs and ten leagues amalgamated (but only) 6 clubs and one league were formed during that period'. Merging or amalgamating with another sport organization presents many governance challenges that are discussed in more detail in the next section.

In some cases, the pressures for governance change may be too great and a sport organization may be forced to close down. A prominent example is the Australian Baseball League (ABL) that was created in 1989 to replace the traditional national championship competition, the Claxton Shield. The national governing body for baseball in Australia, the Australian Baseball Federation (ABF), had licenced the ABL to run a national competition. Governed by a board of directors comprising representatives from the 8 ABL teams and the ABF, the governance structure of the ABL was based on the franchise model of the USA. The structure emphasized autonomy for owners and a decentralized administration. The ABL enjoyed modest success until the mid 1990s when major sponsorship deals were lost and television coverage was reduced to news reports. The ABL suffered from poor financial management and rising costs from 'players demanding more money, high prices for equipment, stadium rental and especially travelling expenses' (Clark, 2006). In 1999, an attempted rescue package from expatriate professional baseball player Dave Nilsson failed to save the ABL after the ABL team owners pulled out of an agreement signed with the ABF, the ABL and the new league entity created by Nilsson, the International Baseball League of Australia. The ABF has since reverted to their former national championship format.

Managing governance change

The management of change to governance structures, systems and processes in sport organizations is usually conducted within the framework of either a formal report which lists a series of recommendations or as part of a wider reform process initiated by a government sport agency. In the former, the review and resulting report may have been commissioned by the sport organization itself or initiated by a government sport agency. The impetus for implementing recommended governance reforms may be greater if a government sport agency stipulates that changes be made in order to meet future funding and service agreement conditions. If the review was commissioned by the sport organization itself, the implementation of changes will be determined largely by the willingness of the board to accept and to act on the recommendations.

In 2003, the UK Sport Modernisation Program outlined a process for sport NGBs to follow that would enable them to assess their competence against a series of criteria articulated in a model framework. The first three steps of the process called for NGBs to be categorized according to their size, to conduct a self assessment of competence against the model framework criteria and to identify gaps in their competencies. The next steps involved NGBs working with their respective Sport Council (e.g. Sport England) to reconcile the differences, to then set development and performance targets, and finally engage in action planning to determine how to meet their targets (UK Sport, 2003).

UK Sport identified that NGBs needed to 'buy into' the modernization programme in order for it to have any impact on their performance. Specific actions recommended by UK Sport that NGBs should implement in relation to governance included implementing specific governance standards and training their board members. They stipulated that the actions of NGBs that their respective Sports Council might determine are needed for improvement would not be compulsory. However, UK Sport (2003: 53) stated that:

> NGBs must recognize the need to change and that they are responsible for their own future. NGBs that fail to change will suffer the same consequences as any other 21st century organization that fails to respond to the changing environment in which they operate.

The UK Sport Modernisation Program was quite prescriptive. It provided NGBs with definite timelines, specific actions and templates for implementing change. In contrast, nonprofit sport organizations that are faced with merging or amalgamating with another entity operate with relatively few guidelines or assistance. In one of the few sources that provide any guidance in this area, La Piana and Hayes (2005) explained the differences between mergers and amalgamations in the corporate and non-profit sectors, the role of the board during an amalgamation process, and the ingredients for a successful amalgamation. They argued that 'the success or failure of a nonprofit merger is largely in the hands of the board members' (La Piana and Hayes, 2005: 11) because boards must take the initial decision to consider a merger, are involved in the negotiations and overall decision-making in relation to mergers, and may form part of the board of the newly formed entity.

La Piana and Hayes (2005) identified six differences between mergers or amalgamations in the corporate and nonprofit sectors. First, the mission of the organization drives the decision to merge, not the underlying pursuit of profit making through acquiring more resources or increasing efficiencies as occurs in the corporate sector. Nonprofit organizations should only merge if they consider a merged entity will be better able to deliver the services and achieve the mission of their respective organizations. Second, nonprofit mergers are considered a real partnership rather than a takeover from a more powerful corporate competitor. Third, the negotiations between nonprofit organizations generally strive for collaboration and attempt to avoid conflict. Fourth, nonprofit organizations serve many stakeholders, who need to be communicated with throughout the merger process. Fifth, as nonprofit organizations operate with scarce resources, the process of amalgamation is a significant drain on resources and boards must be fully committed to expending resources on the process and that it will deliver significant benefits. Finally, they argued that the major benefit of an amalgamation 'may be the enhancement of the new organization's ability to advance its mission' (La Piana and Hayes, 2005: 12), rather than any significant economic gain. Thus, the benefits of the amalgamation process must be clearly communicated 'in order to help individuals – board, staff and volunteers – understand and own its value and benefits' (La Piana and Hayes, 2005: 13).

Not unlike the corporate sector, nonprofit boards undertake a significant role in leading the negotiations for amalgamation. Often this task is delegated to a sub-committee which works on the detail of the proposed amalgamation and then presents a series of reports to the full board for approval. La Piana and Hayes (2005: 13) stated that the negotiation phase can take several months and that it is 'imperative that members of the committee keep their full boards appraised of progress or they may encounter resistance when they bring their recommendation back to their boards for approval'. After approval has been given by each party to amalgamate, the integration phase begins. It is important at this stage that board members 'serve as role models for the staff and volunteers by embracing the opportunities offered by the merger and serving essentially as "champions" for the integration process' (La Piana and Hayes, 2005: 13). The boards of the organizations need to merge as well, which presents an opportunity to review the required size of the board and the skills sets required of board members. La Piana and Hayes (2005) recommend that the new entity should strive to have a new board made up of equal numbers for each of the former organizations.

Two important roles for the new board are to appoint a CEO and to assist in developing the identity and culture for the merged entity. La Piana and Hayes (2005: 14) identified three factors that will lead to the creation of shared culture:

- Consistent communication about the reasons changes are necessary and vital.
- Clear messages about the values and goals of the new organization.
- Clear definition of the aspects of the original cultures that will be honoured and preserved.

Finally, La Piana and Hayes (2005: 16) argued that for a successful amalgamation there must be someone who champions the cause and keeps the process focussed on the mission of the new organization. This role entails having a clear sense of vision for the new organization, explaining why change is necessary, communicating with all stakeholders, developing an integration plan, and respecting the culture of the formerly separate entities.

The principles outlined by La Piana and Hayes (2005) are reflected in a guide for amalgamation for sport organizations produced by the South Australian Office for Recreation and Sport (ORS) (2003). The guide notes that amalgamation between sport organizations usually takes one of two forms. The first, and more common form, is a merger when 'two or more organizations cease to exist in their own right and their resources, assets and roles are consolidated into a new entity which satisfies the needs of the stakeholders' (ORS, 2003: 1). The second form is a takeover when 'one or more organizations cease to exist in their own right and their resources, assets and roles are consolidated into an existing entity. Often a takeover occurs where a larger, more powerful body takes control of a smaller body' (ORS, 2003: 1).

Several reasons sport organizations seek to amalgamate were proffered by ORS (2003). These included reactions to pressures such as 'reduced access to sponsorship, a decreasing number of volunteers, population shifts, deregulated (retail) trading hours and greater accountability expected from funding bodies' (ORS, 2003: 2). A more positive reason for sport organizations seeking amalgamation is to increase the development opportunities for a sport. The guide also highlighted four important issues that could cause an amalgamation between two sport organizations to fail. These were: (1) disputes over the ownership of assets and liabilities the level of membership and capitation fees, and other financial management decisions; (2) mistrust that one organization might be more influential in securing resources and benefits for their members and enjoying higher board representation on the new entity; (3) inequity in decision-making, access to facilities and resources and maintenance of organizational traditions such as life memberships and history and (4) disputes over the boundaries of operations, particularly at club level.

The ORS (2003: 3) emphasized that the 'success of a merger can be totally dependent upon the development of good personal relationships between key people', in particular the board members of the respective organizations. The amalgamation process that sport organizations and their boards should follow as outlined by the ORS (2003) is similar to that provided by La Piana and Hayes (2005) and consists of four stages. The first stage is self-analysis where the board should identify the reasons for amalgamation and potential concerns and then compare objectives, structures, systems, culture and financial information with potential partners. Second, the preparation and planning stage should involve a committee charged with responsibility for reviewing the background of the organization, comparing their constitution and by-laws, receive proposals for how the new body might operate from each organization's perspective, and make recommendations for the governance and operation of the new entity. These would include recommendations on important issues such as 'voting rights, advisory/standing committees, representation and board composition' (ORS, 2003: 4). The third stage entails commitment to the formalization of an agreement covering legal, governance, financial, management issues and a timeline for implementation. The final stage focuses on integration and should involve securing support for the change, communicating a clear vision for the merged entity, and providing as much information as possible to stakeholders.

In taking the view that the 'total integration of separate bodies (particularly mens' and womens' sporting groups) may not provide the best outcomes for all concerned and other options may be more appropriate' (ORS, 2003: 7), the ORS (2003) outlined options other than complete amalgamation. Alternatives might take the form of 'funding, insurance and corporate identification to be handled by a joint committee, whilst leaving separate bodies to manage participation development, programme and competition management' (ORS, 2003: 7). Another alternative is the establishment of a partnership agreement that enables a smaller group, such as a sub-discipline of a sport, to retain control of the delivery of their activities but operate under the auspices of a larger governing organization.

In summary, whether in response to internal or external pressures, the implementation and management of governance change involves the application of a planned approach. To a large extent governance reforms hinge on the board taking an active lead and having some individuals to champion the merits of change. It is important for boards to strike a balance in designing a new entity that will deliver outcomes consistent with the missions of the existing organizations and to retain appropriate cultural and historical elements of those organizations.

Conclusion

This chapter has explored the drivers of governance within sport organizations and the role of boards in managing the change process. Governance change generally manifests as reform of existing systems and structures, the merger or amalgamation with another similar organization, or in some cases the closure of an organization. Boards play a particularly important role in governance changes as their decisions affect the way sport organizations will be structured, the roles and responsibilities of boards and staff within sport organizations, representation systems and voting rights. Matters such as organizational culture, overall strategy, the leadership of the organization and ultimately organizational performance are also important considerations in governance reform processes. Boards should adopt a deliberate and planned approach to managing the complex nature of governance change, particularly amalgamations to ensure that due diligence is carried out in addressing the concerns of the varied stakeholders of sport organizations.

13

Future seasons: sport governance challenges of the 21st century

Overview

The final chapter of the book explores the governance issues that sport organizations are likely to confront as they strive to develop their sport in an increasingly competitive economy and complex external environment. The preceding chapters have explained the core concepts and context of sport governance. They have explored the fundamental elements of governance structures, systems and processes within nonprofit sport organizations. In addition, the preceding chapter profiled the drivers of governance change. Progressive and innovative sport organizations will continue to face up to issues about governance structures, define and redefine the roles of volunteers and staff, develop their unique culture and strategies, manage risks and design governance systems and processes with a view to improving organizational outcomes. To consider future challenges within each of these areas of sport organization governance would be somewhat redundant.

Each of these issues have been addressed in the preceding chapters. Rather, this chapter is devoted to the impact of four broad issues on the governance of nonprofit sport organizations in the years ahead. The issues and the associated regulatory challenges are: maintaining legitimacy, maintaining the values of sport and fostering volunteer involvement in sport governance, dealing with increasingly complex inter-organizational linkages and knowledge management.

Maintaining legitimacy

Sport national governing bodies (NGBs) will operate in an increasingly sophisticated market where they will work closely with professional clubs or franchises, broadcasters and the consumers of their sport, both participants and spectators. They will be challenged to maintain their legitimacy as they strive to preserve traditional control over all aspects of sport development. The commercialization of many sports and the creation of significant broadcast rights revenue from the staging of professional leagues and major sport events present NGBs with both opportunities and threats. The opportunities are: the ability to market their sport through television and other forms of mass and increasingly individualized media with a view to maximizing revenue streams, to invest revenue in community 'grass roots' sport development programmes to grow their participation base, to build or demand better stadia for the hosting of sport competitions and to improve the governance and management of their sport at all levels.

The threats to maintaining legitimacy are somewhat less obvious but have potentially greater impact on the sport. Morgan's (2002) analysis of the issues surrounding the structuring of elite competitions in professional sport provides a good illustration of the likely threats to legitimacy confronting sport NGBs. The major stakeholders for a national elite sport competition are arguably the spectator base, the sport NGB, the leading clubs that provide the playing talent to the competition or league and the corporations holding the broadcast rights. Morgan (2002) noted that the objectives of these stakeholders are rarely fully congruent. Spectators seek exciting sporting contests and to be associated with successful teams. Sport NGBs seek to promote participation in their sport, to be successful in international competitions and to govern in the interests of all their stakeholders. The leading clubs seek to be successful, financially and on the playing field, which requires resources and funding to identify, secure and develop playing talent and associated support systems. Broadcasters seek to profit from their involvement in sport and to secure control over decisions that might affect that profitability. These stakeholders therefore will tend to be in dispute about the best way to structure and govern the competition, the composition of teams, scheduling of games and player contract conditions (Morgan, 2002).

The sport NGB has traditionally been in control of national competitions with its 'authority based on its legitimacy as the elected governing body, its control of key assets such as the national team brand and the national stadium, and its ability to reward members by distributing revenue' (Morgan, 2002: 49). Their ability to retain control will occur only if the 'significant commercial value of the sport is at the top, international level' (Morgan, 2002: 49). In other words, if the sport NGB controls the ability to select teams for international competition and the distribution of associated broadcast and match day revenues, their legitimacy is largely unchallenged. However, other national competition models operate without placing the sport NGB at the centre of decision-making power: the cartel model such as the one adopted by the National Football League (NFL), the promoter-led model in sports such as boxing, car racing and some forms of wrestling and the oligarchy, 'an alternative form of non-market bi-lateral governance' (Morgan, 2002: 50) that operates within English football. The challenge to the legitimacy of a sport NGB emerges over control of domestic elite competitions. Morgan (2002: 54) recognized that sport NGBs need to decide if their role is to be

> solely regulatory, i.e. concerned with the rules of the game, the welfare of players, standards of refereeing and coaching and the running of the national team ... (or should they) ... exert a commercial control over negotiations with sponsors and broadcasters, and the design and marketing of the competition.

In meeting challenges to their legitimacy, sport NGBs must recognize that 'sport is both a marketing channel creating an end-product for a television audience and a network of stakeholders with their own need to survive and prosper' (Morgan, 2002: 58). The challenges for those serving on sport NGBs boards are to be aware of these commercial tensions, to be prepared to decide what role to play in governing the future direction of their sport and to implement the appropriate governance structures and systems which maintain legitimacy amongst significant stakeholders who have a justifiable interest in the sport.

An independent review of European sport commissioned by the UK Presidency of the European Union noted that the independence of sport federations and other governing bodies of sport was legitimized in the Nice Declaration. In 1999, the European Council recognized that 'it is the task of sporting organizations to organize and promote their particular sports, particularly as regards the specifically sporting rules applicable and the make up of national teams' (UK Presidency of the European Union, 2006: 132). The European Council also noted that governing bodies for sport 'must continue to be the key feature of a form of organization providing a guarantee of sporting cohesion and participatory democracy' (UK Presidency of the European Union, 2006: 133).

The Governance in Sport Working Group (2001: 3) stated that governing bodies for sport must earn the right to keep their 'specificity recognized' otherwise 'legislators at both national and international level will come under increasing pressure to legislate and courts will apply laws treating sports bodies like any other commercial organization'. The UK Presidency of the European Union (2006: 23) also noted that sport organizations must remain cognizant that their privileged position of 'self-organization and self-regulation is an important expression and legacy of European civil society from the end of the 19th to the beginning of the 21st century'. The challenge for governing bodies of sport at international and national levels will be to foster good relations with governments so that self-regulation of sport remains 'recognized and protected as a fundamental element of personal liberty' UK Presidency of the European Union (2006: 23) by countries' constitutions.

Maintaining the values of sport and volunteer involvement

The Governance in Sport Working Group (2001: 3) noted that:

> It is undeniable that some sports at some levels now generate substantial revenues through broadcasting rights, sponsorship, ticket revenues and other sources. Nevertheless that remains a small part of sport and should not be allowed to detract from the fact that the main objective of responsible sporting bodies is to promote their sport generally and increase participation at all levels.

Five years later, the UK Presidency of the European Union (2006: 13) highlighted that despite the financial benefits sport has received from the commercialization of competitions and events there was a danger 'that an overly commercial approach to sport will end up compromising important sporting values and undermining the social function of sport'. The review noted that while elite sport receives the majority of media attention and generates increasingly significant revenues, 'throughout the EU, sport is characterized by a flourishing club life, with 70,000 sport clubs and 70 million club members (15% of the EU population)' (UK Presidency of the European Union, 2006: 13). The challenge for nonprofit sport organizations, particularly at the international and national levels, is to strike a balance between the pursuit of commercial opportunities and the associated financial benefits and risks while remaining focussed on the values of sport that drove their commercialization in the first place.

At the state/provincial and local community organization level, the challenge to retain the values of sport takes a different form. Cuskelly, Hoye and Auld (2006: 148) argued that one of the more significant challenges for nonprofit sport organizations was 'responding to the demands of government policy and funding programmes without losing sight of the values and motives that encourage the involvement and interests of volunteers'. They also stated that volunteer board members 'will be faced with decisions about the extent to which they are prepared to engage in government agendas for community change in order to access government funding and support for their (sport organization)' (Cuskelly et al., 2006: 149).

The institutionalized nature of the governance structures of nonprofit sport organizations was discussed in Chapter 1. In particular the work of Kikulis (2000: 297) was used to highlight that volunteer boards had become a 'permanent aspect of governance and decision-making' in nonprofit sport organizations. There are some signs that perhaps this is changing. The increasing numbers of professional staff employed at all levels of nonprofit sport organizations and the associated shift in decision-making power and influence from volunteers to professionals has been well documented. The appointment of independent board members alongside elected board members represents a watering down of the traditional membership-only based board. The question is whether such changes make any difference to the execution of the governance function and if so, do they deliver better outcomes for sport organizations and their members?

Cuskelly et al., (2006: 146) stated that 'it is almost inconceivable to visualize sport in the past, present or future without volunteers'. In the EU alone it is estimated that there are approximately 10 million sport volunteers (UK Presidency of the European Union, 2006: 13). The vast numbers of people who volunteer as coaches, officials and administrators in sport suggests that there will always be individuals who wish to fulfil governance roles on the boards of local sport clubs, as well as regional, state/provincial, national and international sport organizations. However, in an increasingly litigious society and in light of the rising demands and expectations being placed on the individuals who serve on volunteer boards, it is somewhat questionable whether existing levels of volunteer involvement in the governance of non-profit sport organizations are sustainable.

Given the consistent criticisms from government sport agencies including the Australian Sports Commission (ASC), Sport and Recreation New Zealand (SPARC) and UK Sport about the quality of governance being provided by volunteer boards, the question must be asked, has the time come to consider an alternative to having volunteers govern these organizations? Directors serving on corporate boards are paid for their time and expertise therefore, it might be argued, those who serve on the boards of sport organizations should also be paid. However, most sport organizations do not have sufficient financial resources to pay board members without substantially increasing the costs to participants. Furthermore, paying volunteer board members for their time would set a precedent for paying other categories of volunteers.

The challenge is therefore to maintain volunteer involvement in the governance of sport organizations while improving performance standards. Developing the skills, knowledge and experience levels of volunteer board members will contribute ultimately to their ability to improve organizational outcomes. The volunteer traditions of nonprofit sport organizations assist in maintaining and conveying many of the values fundamental to sport participation and involvement. Nonprofit sport organizations need to focus on maintaining such values (i.e. civic engagement, fair play, commitment) while utilizing the expertise of professional staff in managing the provision of services and programmes. Maximizing the benefits of the relationship between volunteer boards and paid staff and the duality of leadership within these organizations requires the roles and responsibilities of volunteers and staff to be clearly defined, for governance structures to fully integrate staff and volunteer roles, and for organizational cultures to recognize and accept the value they each provide to their organization. Successfully achieving this may present a significant challenge for those nonprofit sport organizations and volunteer board members who have been slow to accept the introduction of professional staff into the nonprofit sport sector.

Inter-organizational linkages

As highlighted in Chapter 3, nonprofit sport organizations are involved in highly complex inter-organizational relationships where the relationships between International Sports Federations (ISFs), NGBs and state or provincial, regional and local level sport organizations do not operate as top-down power hierarchies. This complexity manifests in a range of governance issues including: structural inefficiencies, the nature of paid staff and volunteer relationships, resource exchange between national and state organizations, compliance with national initiatives, decision-making and strategic planning and meeting government funding requirements. The boards of these organizations must cooperate with each other in order to make the overall sport system operate effectively and efficiently.

The challenge for nonprofit sport organizations, particularly at the international and national levels is to ensure compliance from their member organizations in areas such as delivering prescribed programmes, adhering to policy directives and reporting progress. Decisions to comply with directives and requests designed to achieve organizational goals developed at national or international levels requires the boards at lower hierarchical levels to recognize the value of sometimes quite abstract goals. This may be a significant challenge for volunteer board members to behave in the best interests of the sport rather than in the interests of their own organization.

Nonprofit sport organizations are involved in inter-organizational relationships and more formalized contractual relationships with other sport organizations, funding agencies, sponsors, broadcasters, corporate partners, stadia operators, event organizations and other public and nonprofit organizations. Thibault and Harvey (1997: 60) argued that these linkages may result in 'power struggles, loss of autonomy on the part of organizations, asymmetrical relationships, different levels of commitment in the relationship, conflicting loyalties, changes in resource allocation, resource imbalances, goal displacement and resistance to change'. From time to time these issues will emerge as significant challenges to the boards and chief executive officers (CEOs) of nonprofit sport organizations. They are likely to face decisions about balancing the potential benefits of strategic and innovative relationships with responsibilities for the management of risks associated with these relationships.

Knowledge development

In the early 1990s, Hollister (1993: 310) noted that 'the functioning of boards will be the most promising point of leverage for strengthening the (nonprofit) sector'. He noted that despite the development of an impressive body of knowledge about board development and board–staff relations there were significant problems. Specifically he identified that 'the pervasive weakness of many boards and dysfunctional board–staff relations are a major problem both for individual organizations and for the sector as a whole' (Hollister, 1993: 310). These criticisms could arguably be levelled at the state of governance in nonprofit sport organizations. A contributing factor to the perceived poor governance standards in sport could be the lack of directly relevant empirical research in the area which could potentially inform governance practice within sport organizations.

Ostrower and Stone (forthcoming) noted there are still gaps in our theoretical and empirical knowledge about the functioning of nonprofit boards. These gaps are far wider in relation to our understanding of the workings of sport organization boards. The body of research devoted to the study of governance within any form of sport organization is in its infancy. Published studies thus far have tended to describe the unique nature of governance in sport and have tended to focus on issues such as board–staff relations, board roles, board performance and, to a limited extent, the

203

behaviour of individual board members. One of the more significant challenges for nonprofit sport organizations is to develop a greater understanding of the behaviour of board members and staff in the performance of their governance roles along with the utility of prescribed governance practices in driving improvements in board and organizational performance. There is still much to discover about how board structures, culture, democratic processes and deeply held values in sport impact on the functioning of sport boards. There has also been little research into how and why boards make meaningful contributions to the strategy of sport organizations and whether such contributions influence organizational outcomes.

There is scope to reverse the current trend of sport organizations borrowing from the lessons of the corporate sector and the wider nonprofit sector. As discussed in several chapters, many of the guidelines developed to assist sport organizations improve their governance practices are based on corporate or nonprofit governance principles. While financial success may be less of an imperative for the majority of sport organizations than it is for for-profit corporations, the governance of sport organizations is arguably more complex than the governance of corporations or even charitable organizations. The time may come when the knowledge base in nonprofit sport organizations is sufficiently developed to inform the governance of corporations and nonprofit organizations other than those in the sport sector.

Conclusion

This book has explored the elements of structure, culture, strategy, leadership, change and performance in relation to the governance of nonprofit sport organizations. It has reviewed a number of challenges and drivers of governance change that compel sport organizations to continually examine and evolve their governance structures and practices in order to meet ever increasing expectations and standards of transparency, accountability and performance from a wide range of stakeholders. The boards of nonprofit sport organizations are vital for the continued effective delivery of sport opportunities to members, participants, spectators and the wider community because they are the core decision-making authority with responsibility for organizational strategies and the management of risk. Sport organization boards are central to the development of organizational culture, leadership and ultimately organizational performance. It is therefore important that we understand how and be able to explain why they work as they do. This book has endeavoured to emphasize the importance of approaches other than traditional legal and financial perspectives to understanding sport organization governance. In particular it has examined governance from the perspectives of the structural attributes of sport organization boards, the roles and responsibilities of board and staff members, the efficacy of member representation and voting systems, assessing and improving the performance of individual board members, shared leadership between volunteers and paid staff and the impact of boards on organizational performance.

At the heart of the effective delivery of sport are the concepts of governance and accountability. As outlined by the Panel on Accountability and Governance in the Voluntary Sector (1999: 6–7):

> Governance entails the processes and structures that an organization uses to direct and manage its general operations and programme activities. Without good governance, an organization cannot expect to perform effectively and to have the capacity to adapt readily to change. Accountability for how an organization's activities and responsibilities have been carried out is critical to ensuring its credibility and to maintaining public confidence in it.

The future of the nonprofit sport sector is arguably dependent on the ability of sport organizations to govern themselves well and to demonstrate accountability to their many stakeholders. It is vital that nonprofit sport organizations strive to adopt governance standards that are considered good practice in readiness for the many challenges they will face in achieving their strategic goals. This book has sought to assist volunteers, practicing and future professionals and researchers understand the nature of sport governance and to assist them in dealing with the various issues associated with the execution of governance within nonprofit sport organizations.

Bibliography

Alexander, J.A. & Weiner, B.J. (1998). The adoption of the corporate governance model by nonprofit organizations. *Nonprofit Management and Leadership*, 8, 223–242.

Amis, J. & Slack, T. (1996). The size–structure relationship in voluntary sport organizations. *Journal of Sport Management*, 10, 76–86.

Amis, J., Slack, T. & Berrett, T. (1995). The structural antecedents of conflict in voluntary sport organizations. *Leisure Studies*, 14, 1–16.

Amundson, W. (2004). *Enhancing the board's monitoring role: Without micromanaging*. Calgary, Canada: The Canadian Association. Available online at http://www.axi.ca/tca/Mar2004/featurearticle.shtml (accessed 1 March 2006).

Anheier, H.K. (2005). *Nonprofit organizations: Theory, management, policy*. London: Routledge.

Associations Incorporations Act 1981. Government of Victoria.

Associations Incorporations Regulations 1998. Government of Victoria.

Auditor General South Australia (2004). *Report of the Auditor-General on the Basketball Association of South Australia Incorporated*. Adelaide: South Australia Government Printer.

Auld, C. (1997). Professionalisation of Australian sport: The effects on organisational decision-making. *European Journal for Sport Management*, 4(2), 17–39.

Auld, C. & Godbey, G. (1998). Influence in Canadian national sport organizations: Perceptions of professionals and volunteers. *Journal of Sport Management*, 12, 20–38.

Australian Sports Commission (n.d.). *Risk management for directors and board members of National Sporting Organisations*. Canberra, Australia: Australian Sports Commission.

Australian Sports Commission (1999a). *Governing sport: The roles of the board and CEO*. Canberra, Australia: Australian Sports Commission.

Australian Sports Commission (1999b). *The Australian Sports Commission – Beyond 2000*. Canberra, Australia: Australian Sports Commission.

Australian Sports Commission (2002). *National Sporting Organisations Governance: Principles of best practice*. Canberra, Australia: Australian Sports Commission.

Australian Sports Commission (2003). *Independent soccer review: Report of the independent soccer review committee into the structure, governance and management of soccer in Australia*. Canberra: Australian Sports Commission.

Australian Sports Commission (2004). *Sport innovation and best practice – governance*. Canberra: Australian Sports Commission. Available online at http://www.ausport.gov.au/ibp/governance.asp.

Australian Sports Commission (2005). *Governing sport: The role of the board, a good practice guide for sporting organisations.* Canberra, Australia: Australian Sports Commission.

Australian Stock Exchange (2003). *Principles of good corporate governance and best practice recommendations.* Sydney: Australian Stock Exchange.

Balser, D. & McClusky, J. (2005). Managing stakeholder relationships and nonprofit organization effectiveness. *Nonprofit Management and Leadership*, 15, 295–315.

Bart, C. (2004). The governance role of the board in corporate strategy: An initial progress report. *International Journal of Business Governance and Ethics*, 1(2/3), 111–125.

Bart, C. & Deal, K. (2006). The governance role of the board in corporate strategy: A comparison of board practices in 'for profit' and 'not for profit' organisations. *International Journal of Business Governance and Ethics*, 1(1/2), 2–22.

Bieber, M. (2003). Governing independent museums: How trustees and directors exercise their powers. In C. Cornforth (Ed.), *The governance of public and non-profit organisations: What do boards do?* Oxford: Routledge, pp. 164–184.

Ben-Ner, A. & Van Hoomisen, T. (1994). The governance of nonprofit organisations: Law and public policy. *Nonprofit Management and Leadership*, 4, 393–414.

Berger, P. & Luckmann, T. (1967). *The social construction of reality: A treatise on the sociology of knowledge.* London: Penguin.

Block, S.R. (1998). *Perfect nonprofit boards: Myths, paradoxes and paradigms.* Needham Heights, MA: Simon Sz Schuster.

Bradshaw, P., Murray, V. & Wolpin, J. (1992). Do nonprofit boards make a difference? An exploration of the relationships among board structure, process, and effectiveness. *Nonprofit and Voluntary Sector Quarterly*, 21, 227–249.

Bridgman, P. & Davis, G. (2000). *The Australian policy handbook*, 2nd edn. Crows Nest, NSW: Allen and Unwin.

Brown, W.A. (2002). Inclusive governance practices in nonprofit organizations and implications for practice. *Nonprofit Management and Leadership*, 12, 369–385.

Brown, W.A. (2005). Exploring the association between board and organizational performance in nonprofit organizations. *Nonprofit Management and Leadership*, 15, 317–339.

Brown, W.A. & Iverson, J.O. (2004). Exploring strategy and board structure in nonprofit organizations. *Nonprofit and Voluntary Sector Quarterly*, 33, 377–400.

Bugg, G. & Dallhoff, S. (2006). *National study of board governance practices in the non-profit and voluntary sector in Canada.* Ottawa, Canada: Strategic Leverage Partners.

Callen, J.L., Klein, A. & Tinkelman, D. (2003). Board composition, committees and organizational efficiency: The case of nonprofits. *Nonprofit and Voluntary Sector Quarterly*, 32, 493–520.

Canadian Amateur Rowing Association (2005). *Constitution*.

Carbery, R., Garavan, T. H., O'Brien, F. & McDonnell, J. (2003). Predicting hotel managers' turnover cognitions. *Journal of Managerial Psychology*, 18, 649–679.

Canadian Centre for Sport and Law (2005). Topics. Ontario: Canadian Centre for Sport and Law. Available online at http://www.sportlaw. ca/index.htm (accessed 1 March 2006).

Canadian Cycling Association (2003). *Policy on Organization Structure*.

Canadian Cycling Association (2004). *Constitution and By-Laws*.

Canadian Olympic Committee (1997). *White Paper on Governance*.

Canadian Olympic Committee (2006). *Canadian Olympic Committee Governance Structure*. Toronto: COC. Available online at http://www. olympic.ca/EN/organization/governance/index.shtml (accessed 1 March 2006).

Carpenter, M.A. & Westphal, J.D. (2001). The strategic context of external network ties: Examining the impact of director appointments on board involvement in strategic decision making. *Academy of Management Journal*, 44(4), 639–660.

Carver, J. (1997). *Boards that make a difference: A new design for leadership in nonprofit and public organisations*, 2nd edn. San Francisco, CA: Jossey-Bass.

Centre for Corporate Law and Securities Regulation (2004). *A better framework: Reforming not-for-profit regulation*. Melbourne, Australia: University of Melbourne.

Chait, R., Holland, T.P. & Taylor, B.E. (1996). *Improving the performance of governing boards*. Phoenix, AZ: Oryx Press.

Chelladurai, P. & Haggerty, T.R. (1991). Differentiation in national sport organizations in Canada. *Canadian Journal of Sport Science*, 16(2), 117–125.

Clarke, J. (2006). Australian Baseball History. Sydney: Author. Available online at http://www.australianbaseballhistory.webcentral.com.au/ Baseball%20Web%20Pages/Default.htm (accessed 7 April 2006).

Clarke, T. (Ed.) (2004). *Theories of corporate governance: The philosophical foundations of corporate governance*. London: Routledge.

Clifford, P.W. & Evans, R.T. (1996). The state of corporate governance practices in Australia. *Corporate Governance*, 4(2), 60–70.

Commonwealth Games Federation (2006). *Constitution, Regulations, Code of Conduct*. London: Commonwealth Games Federation.

Cornforth, C. (2001). What makes boards effective? An examination of the relationships between board inputs, structures, processes and effectiveness in non-profit organisations. *Corporate Governance*, 9, 217–227.

Cornforth, C. (2003a). Conclusion: Contextualising and managing the paradoxes of governance. In C. Cornforth (Ed.), *The governance of public and non-profit organisations: What do boards do?* London: Routledge, pp. 237–253.

Cornforth, C. (2003b). Introduction: The changing context of governance – emerging issues and paradoxes. In C. Cornforth (Ed.), *The governance of public and non-profit organisations: What do boards do?* London: Routledge, pp. 1–19.

Cornforth, C. (Ed.) (2003c). *The governance of public and non-profit organisations: What do boards do?* London: Routledge.

Crittenden, W.F., Crittenden, V.L., Stone, M.M. & Robertson, C.J. (2004). An uneasy alliance: Planning and performance in nonprofit organizations. *International Journal of Organization Theory and Behaviour*, 6(4), 81–106.

Cuskelly, G. (1995). The influence of committee functioning on the organizational commitment of volunteer administrators in sport. *Journal of Sport Behaviour*, 18, 254–269.

Cuskelly, G., Hoye, R. & Auld, C. (2006). *Working with Volunteers in Sport: Theory and Practice.* London: Routledge.

Cuskelly, G., McIntyre, N. & Boag, A. (1998). A longitudinal study of the development of organizational commitment amongst volunteer sport administrators. *Journal of Sport Management*, 12, 181–202.

Daley, J.M. & Angulo, J. (1994). Understanding the dynamics of diversity within nonprofit boards. *Journal of the Community Development Society*, 25, 173–188.

Dansereau, F., Graen, G. & Haga, B.A. (1975). A vertical-dyad linkage approach to leadership within formal organizations: A longitudinal investigation of the role making process. *Organizational Behavior and Human Performance*, 13, 46–78.

Dart, R., Bradshaw, P., Murray, V. & Wolpin, J. (1996). Boards of directors in nonprofit organizations: Do they follow a lifecycle model? *Nonprofit Management and Leadership*, 6, 367–379.

Dawley, D.D., Stephens, R.D. & Stephens, D.B. (2005). Dimensionality of organizational commitment in volunteer workers: Chamber of commerce board members and role fulfilment. *Journal of Vocational Behaviour*, 67, 511–525.

Dawson, I. & Dunn, A. (2006). Governance codes of practice in the not-for-profit sector. *Corporate Governance*, 14, 33–42.

DeSchriver, T. & Stotlar, D. (1996). An economic analysis of cartel behaviour within the NCAA. *Journal of Sport Management*, 10, 388–400.

DiMaggio, P.J. & Powell, W.W. (1983). The iron cage revisited: Institutional isomorphism and collective rationality in organizational fields. *American Sociological Review*, 48, 147–160.

Doherty, A.J. (1998). Managing our human resources: A review of organisational behaviour in sport. *Sport Management Review*, 1, 1–24.

Doherty, A. (2005). *A profile of community sport volunteers.* Ontario: Parks and Recreation Ontario and Sport Alliance of Ontario. Available online at http://216.13.76.142/PROntario/PDF/reports/finalReport_phase One2005.pdf (accessed 16 January 2006).

Doherty, A.J. & Carron, A.V. (2003). Cohesion in volunteer sport executive committees. *Journal of Sport Management*, 17, 116–141.

Doherty, A., Patterson, M. & Van Bussel, M. (2004). What do we expect? An examination of perceived committee norms in non-profit sport organizations. *Sport Management Review*, 7, 109–132.

Drucker, P.F. (1990a). Lessons for successful nonprofit governance. *Nonprofit Management and Leadership*, 1, 7–14.

Drucker, P.F. (1990b). *Managing the non-profit organization*. Oxford: Butterworth-Heinemann.

Duchon, D., Green, S. & Taber, T. (1986). Vertical dyad linkage: A longitudinal assessment of antecedents, measures and consequences. *Journal of Applied Psychology*, 71, 56–60.

du Plessis, J.J., McConvill, J. & Bagaric, M. (2005). *Principles of contemporary corporate governance*. Melbourne: Cambridge University Press.

Edwards, C. & Cornforth, C. (2003). What influences the strategic contribution of boards? In C. Cornforth (Ed.), *The governance of public and non-profit organisations: What do boards do?* London: Routledge, pp. 77–96.

Eisenhardt, K.M. (1989). Building theories from case study research. *Academy of Management Review*, 14, 532–550.

Farrar, J. (2005). *Corporate governance: Theories, principles, and practice*, 2nd edn. Melbourne: Oxford University Press.

Ferkins, L., Shilbury, D. & McDonald, G. (2005). The role of the board in building strategic capability: Towards an integrated model of sport governance research. *Sport Management Review*, 8, 195–225.

Fishel, D. (2003). *The book of the board: Effective governance for non-profit organisations*, Sydney: Federation Press.

Fleisher, C.S. (1991). Using an agency-based approach to analyse collaborative federated interorganizational relationships. *Journal of Applied Behavioral Science*, 27(1), 116–130.

Fletcher, K. (1992). Effective boards: How executive directors define and develop them. *Nonprofit Management and Leadership*, 2, 283–293.

Fletcher, K. (1999). Four books on nonprofit boards and governance. *Nonprofit Management and Leadership*, 9, 435–441.

Football Association (2005). *Structural review: A review of comparator sporting organisations*. London: Football Association.

Football Association (2006). *The Organisation*. London: Football Association. Available online at http://www.thefa.com/TheFA/Postings/2004/03/THE_ORGANISATION.htm (accessed 1 March 2006).

Football Governance Research Centre (2004). *The state of the game: The corporate governance of football clubs 2004*, Research paper 2004 No. 3. Football Governance Research Centre, Birkbeck, University of London.

Football Governance Research Centre (2005). *The state of the game: The corporate governance of football clubs 2005*, Research paper 2005 No. 3. Football Governance Research Centre, Birkbeck, University of London.

Forbes, D.P. (1998). Measuring the unmeasurable: Empirical studies of nonprofit organization effectiveness from 1977 to 1997. *Nonprofit and Voluntary Sector Quarterly*, 27, 183–202.

Forster, J. (2006). Global sports organisations and their governance. *Corporate Governance*, 6(1), 72–83.

French, Jr. J.R.P. & Raven B., (1959). The bases of social power. In D. Cartwright (Ed.), *Studies in social power* (pp. 150–167). Ann Arbor: University of Michigan Press.

Friedman, A. & Phillips, M. (2004). Balancing strategy and accountability: A model for the governance of professional associations. *Nonprofit Management and Leadership*, 15, 187–204.

Frisby, W. (1986). The organizational structure and effectiveness of voluntary organizations: The case of Canadian national sport governing bodies. *Journal of Park and Recreation Administration*, 4, 61–74.

Fuller, J.B., Barnett, T., Hester, K. & Relyea, C. (2003). A social identity perspective on the relationship between perceived organizational support and organizational commitment. *Journal of Social Psychology*, 143, 789–791.

Gill, M. (2001). *Governance do's & don'ts: Lessons from case studies on twenty Canadian non-profits: Final report*. Ottawa, Canada: Institute on Governance.

Golensky, M. (1993). The board–executive relationship in nonprofit organizations: Partnership or power struggle? *Nonprofit Management and Leadership*, 4, 177–191.

Gomez, C. & Rosen, B. (2001). The leader–member exchange as a link between managerial trust and employee empowerment. *Group and Organization Management*, 26(1), 53–69.

Gopinath, C., Sicilian, J.I. & Murray, R.L. (1994). Changing role of the board of directors: In search of a new strategic identity? *The Mid-Atlantic Journal of Business*, 30(2), 175–185.

Governance in Sport Working Group (2001). *The rules of the game: Conference report and conclusions*. Brussels: Governance in Sport Working Group.

Graen, G.B. & Uhl-Bien, M. (1995). Relationship-based approach to leadership: Development of leader–member exchange (LMX) theory of leadership over 25 years: Applying a multi-level multi-domain perspective. *Leadership Quarterly*, 6(2), 219–247.

Green, M. (2004). Changing policy priorities for sport in England: The emergence of elite sport development as a key policy concern. *Leisure Studies*, 23, 365–385.

Green, M. (2005). Integrating macro and meso-level approaches: A comparative analysis of elite sport development in Australia, Canada and the United Kingdom. *European Sport Management Quarterly*, 5, 143–166.

Green J.C. & Griesinger, D.W. (1996). Board performance and organizational effectiveness in nonprofit social services organizations. *Nonprofit Management and Leadership*, 6, 381–402.

Grossman, A. & Rangan, V.K. (2001). Managing multisite nonprofits. *Nonprofit Management and Leadership*, 11(3), 321–337.

Hamil, S., Holt, M., Michie, J., Oughton, C. & Shailer, L. (2004). The corporate governance of professional football clubs. *Corporate Governance*, 4(2), 44–51.

Harris, M. (1989). The governing body role: Problems and perceptions in implementation. *Nonprofit and Voluntary Sector Quarterly*, 18, 317–323.

Harris, M. (1993). Exploring the role of boards using total activities analysis. *Nonprofit Management and Leadership*, 3, 269–281.

Healey, D. (2005). *Sport and the Law*. Sydney: University of New South Wales Press.

Heimovics, R.D. & Herman, R.D. (1990). Responsibility for critical events in nonprofit organizations. *Nonprofit and Voluntary Sector Quarterly*, 19, 59–72.

Heimovics, R.D., Herman, R.D. & Jurkiewicz, C.L. (1995). The political dimension of effective nonprofit executive leadership. *Nonprofit Management and Leadership*, 5(3), 233–248.

Henry, I. & Theodoraki, E. (2000). Management, organizations and theory in the governance of sport. In J. Coakley, & E. Dunning (Eds), *Handbook of Sports Studies* (pp. 490–503). London: Sage.

Herman, R.D. & Heimovics, R. (1990a). An investigation of leadership skill differences in chief executives of nonprofit organizations. *American Review of Public Administration*, 20, 197–204.

Herman, R.D. & Heimovics, R. (1990b). The effective nonprofit executive: Leader of the board. *Nonprofit Management and Leadership*, 1, 167–180.

Herman, R.D. & Heimovics, R. (1991). *Executive leadership in nonprofit organizations*. San Francisco, CA: Jossey-Bass.

Herman, R.D. & Heimovics, R. (1994). Executive leadership. In R.D. Herman, & Associates (Eds), *The Jossey-Bass handbook of nonprofit leadership and management* (pp. 137–153). San Fransisco: Jossey-Bass.

Herman, R.D. & Renz, D.O. (1997). Multiple constituencies and the social construction of nonprofit organizational effectiveness. *Nonprofit and Voluntary Sector Quarterly*, 26, 185–206.

Herman, R.D. & Renz, D.O. (1998). Nonprofit organizational effectiveness: Contrasts between especially effective and less effective organizations. *Nonprofit Management and Leadership*, 9, 23–38.

Herman, R.D. & Renz, D.O. (2000). Board practices of especially effective and less effective local nonprofit organizations. *American Review of Public Administration*, 30, 146–160.

Herman, R.D. & Tulipana, F.P. (1989). Board–staff relations and perceived effectiveness in nonprofit organizations. In R.D. Herman & J.V. Til (Eds), *Nonprofit boards of directors: Analyses and applications* (pp. 48–59). New Brunswick, NJ: Transaction.

Herman, R.D., Renz, D.O. & Heimovics, R. (1997). Board practices and board effectiveness in local nonprofit organizations. *Nonprofit Management and Leadership*, 7, 373–385.

Hilmer, F.G. (1993). *Strictly boardroom: Improving governance to enhance company performance: Report of the independent working party into corporate governance.* Melbourne: The Sydney Institute and Information Australia.

Hodgkin, C. (1993). Policy and paper clips: Rejecting the lure of the corporate model. *Nonprofit Management and Leadership*, 3, 415–428.

Holland, T.P. (1991). Self-assessment by nonprofit boards. *Nonprofit Management and Leadership*, 2, 25–36.

Holland, T.P. & Jackson, D.K. (1998). Strengthening board performance: Findings and lessons from demonstration projects. *Nonprofit Management and Leadership*, 9, 121–134.

Holland, T.P., Leslie, D. & Holzhalb, C. (1993). Culture and change in nonprofit boards. *Nonprofit Management and Leadership*, 4, 141–155.

Hollister, R.M. (1993). Developing a research agenda for nonprofit management. In D.R. Young, R.M. Hollister & V.A. Hodgkinson (Eds), *Governing, leading, and managing nonprofit organizations: New insights from research and practice.* (pp. 306–323). San Francisco, CA: Jossey-Bass.

Houle, C.O. (1960). *The effective board.* New York: Association Press.

Houle, C.O. (1997). *Governing boards: Their nature and nurture.* San Francisco, CA: Jossey-Bass.

House, R.J. (1991). The distribution and exercise of power in complex organizations: A meso theory. *Leadership Quarterly*, 2, 23–58.

Hoye, R. (2004). Leader-member exchanges and board performance of voluntary sport organisations, *Nonprofit Management and Leadership*, 15(1), 55–70.

Hoye, R. (2006a). Governance reform in Australian horse racing. *Managing Leisure*, 11, 129–138.

Hoye, R. (2006b). Leadership within voluntary sport organization boards. *Nonprofit Management and Leadership*, 16(3), 297–313.

Hoye, R. & Auld, C. (2001). Measuring board performance in nonprofit voluntary sport organisations. *Australian Journal on Volunteering*, 6(2), 108–116.

Hoye, R. & Cuskelly, G. (2003a). Board power and performance in voluntary sport organisations, *European Sport Management Quarterly*, 3(2), 103–119.

Hoye, R. & Cuskelly, G. (2003b). Board–executive relationships within voluntary sport organisations, *Sport Management Review*, 6(1), 53–73.

Hoye, R. & Cuskelly, G. (2004). Board member selection, orientation and evaluation: Implications for board performance in member-benefit voluntary sport organisations. *Third Sector Review*, 10(1), 77–100.

Hoye, R. & Inglis, S. (2003). Governance of nonprofit leisure organisations. *Society and Leisure*, 26(2), 369–387.

Hoye, R., Smith, A., Westerbeek, H., Stewart, B. & Nicholson, M. (2006). *Sport Management: Principles and Application.* Oxford: Elsevier Butterworth-Heinemann.

Hung, H. (1998). A typology of theories of the roles of governing boards. *Corporate Governance*, 6(2), 101–111.

Iecovich, E. (2004). Responsibilities and roles of boards in nonprofit organizations: The Israeli case. *Nonprofit Management and Leadership*, 15, 5–24.

Ingley, C.B. & van der Walt, N.T. (2003). Board configuration: Building better boards. *Corporate Governance*, 3(4), 5–17.

Inglis, S. (1997a). Roles of the board in amateur sport organizations. *Journal of Sport Management*, 11, 160–176.

Inglis, S. (1997b). Shared leadership in the governance of amateur sport: Perceptions of executive directors and board members. *Avante*, 3, 14–33.

Inglis, S., Alexander, T. & Weaver, L. (1999). Roles and responsibilities of community nonprofit boards. *Nonprofit Management and Leadership*, 10, 153–167.

Inglis, S. & Weaver, L. (2000). Designing agendas to reflect board roles and responsibilities: Results of a study. *Nonprofit Management and Leadership*, 11, 65–77.

International Cricket Council (2005). *Annual Report 2004–2005*.

International Rugby Board (2004). *Bye Laws of the Board*.

Jackson, D.K. & Holland, T.P. (1998). Measuring the effectiveness of nonprofit boards. *Nonprofit and Voluntary Sector Quarterly*, 27, 159–182.

Judge, Jr. W.Q. & Zeithaml, C.P. (1992). Institutional and strategic choice perspectives on board involvement in the strategic decision process. *Academy of Management Journal*, 35(4), 766–794.

Kent, A. & Chelladurai, P. (2001). Perceived transformational leadership, organizational commitment, and citizenship behaviour: A case study in intercollegiate athletics. *Journal of Sport Management*, 15, 135–159.

Kikulis, L.M. (2000). Continuity and change in governance and decision making in national sport organizations: Institutional explanations. *Journal of Sport Management*, 14, 293–320.

Kikulis, L.M., Slack, T. & Hinings, B. (1992). Institutionally specific design archetypes: A framework for understanding change in national sport organizations. *International Review for the Sociology of Sport*, 27, 343–367.

Kikulis, L.M., Slack, T. & Hinings, B. (1995a). Does decision making make a difference? Patterns of change within Canadian national sport organizations. *Journal of Sport Management*, 9, 273–299.

Kikulis, L.M., Slack, T. & Hinings, B. (1995b). Toward an understanding of the role of agency and choice in the changing structure of Canada's national sport organizations. *Journal of Sport Management*, 9, 135–152.

Kikulis, L.M., Slack, T. & Hinings, B. (1995c). Sector-specific patterns of organizational design change. *Journal of Management Studies*, 32(1), 67–100.

Kikulis, L.M., Slack, T., Hinings, B. & Zimmermann, A. (1989). A structural taxonomy of amateur sport organizations. *Journal of Sport Management*, 3, 129–150.

Koski, P. & Heikkala, J. (1998). Professionalization and organizations of mixed rationales: The case of Finnish national sport organizations. *European Journal for Sport Management*, 5(1), 7–29.

La Piana, D. & Hayes, M. (2005). M&A in the nonprofit sector: Managing merger negotiations and integration. *Strategy and Leadership*, 33(2), 11–16.

Leisure Industries Research Centre (2003). *Sports Volunteering in England 2002*. England: London.

Leiter, J. (2005). Structural isomorphism in Australian nonprofit organizations. *Voluntas: International Journal of Voluntary and Nonprofit Organizations*, 16, 1–31.

London Stock Exchange (2004). *Corporate governance: A practical guide*. London: London Stock Exchange.

Mathiasen, K. (1990). *Board passages: Three key stages in a nonprofit board's lifecycle*. Governance series paper. Washington, DC: National centre for Nonprofit Boards.

McGregor-Lowndes, M. (2003). Keeping to the straight and narrow. In D. Fishel, *The book of the board: Effective governance for non-profit organisations*, (pp. 55–69). Sydney: Federation Press.

Meyer, J.W. & Allen, N.J. (1991). A three component conceptualization of organizational commitment. *Human Resource Management Review*, 1, 61–89.

Meyer, J. & Allen, N. (1997). *Commitment in the workplace. Theory, research, and application*. Thousand Oaks, CA: Sage.

Middleton, M. (1987). Nonprofit boards of directors: Beyond the governance function. In W.W. Powell (Ed.), *The nonprofit sector: A research handbook*, (pp. 141–153). New Haven, CT: Yale University Press.

Miller, J.L. (2002). The board as a monitor of organizational activity: The applicability of agency theory to nonprofit boards. *Nonprofit Management and Leadership*, 12, 429–450.

Miller-Millesen, J.L. (2003). Understanding the behaviour of nonprofit boards of directors: A theory-based approach. *Nonprofit and Voluntary Sector Quarterly*, 32(4), 521–547.

Milliken, F.K. & Martins. L.L. (1996). Searching for common threads: Understanding the multiple effects of diversity in organizational groups. *Academy of Management Review*, 21, 402–433.

Mitchell, R., Crosset, T. & Barr, C. (1999). Encouraging compliance without real power: Sport associations regulating teams. *Journal of Sport Management*, 13, 216–236.

Morgan, M. (2002). Optimizing the structure of elite competitions in professional sport: Lessons from Rugby Union. *Managing Leisure*, 7, 41–60.

Murray V., Bradshaw, P. & Wolpin, J. (1992). Power in and around nonprofit boards: A neglected dimension of governance. *Nonprofit Management and Leadership*, 3, 165–182.

Nadler, D.A. (2004). What's the board's role in strategy development? Engaging the board in corporate strategy. *Strategy and Leadership*, 32(5), 25–33.

Najam, A. (2000). The four Cs of third sector-government relations: Cooperation, confrontation, complementarity, and co-optation. *Nonprofit Management and Leadership*, 10(4), 375–396.

National Council for Voluntary Organisations (2005). *Good governance: A code for the voluntary and community sector*. London, UK: National Council for Voluntary Organisations.

New York Stock Exchange (2004). *Section 303A Corporate governance listing standards*. New York: New York Stock Exchange.

New Zealand Orienteering Federation (2005). *Stakeholder relationship strategies for the sport of orienteering*. Wellington, NZ: New Zealand Orienteering Federation.

New Zealand Securities Commission (2004). *Corporate governance in New Zealand: Principles and Guidelines: A handbook for directors, executives and advisers*. Wellington: New Zealand Securities Commission.

Nicholson, G.J. & Kiel, G.C. (2004). Breakthrough board performance: How to harness your board's intellectual capital. *Corporate Governance*, 4, 5–23.

Northouse, P.G. (2001). *Leadership theory and practice*, 2nd edn. California: Sage.

Oakley, B. & Green, M. (2001). Still playing the game at arm's length? The selective re-investment in British sport, 1995–2000. *Managing Leisure*, 6, 74–94.

Office for Recreation and Sport (2003). *Amalgamation: A guide for recreation and sporting organisations*. Adelaide, Australia: Office for Recreation and Sport.

Office for Recreation and Sport (2004). *South Australian Cycling Federation Governance Review*. Adelaide, Australia: Office for Recreation and Sport.

Oliver, C. (1990). Determinants of interorganizational relationships: Integration and future directions. *Academy of Management Review*, 15, 241–265.

Oliver, C. (1991). Strategic responses to institutional processes. *Academy of Management Review*, 16, 145–179.

O'Regan, K. & Oster, S. (2002). Does government funding alter nonprofit governance? Evidence from New York City contractors. *Journal of Policy Analysis and Management*, 21, 359–379.

O'Regan, K. & Oster, S. (2005). Does the structure and composition of the board matter? The case of nonprofit organizations. *Journal of Law, Economics, and Organization*, 21, 205–227.

Organisation for Economic Co-operation and Development (2004). *OECD Principles of Corporate Governance*. Paris: OECD.

Oster, S.M. (1992). National organizations as franchise operations. *Nonprofit Management and Leadership*, 2(3), 223–238.

Oster, S.M. (1996). Nonprofit organizations and their local affiliates: A study in organizational forms. *Journal of Economic Behaviour and Organization*, 30, 83–96.

Ostrower, F. & Stone, M.M. (forthcoming, 2006). Governance: Research trends, gaps, and future prospects. In W.W. Powell & R. Steinberg (Eds), *The nonprofit sector: A research handbook*, 2nd edn (pp. 1–13). New Haven CT: Yale University Press.

217

Padilla, A. & Baumer, D. (1994). Big-time college sports: Management and economic issues. *Journal of Sport and Social Issues*, 18(2), 123–143.

Panel on Accountability and Governance in the Voluntary Sector (1999). *Building on strength: Improving governance and accountability in Canada's voluntary sector*. Vancouver: Panel on Accountability and Governance in the Voluntary Sector.

Papadimitriou, D. (1999). Voluntary boards of directors in Greek sport governing bodies. *European Journal for Sport Management*, 6, 78–103.

Pfeffer, J. (1992). Understanding the role of power in decision making. In J.M. Shafritz & J.S. Ott (Ed.), *Classics of organization theory*, 3rd edn (pp. 404–423). Pacific Grove, CA: Brooks/Cole (Reprinted from Pfeffer, J. (1981). *Power in organizations*, pp. 1–32, Marshfield, MA: Pitman.)

Pfeffer, J. & Salancik, G. (1978). *The external control of organizations: A resource dependence perspective*. New York: Harper & Row.

Preston, J.B. & Brown, W.A. (2004). Commitment and performance of nonprofit board members. *Nonprofit Management and Leadership*, 15(2), 221–238.

Provan, K.G. (1980). Board power and organizational effectiveness among human service agencies. *Academy of Management Journal*, 23, 221–236.

Robbins, S.P., Millett, B., Cacioppe, R. & Waters-Marsh, T. (2001). *Organizational Behaviour: Leading and Managing in Australia and New Zealand*. Sydney: Prentice Hall.

Roche, M. (1993). Sport and community: Rhetoric and reality in the development of British sport policy. In J.C. Binfield & J. Stevenson (Eds), *Sport, Culture and Politics*. Sheffield: Sheffield Academic Press, pp. 72–112.

Rochester, C. (2003). The role of boards in small voluntary organisations. In C. Cornforth (Ed.), *The governance of public and non-profit organisations: What do boards do?* Oxford: Routledge, pp. 115–130.

Rowing Canada Aviron (2004). *Board of directors code of conduct and conflict of interest policy*. Victoria, Canada: Rowing Canada Aviron.

Rural and Regional Services Development Committee (2004). *Inquiry into Country Football*. Melbourne: Government Printer for the State of Victoria.

Saidel, J.R. (2002). *Guide to the literature on governance: An annotated bibliography*. Washington, DC: Boardsource.

Schein, E.H. (1990). Organizational culture, *American Psychologist*, 45(2), 109–119.

Schein, E.H. (1996). Culture: The missing concept in organization studies. *Administrative Science Quarterly*, 41(2), 229–240.

Scherrer, P.S. (2003). Director's responsibilities and participation in the strategic decision making process. *Corporate Governance*, 3(1), 86–90.

Shilbury, D. (2001). Examining board member roles, functions and influence: A study of Victorian sporting organizations. *International Journal of Sport Management*, 2, 253–281.

Siciliano, J.I. (1996). The relationship of board member diversity to organizational performance. *Journal of Business Ethics*, 15, 1313–1320.

Slack, T. (1985). The bureaucratization of a voluntary sport organization. *International Review for the Sociology of Sport*, 20, 145–165.

Slack, T. (1996). From the locker room to the board room: Changing the domain of sport management. *Journal of Sport Management*, 10, 97–105.

Slack, T. & Hinings, B. (1992). Understanding change in national sport organizations: An integration of theoretical perspectives. *Journal of Sport Management*, 6, 114–132.

Slack, T. & Hinings, B. (1994). Institutional pressures and isomorphic change: An empirical test. *Organization Studies*, 15(6), 803–827.

Slesinger, L.H. (1991). *Self-assessment for nonprofit governing boards.* Washington, DC: National Centre for Nonprofit Boards.

Smith, D.H. (1993). Public benefit and member benefit nonprofit, voluntary groups. *Nonprofit and Voluntary Sector Quarterly*, 22, 53–68.

Smith, D.H. (1999). *Grassroots associations.* Thousand Oaks, CA: Sage.

Sport and Recreation New Zealand (2004). *Nine steps to effective governance: Building high performing organisations.* Wellington, New Zealand: Sport and Recreation New Zealand.

Standards Australia (2003). *Australian Standard AS 8000-2003 Good governance principles.* Sydney: Standards Australia.

Standing Committee on Recreation and Sport Working Party on Management Improvement (1997). *Report to the Standing Committee on Recreation and Sport July 1997.* Canberra, Australia: Standing Committee on Recreation and Sport Working Party on Management Improvement.

Stephens, R.D., Dawley, D.D. & Stephens, D.B. (2004a). Commitment on the board: A model of volunteer directors' levels of organizational commitment and self-reported performance. *Journal of Managerial Studies*, 16, 483–504.

Stephens, R.D., Dawley, D.D. & Stephens, D.B. (2004b). Director role potential as antecedents of normative and affective commitment on nonprofit boards. *Organisational Analysis*, 12, 395–413.

Stern, R. (1979). The development of an interorganizational control network: The case of intercollegiate athletics. *Administrative Science Quarterly*, 24, 242–266.

Stewart, B., Nicholson, M., Smith, A. & Westerbeek, H. (2004). *Australian Sport: Better By Design? The Evolution of Australian Sport Policy.* London: Routledge.

Stone, M.M., Bigelow, B. & Crittenden, W. (1999). Research on strategic management in nonprofit organizations. *Administration and Society*, 31, 378–423.

Surf Life Saving Australia (2003). *Governance Policy.* Sydney: Surf Life Saving Australia.

Taylor, P. (2004). Driving up participation: Sport and Volunteering. In *Driving Up Participation: The Challenge For Sport.* London: Sport England.

Taylor, B.E., Chait, R.P. & Holland, T.P. (1991). Trustee motivation and board effectiveness. *Nonprofit and Voluntary Sector Quarterly*, 20, 207–224.

Theodoraki, E.I. & Henry, I.P. (1994). Organisational structures and contexts in British national governing bodies of sport. *International Review for the Sociology of Sport*, 29, 243–263.

Thibault, L. & Babiak, K. (2005). Organizational changes in Canada's sport system: Toward an athlete-centred approach. *European Sport Management Quarterly*, 5, 105–132.

Thibault, L. & Harvey, J. (1997). Fostering interorganizational linkages in the Canadian sport delivery system, *Journal of Sport Management*, 11, 45–68.

Thibault, L., Slack, T. & Hinings, B. (1991). Professionalism, structures and systems: The impact of professional staff on voluntary sport organizations. *International Review for the Sociology of Sport*, 26, 83–97.

Thibault, L., Slack, T., & Hinings, B. (1993). A framework for the analysis of strategy in nonprofit sport organizations. *Journal of Sport Management*, 7, 25–43.

Trice, H.M. & Beyer, J.M. (1993). *The cultures of work organizations*. Englewood Cliffs, NJ: Prentice Hall.

Tricker, R.I. (1984). *Corporate governance*. London: Gower.

Tricker, R.I. (1993). Corporate governance – the new focus of interest. *Corporate Governance*, 1(1), 1–3.

Tricker, R.I. (1994). Editorial. *Corporate Governance*, 2(1), 1–3.

UK Presidency of the European Union (2006). *Independent European Sport Review*.

UK Sport (2003). *Investing in change: High level review of the modernization programme for governing bodies of sport*. London: UK Sport.

UK Sport (2004). *Good governance guide for national governing bodies*. London: UK Sport.

Victorian Golf Association (2004). *Issues and challenges for golf clubs in Victoria*. Melbourne: VGA.

Volunteer Canada (2002). *Directors' liability: A discussion paper on legal liability, risk management and the role of directors in non-profit organizations*. Ottawa, Canada: Volunteer Canada.

Warburton, J. & Mutch, A. (2000). Will people continue to volunteer in the next century? In J. Warburton & M. Oppenheimer (Eds), *Volunteers and volunteering*. Leichardt, NSW: Federation Press, pp. 32–43.

Watt, D. (2003) *Sports management and administration*, 2nd edn. London: Routledge.

Westerbeek, H.M. & Smith, A.C.T. (2003). *Sport Business in the Global Marketplace*. London: Palgrave Macmillan.

Widmer, C. (1993). Role conflict, role ambiguity, and role overload on boards of directors of nonprofit human service organizations. *Nonprofit and Voluntary Sector Quarterly*, 22, 339–356.

Widmer, C. (1996). Volunteers with the dual roles of service provider and board member: A case study of role conflict. *Organizational Development Journal*, 14(3), 54–60.

Wood, M.M. (1992). Is governing board behaviour cyclical? *Nonprofit Management and Leadership*, 3, 139–163.

Young, D. (1989). Local autonomy in a franchise age: Structural change in national voluntary associations. *Nonprofit and Voluntary Sector Quarterly*, 22(4), 339–356.

Young, D., Bania, N. & Bailey, D. (1996). Structure and accountability: A study of national nonprofit associations. *Nonprofit Management and Leadership*, 6(4), 347–365.

Zahra, S.A. & Pearce, J.A. (1989). Boards of directors and corporate financial performance: A review and integrative model. *Journal of Management*, 15, 291–334.

Index

Index